Advance praise for *My Black Fam*
Journey Through the Nation's Ra

No one who reads this extraordinary saga of one man's intimate involvement in the conflicts and contradictions of race in America will ever be the same in terms of his or her personal feelings on this issue which, whether we admit it or not, vitally affects all of us. In the many years that I have known and worked with Mike Wenger, he has been my inspiration and mentor in enabling me to overcome my own biases and misunderstandings. His passion for helping build a society that is free of racist thoughts and deeds is reflected in all of his diverse life experiences. The reading of this account of his tireless efforts toward that end will serve to inform and inspire each of us as to what we can do to help achieve that noble purpose. This book needs to be read by every citizen of our country.
Honorable William F. Winter, former Governor of Mississippi and Member of President Clinton's Advisory Board on Race

Extraordinarily honest, beautifully written and compelling, Mike Wenger's journey through difference and diversity to racial healing is a gift to readers. Here is a white, male, American willing to acknowledge his privilege and leverage it on behalf of a better tomorrow for his children and future generations. "My Black Family, My White Privilege" is a timely and needed contribution to the national discourse on racism and its legacy in America. Mike Wenger is well qualified personally and professionally to make this vital contribution. His book is a must read for anyone who cares that America heal its racial divides.
Gail C. Christopher, DN, Vice President for Program Strategy, W.K. Kellogg Foundation

At a time when it often seems that our divisions trump what unites us as Americans, Michael Wenger offers a deeply personal perspective on race relations that will help point the way toward bridging divides and bringing us together. He is a keen social observer who himself has traveled on a unique journey through both privilege and disadvantage, woven with the racial and ethnic experiences that have defined our nation's recent history. Americans of every color and creed can learn from the author's honest and deeply felt assessments of the unique diversity that has characterized his life, and from the energy and intellect he has invested in contemplating ways to change things for the better. Mr. Wenger has made an honest assessment of where race relations is heading and on how we as Americans can work together to better understand our common values and to appreciate the unique strengths and attributes each of us possesses.
Ralph B. Everett, Esq., President & CEO, Joint Center for Political and Economic Studies

MY BLACK FAMILY, MY WHITE PRIVILEGE

*A White Man's Journey Through
the Nation's Racial Minefield*

Michael R. Wenger

iUniverse, Inc.
Bloomington

MY BLACK FAMILY, MY WHITE PRIVILEGE
A White Man's Journey Through the Nation's Racial Minefield

iUniverse books may be ordered through booksellers or by contacting:

iUniverse
1663 Liberty Drive
Bloomington, IN 47403
www.iuniverse.com
1-800-Authors (1-800-288-4677)

ISBN: 978-1-4759-4498-3 (sc)
ISBN: 978-1-4759-4499-0 (hc)
ISBN: 978-1-4759-4500-3 (ebk)

Library of Congress Control Number: 2012915326

Printed in the United States of America

iUniverse rev. date: 11/14/2012

CONTENTS

This book is dedicated to my parents, Rose and Emanuel Wenger, without whom my journey would not have been possible.

ACKNOWLEDGEMENTS

At every stage of my journey I have benefited from the influence and guidance of countless people too numerous to mention here. In fact, the more I wrote, the more I realized how many people I should thank. But, with apologies to those who are not mentioned, there are some who have exerted special influence on the path I have traveled.

First and foremost, of course, are my parents, Rose and Emanuel Wenger, who lived lives of commitment and passion and taught me and my sister Alice to do the same. They were a team, and they established the foundation from which my journey sprung. And my sister has always been my biggest booster.

At Queens College I came under the influence of three faculty members—Sid Simon, Rachel Weddington, and Mickey Brody—who taught me the importance of doing what I value, valuing what I do, and combining commitment with responsibility. Stan Shaw, Ron Pollack, and Hanoch McCarty, among many other fellow students, were my daily allies as we launched our respective journeys. Although Drs. Weddington and Brody are no longer with us, Sid, Stan, Ron, and Hanoch remain integral parts of my life.

In West Virginia I learned from both then-Governor and now U.S. Senator John D. Rockefeller IV and former Charleston Mayor John G. Hutchinson that you cannot judge a book by its cover or a person by his or her background and that elected public officials can succeed without sacrificing their integrity. My colleagues at Charleston's City Hall, Jim Johnson, Tom Carroll, and Cookie Chance, taught me the value of operating as a team. Both Don and Sally Richardson have had unique and important influences on my career path, and Sally introduced me to my wife Jackie, to whom I've been joyfully married for 23 years. Rick and Rita Bank sustained me during my first few years in West Virginia, accepted my first marriage with enthusiasm, and took care of our daughters on more than one occasion. Dick Yannantuono was a strong and supportive roommate, and Jeff Monroe was a trusted friend and advisor. And I regularly learned lessons of daily life from the people I met in West Virginia who struggled every day to make life better for others; among them were Robert Guerrant, Martha Crider, Ethel and Popeye Goss, Harold and Garnet Meadows, Allen Dailey, Chester Workman, and Frances Fourney.

In Washington, D.C., I have encountered several people who have had profound influences on my professional journey. My former colleagues at the Appalachian Regional Commission introduced me to the internal workings of Washington, D.C. Former Mississippi Governor William Winter, a member of President Clinton's Advisory Board on Race, has been for me a role model of integrity who demonstrates every day that the term "courageous politician" need not be an oxymoron. Judith Winston, Executive Director of President Clinton's Initiative on Race, set a standard for grace under pressure that I doubt will ever be matched. David Campt is among the smartest people I know and the inspiration for this book. Eddie Williams, former President and CEO of the Joint Center for Political and Economic Studies, gave me a chance to continue my newly minted career in race relations. My good friend Milton Morris, former Vice President for Research at the Joint Center, introduced me to Eddie Williams and possesses the most insightful political mind I know. Margaret Simms, formerly Acting President and CEO of the Joint Center, and Ralph B. Everett, current President and CEO, have enabled me to continue my career at the Joint Center. Ngozi Robinson, Maggie Potapchuk, Sheila Collins, and Muriel Warren were my teammates in creating the Network of Alliances Bridging Race and Ethnicity (NABRE) at the Joint Center. Gail Christopher taught me how to translate dreams into realities and has set a standard for making a difference that I can only gaze upon with admiration and awe. Steve Tuch and Greg Squires opened the door at George Washington University.

With regard to the chronicling of my journey I am grateful to Joann Prichard Morris, William Winter, Stan Shaw, Gail Christopher, Carole Henderson Tyson, Maggie Potapchuk, Susan Glisson, and Marc DeFrancis, all of whom have read the manuscript at various stages of its progress and offered helpful suggestions. The cover was beautifully designed by Kara Budd.

At every stop along my journey, I have encountered many other people who have made my journey more fulfilling and eye-opening. Nobody has been more important in opening my eyes to different perspectives than my first wife and the mother of my children, Tempie Bellamy Liffridge. Although space does not permit naming everyone else, I hope you know who you are, for I am grateful to all of you.

Finally, and most importantly, I could not have made it to this point in my journey without the love and support of my wife and children. Jackie's willingness to listen to and make sense of my musings is largely responsible for President Clinton's Initiative on Race and for the past 16 years of my career. More to the point, her love and support is responsible for the life of bliss I currently lead. Our three children, Regina Cherree, Arnya Lionette, and Ian Kimani, have shown uncommon strength in confronting and overcoming barriers to success that have been placed in their paths; our four wonderful grandchildren, Arian Cherree, Alexis Dominique, Michael Ian, and Lana Simone, are each, in their own way, the apples of their grandfather's eye; and our great grandson, Noah, initiates the next generation with an engaging smile, a lively curiosity, and an outgoing personality. I love you all for the richness you have given my life. Life would not be worth living without you.

Mike Wenger
Mitchellville, Maryland
August, 2012

INTRODUCTION

A BLESSED JOURNEY

I awoke with a start, bathed in perspiration. I looked at Tempie sleeping alongside me. She stirred uncomfortably. Daylight intruded through the thin curtains that fluttered in the hot morning breeze. In the adjoining room, the girls had yet to stir. Dishes rattled in the kitchen. Mama was getting ready to prepare breakfast. It was Easter Sunday, 1970, and we were visiting Tempie's parents in the small, still-segregated town in central North Carolina where they had lived since before she was born.

We had arrived on Saturday in midafternoon with our two daughters, Regina and Arnya, ages eight and six. After unloading the car and making small talk with Tempie's parents, we had made the rounds up and down dry, dusty Maple Street to see Tempie's family and friends, snacking at every house along the way—corn bread and fried chicken at one house, sweet corn at another, chocolate-chip cookies and yellow pound cake at a third. By the time we'd finished our rounds, Mama was waiting for us with a dinner of pork chops, greens, sweet potatoes, and corn bread. One thing was certain: we'd never be hungry while we were in North Carolina. After dinner, Tempie and I had lounged on the front porch of the aging, white four-room frame house and made small talk with Mama and Daddy and Aunt Louise, who lived next door. Regina and Arnya played jump rope in the front yard. At about 10 p.m., our food digested and the girls safely tucked into bed, Tempie and I decided to go to a local club. We left the house with Mama's stern warning that she expected all of us to accompany them to church the next morning. We got back at about 4 a.m., still humming tunes from the Ray Charles and James Brown recordings to which we'd danced while talking, laughing, and drinking with a few of Tempie's cousins and friends she hadn't seen since high school. Mama's warning had been long forgotten.

But Mama had not forgotten. At about 7 a.m., as Tempie and I tried to sleep off our modest overindulgence in alcohol from just a few hours earlier, Mama began stoking the wood-burning stove that sat within an arm's length of our bed. It was an eighty-degree North Carolina morning, and the fully fired stove pushed the temperature to over one hundred degrees where we lay. Mama intended to roast us out of bed, and there was no escape. Our headaches, sleep deprivation, and weak stomachs notwithstanding, we did not miss a minute of church that Easter Sunday—or, for that matter, on any Easter Sunday when we visited.

A few years ago, a good friend of mine, an African American man, asked me what I had learned as a result of the unique diversity that has characterized my life. His question reminded me of how startled I'd been by my mother-in-law's behavior on that toasty morning more than forty years ago. Having grown up in a white, working-class environment in New York City and on Long Island, I knew little of using potbellied stoves to heat homes. Having grown up in a Jewish family that disdained organized religion, I was ignorant of the importance of attending church on Easter Sunday. And having grown up in a household in which democratic decision-making was valued, I was totally unprepared for the iron hand Mama wielded. More importantly, my friend's question reminded me of how blessed I've been by the wide range of unique relationships and experiences in my life. I was married for eleven years to Tempie, an African American woman with a strict Baptist upbringing in the rural, segregated South. I have three African American children (two daughters from Tempie's first marriage and a son born of our union), four African American grandchildren, and an African American great-grandson who was born on August 28, 2011, the forty-eighth anniversary of Dr. Martin Luther King, Jr.'s "I Have a Dream" speech in front of the Lincoln Memorial. Tempie and I divorced in 1981, and in 1988 I married Jackie, a white New England woman who was raised Catholic and became a born-again Christian as an adult.

I've been a sports writer for a Brooklyn newspaper and a newspaper columnist on race relations issues for a Washington, D.C.-area newspaper. I've taught white children in the wealthy suburbs of New York City, black children in poor, rural Southside, Virginia, and diverse groups of college students in Washington, DC. I've organized college students to tutor children in one of New York City's ghettos, and adults to challenge the power structure in rural, southern West Virginia. I've worked as a neighborhood troubleshooter for a young mayor and as a cabinet official for a young governor in West Virginia. I've served as a deputy director for President Clinton's Initiative on Race after serving as the Washington, D.C., representative for Appalachian governors ranging in philosophy from Mario Cuomo to George Wallace. And for more than a decade, I've served in various policy-making positions at the Joint Center for Political and Economic Studies, a Washington, D.C., think tank focusing on issues of particular concern to African Americans. I also teach classes on race relations and institutional racism to both undergraduate and graduate students at George Washington University, and I've helped the W. K. Kellogg Foundation develop and implement its recently launched America Healing initiative, which is designed to confront structural racism and promote racial healing.

I've worked and lived in both predominantly white and predominantly black environments and have gone to school with both the rich and the working class. I go to a female Liberian-born family doctor, a male African American dentist, and an eye doctor of Middle Eastern ancestry (Lebanese, I believe). I was raised in a home where Adlai Stevenson, Hubert Humphrey, and Ted Kennedy were considered insufficiently liberal. On the other hand, I have a brother-in-law whom I love and respect and who regularly listens to and approvingly quotes Rush Limbaugh.

Yet my friend's question caught me off guard. I had not thought much about what I'd learned from the diversity in my life, particularly in terms of race. I've had the privilege of being able to take life as it comes and to pursue my interests without stopping to examine the meaning of my experiences. So my immediate answer was, "Well, I guess I've learned we're all the same."

We are all the same, of course, in many essential ways. Most of us, no matter what our skin color, cherish common values: freedom, justice, fairness, honesty, hard work. We possess common aspirations: a decent and affordable home, a fulfilling job, healthy and educated children, and a life that is long enough to enjoy our grandchildren, and perhaps even the early years of their children. We all feel the same emotions: joy at the birth of a child, sadness at the death of a loved one, love for our family, anger at people who disrespect us, hope for the future, frustration at the daily barriers we encounter.

However, as I reflected further, it became clear to me that "we're all the same," the mantra of most fair and open-minded white people, is simply too glib when it comes to race. We may be essentially the same in a biological sense, as recent human genome research has confirmed. But "we're all the same" ignores our nation's unique history, the different tracks on which our lives have traveled, and the special challenges our individual experiences have presented. We are shaped by the racial, religious, economic, and cultural environments in which we've grown up. Mama cherished many of the same values I cherished, possessed many of the same aspirations, was moved to laughter or tears by events that evoked the same emotions in me. But we were from two very different worlds and had journeyed through life on two very different tracks. And, of course, so had Tempie and I.

As I look back on it now, that Easter Sunday experience began to teach me how significantly our backgrounds shape our lives and how much we can learn from people with backgrounds different from our own. That morning, for example, Mama taught me that racial oppression and economic deprivation may create victims, but they do not necessarily create a victim's mentality. On my frequent visits to Maple Street, I also learned about the importance of a close-knit community, the strength and sanctuary of extended family and loyal friends, and the role faith can play in life.

We constantly struggle with the issue of race. It generates intense emotions and often puzzling contradictions. Despite the fact that we are a half-century beyond the civil rights struggles of the 1950s and 1960s, finding common ground and common understanding remain ongoing challenges. Confronting these challenges is increasingly important because the current demographic revolution in the United States will force most of us to live and work in environments more diverse than we have ever experienced. By the time my nineteen-year-old granddaughter is old enough to be President, around midcentury, white (read: European) Americans will likely comprise less than half of the U.S. population, as is already the case in states like California and Texas. Less than 40 percent of today's labor force are white males, and this percentage is declining rapidly. Want more concrete evidence? One of the most popular boy's names in both California and Texas is "Jose," and salsa now outsells ketchup in the United States.

Understanding the unique life journeys of people from diverse backgrounds is becoming essential to effectively negotiating the various challenges of our daily life—relating to coworkers and friends, dealing with salesclerks and home repair people, and guiding our children through their school and neighborhood experiences. Being deceived by the old stereotypes is increasingly self-defeating, and insulation from people who are not just like us is becoming virtually impossible. Stroll down the street in any big city, stride through any major airport, or scan the employment ranks of most big companies. The diversity is already inescapable.

Many of us talk with great sincerity about the value of this growing diversity. But we usually talk about it in abstract terms: food, music, art, literature, etc. Too many white folks think that if we eat soul food, listen to Ray Charles, Stevie Wonder, and Michael Jackson, and perhaps read Toni Morrison, we've got it. I thought after I'd eaten chitterlings (pig's intestines) for the first time, I had arrived—although my taste buds were mightily offended until I tried Aunt Mary's chitterlings (pronounced *chitlins*) many months later. Of course, I knew as much about being black after eating chitterlings as Tempie knew about being Jewish after eating my mother's chicken soup. Stymied by key institutions of our society—primarily our schools, the media, and public officialdom—that continue to foster racial and ethnic divisions, we find it difficult to develop the kinds of relationships that would allow us to better understand our common values and aspirations and to appreciate the unique strengths and attributes each of us possesses. We journey through life on very different paths, rarely taking our eyes off our own path to glance at the pathways of others. We all encounter barriers along the way, but we are ignorant of how vastly different those barriers are in intensity and frequency. We who are white are privileged to be born into a society that has been controlled for hundreds of years by people who look just like us; we have the luxury of avoiding and being oblivious to many of the barriers that others must confront.

The truth is that although black people and white people have shared this land for hundreds of years, we remain a "country of strangers," as the title of David Shipler's 1997 book asserts. We may work together during the day, perhaps share an occasional beer after work, or encounter each other and even high-five each other in shopping malls or at football games, but we don't know each other. We may have voted for Barack Obama for President, but communication and interaction between us is usually superficial. We see each other on television, and we read about each other in the newspapers, absorbing the prevailing stereotypes. But for the most part, we don't live in the same communities, don't attend the same schools, don't socialize in the same venues, and don't worship in the same churches, synagogues, or mosques.

This book is an attempt to answer my friend's question and, at the same time, to share my discoveries with as many people as possible, of all racial and ethnic backgrounds. I've been on a unique journey for most of my life, and I've had glimpses into a world most white people never see. But I, too, blinded by the privilege of my skin color, have seen precious little. I've been able to stride through the episodes of my life without giving them much more thought than I give the stations I pass when I ride the Washington, D.C., Metro. At times, these episodes have evoked intense emotions: joy, love, gratitude, as well as anger, frustration, and pain. But after they were over, I had the luxury of moving beyond them, bringing them to mind only when it suited me. So discovering the answer to my friend's question has been personally revealing and rewarding. I have tried to explore the episodes of my life more deeply, not only recalling how I reacted to them in the moment, but also attempting to understand what I should have learned from them. This is an exploration that African Americans must engage in every day. My former wife, my three children, and now my four grandchildren confront the issue of skin color on a daily basis. Until now, I have been mostly oblivious to their reality. I've verbally acknowledged their experiences without truly feeling the pain they were enduring. And when I did share their hurt, it was transitory.

I've had my own challenges, but they have been challenges over which I have had some control. Overcoming them has depended largely on my efforts. Some people may be more capable than I am. Others may have been born to greater economic privilege. But for the most part, I have had the privilege of knowing that I would rise or fall based primarily on my own ability and effort. The members of my family who are black do not enjoy that same privilege. Their abilities and their efforts have often been overshadowed by the negative stereotypes that many white people attribute to them simply from looking at them. Children in many black homes are warned, as they were in our home, that they will have to be twice as good as a white person in order to have any hope of achieving their dreams. And if they do succeed, they may well have to suffer through the usually unwarranted assumption that their success is due only to affirmative action.

Even after the election of a President with African ancestry, life in this country is lived in a white man's environment. White people control the context, and whatever happens is within our collective power to change. We own most of the businesses, run most of the schools, command most of the power levers of government, and control most of the media. Not most of us, of course, as individuals, but people who look like us, think like us, have had experiences similar to ours, and share perspectives that we intuitively understand. Because their perspectives seem so normal to us, most of us simply don't recognize how different—and more difficult—it is for people who do not share our perspectives, our history, or our experiences. Consumed by our own challenges, we don't see the hurdles that African Americans (not to mention Hispanic Americans, Asian Americans, and Native Americans) confront in their journeys. They bear a burden of which we are largely unaware, a burden that is the legacy of often intentional government policies ranging from slavery to the subprime mortgage bubble and to which our privilege contributes in a mighty way.

We may be oblivious to these inequities, but ultimately we cannot escape their consequences. As our nation becomes increasingly diverse, restoring and maintaining the health of our economic engine, sustaining the stability of our political process, and strengthening the credibility of our moral stature will depend on confronting these inequities in a concerted and cooperative manner. We must become not a country of strangers, but a nation of friendly travelers on the road to our individual visions of the American dream. In the unique cul-de-sac where I live, our neighbors are white families, African American families, and Asian American families. They are business owners, attorneys, doctors, and government managers. Every day can be a learning experience as we watch each other's children and grandchildren grow, chat with each other, browse the merchandise at local clothing and book stores, shop at the local grocery stores, and eat at the local restaurants. Drinking in the richness of the diversity that surrounds us, we grow in our mutual understanding, in our awareness of and appreciation for our varying perspectives, and in our grasp of the issues we confront.

This is an experience that eludes most white people. Rarely, if ever, is the color of their skin a factor in their lives. Rarely, if ever, are they even reminded of their skin color. When they do think about race, they perceive with satisfaction that racial discrimination is a relic of the past thanks to Martin Luther King, Jr., and Rosa Parks. They believe in fairness and justice for all regardless of skin color, and they presume that it is today's norm. They would recoil at being labeled racist. They shake their heads in disbelief when they hear about the Texaco tapes on which top executives are heard using racial epithets, or read about the shootings of Amadou Diallo and Sean Bell and the brutalization of Abner Louima in New York City, or witness the aftermath of Hurricane Katrina in New Orleans. Yet, they regard these as isolated incidents that do not reflect the reality of our society. A Gallup poll co-commissioned by the AARP and the Leadership Conference on Civil Rights on the fortieth anniversary of the 1964 Civil Rights Act found that 75 percent of white Americans believe that blacks are treated fairly, and 56 percent believe all or most of the goals of Martin Luther King, Jr., have been achieved. However, that same poll found that only 38 percent of African Americans believe they are treated fairly, and only 21 percent feel that all or most of the goals of Dr. King have been achieved. More recent polls yield similar findings. Clearly, there is a disconnect.

It is this disconnect that I hope to bridge with this book. The fact that, as a member of the most privileged group of the human species—white, male, and American—I have been able to glimpse what life can be like for those who are not similarly privileged does not make me any less guilty or less responsible for the words and actions that sustain our racist society. However, I may be more aware of the pain that well-meaning white Americans unwittingly inflict every day on people of color. I may also be more aware of the urgency of addressing the causes of this pain and of the political, economic, and human consequences of failing to do so.

On election night in 2008, my wife and I sat in front of the television, tears of joy streaming down our faces as the President-elect and his family emerged from behind that curtain in Chicago's Grant Park. We had purposely remained home alone so we could savor this moment and its true meaning. We received telephone calls from my sister and her husband, each of my three children, and my black ex-wife. Each of the conversations began the same way. "Isn't this unbelievable?" The joy and disbelief in their voices were palpable. In fact, it seems unbelievable that so many of us were able to overcome the fears and apprehensions of a lifetime to vote for a presidential candidate whose lineage is African and European. It is testimony to the progress we've made and a justification for optimism about our future. But it does not, as some claim, portend a post-racial society.

My children and grandchildren, the people with whom I work and socialize, and the students I encounter verify in countless ways that our journey remains long and arduous. But they also reveal how each of us can be meaningful participants. So, allow me to share my journey with you in the hope that it will help to enrich your own journey and strengthen your contribution to achieving a society in which we cherish our individual uniqueness and glory in the common threads that bind us all together, a society in which skin color is not in any way a factor in an individual's ability to achieve his or her vision of the American dream.

I

GROWING UP WHITE

In 1999, at a reception in Washington, D.C., for members of the Joint Center Board of Governors, a rather portly and well dressed African American gentleman approached me.

"Hello." He smiled as he stuck out his hand. "My name is Hector Hyacinthe." I had never met him, but I recognized his name from the list of board members and knew he was a prominent businessman from Westchester County, New York. "Mike Wenger," I replied as we shook hands.

"Good to meet you, Mike. Are you from D.C.?"

"Nope, originally from Brooklyn," I replied.

"Really? What part?"

"East New York."

"Really? What street?"

"Bradford Street."

"What number?"

"Three hundred."

"Three-eighty!" he proclaimed triumphantly.

"That's right across the street from my grandparents' house. They lived at three-eighty-one."

Hector nodded. "Yep, lived there until I finished high school."

We spent the next several minutes comparing notes on the old neighborhood. Then I spent the remainder of the evening trying to reconcile my surprise at what I'd just learned about Hector with what I'd suddenly realized was the subconscious mixed message of my childhood. Simply stated: "Blacks deserve equal rights but they are not really our equals." More importantly, I was left to ponder how this mixed message conspired to make us liberal white people complicit in the pervasive racial discrimination that we so glibly condemn.

My family's story is typical of most European immigrants. Like millions of others, I am descended from people who came to our shores voluntarily. They came to escape famine, to flee religious or political persecution, to avoid war, or to find economic opportunity. Philip and Anna Kaplan, my maternal grandparents, fled from oppressive conditions in Russia as a young couple with a baby. They arrived in 1910 with few possessions but with a sense of pride in their heritage and excitement about the opportunities that lay ahead in a new country. Once here, they had to endure a period of adjustment and discrimination. They were called "kikes" and "Christ-killers" and were barred from living in certain neighborhoods. Because he was Jewish, my grandfather was denied jobs and victimized by hiring quotas. He and my grandmother persevered, however, driven by a faith in the future and inspired by the examples of other immigrants who had made it. In time, they were able to draw on their culture, skills, and sense of identity to carve out a decent life for themselves and their offspring. And they were able to melt into American life.

They were never rich. In fact, they viewed those with wealth as somehow immoral "as long as there are people starving in Europe." But they could always put food on the table and clothes, albeit often hand-me-downs, on their children's backs. They settled in Brooklyn, New York, and my mother was born in 1913, the second eldest of four sisters. The eldest sister became a teacher, my mother and her youngest sister became registered nurses, and the third-born sister became a librarian. All four married. I am the second-eldest of the six cousins, and the oldest male.

My grandfather was a shoemaker, and he found work at a shoe factory in Brooklyn about five miles from their house. As the story goes, he walked to and from work each day. Whether or not that is true, he undeniably worked hard, and he saved his money.

Some years later, he and my grandmother bought a two-family house on Bradford Street in Brooklyn's East New York section, a neighborhood then populated by Eastern European immigrants like themselves. They lived upstairs, and my mother's older sister and husband and their daughter, my oldest maternal cousin, moved in downstairs.

My father and his mother arrived in Brooklyn from Poland in 1920. He was thirteen years old, the youngest of nine brothers and sisters, and the last of them to emigrate. The others had come in groups of twos and threes in the preceding several years. My father had to be smuggled out of Poland disguised as a girl, because the authorities did not allow teenage boys to leave the country. My grandfather, a tailor, was in his eighties when my father left (yes, he was over seventy when my father was born), and he never made it out of Poland. Because he spoke little English, my father was initially put into the third grade. But he was bright and hard-working, and with the help of his family and kind teachers, he graduated from Thomas Jefferson High School in 1926, at the age of eighteen. His three older brothers were already working in Manhattan's Garment District, so he joined them and became an embroiderer. Like my mother's family, he had a deep distrust of the wealthy. He was a union man, and he used to tell me that in those dark depression days of the 1930s, he was convinced that "the (socialist) revolution was just around the corner."

He met my mother at a political rally in Brooklyn. Mutually attracted by their common political passion and perhaps by their similar stature (my father was just over five feet tall and my mother was four-foot-eight), they married in 1938 and moved to a house on Bradford Street two blocks from where my grandparents lived. In 1942, my father joined the Navy, but because of his short stature, he remained stateside during World War II, serving as an x-ray technician and ambulance driver at the naval base in Norfolk, Virginia. When he was discharged in 1945, he returned to the embroidery trade.

I came along in 1942, just before my father left for basic training. Until we moved out of Brooklyn when I was about seven years old, my mother, my sister Alice (born in 1945), and I visited my grandparents every day. My grandmother was always in the kitchen. On most days the smell of chicken soup greeted us at the door. Occasionally, the aroma of frying potatoes overwhelmed the chicken soup, which meant that she was making potato latkes, to this day my favorite food. I'd rush into the kitchen for a "tastee." On other days, I'd immediately look for my grandfather, who was retired by then. He'd either be rolling cigarettes in a small room at the top of the steps or playing checkers in the park on the next block. My reward for hugging him was a nickel for penny candy. On Sundays it might be a quarter, which my parents required that I "save for a rainy day."

All the neighbors on my grandparents' side of the street had similar backgrounds. They were primarily older Russian and Polish immigrant families who had bought their homes many years earlier and raised their children on that block. Now, they yearned for nothing more than to finish their lives in these familiar surroundings, the men playing checkers in the park, the women preparing for daily or weekly visits from children and grandchildren, most of whom had not strayed far from the old neighborhood. They feared, however, that their modest dream was being challenged by an influx of black families with young children. Many were from the South, and they now occupied every house on the other side of the street, two or three families to an apartment, in some cases. Although they were separated only by the width of a tree-lined city street, these two groups had virtually no contact with each other. Not even the Berlin Wall that divided colorful and lively West Berlin from gray and dreary East Berlin when I was there in 1983 could have made the divide any more explicit.

The houses on my grandparents' side of the street were all owner-occupied and had the look of being lovingly cared for as the prized possessions they were. Their red brick exteriors were clean and bright, and screens hung in every window frame.

Meticulously trimmed hedges defined each owner's postage stamp front yard. Across the street, nearly all the families were renters, the prevailing ambiance was drab, window screens were the exception, and little healthy shrubbery was visible in the front yards, many of which were paved over. There was no obvious hostility between the two sides of the street, but there was no communication, either. Rarely did anybody on my grandparents' side of the street even park their car on the other side of the street. As children, we understood that we were not to walk on the other side of the street. I spent a major portion of my childhood at my grandparents' house, but until I met Hector, when I was fifty-seven years old, I'd never actually met anyone who lived across the street.

The block on which we lived at the time was not yet changing so dramatically. Working-class Jewish families, many of them second-generation Americans, lived on both sides of the street. Most were renters, and there was a fair amount of transience on the block; families headed for the newly developing suburbs as soon as they were financially able, to be replaced by other working-class Jewish families who were a step behind on their journey toward the middle class. My family followed the same pattern. In 1948, my father, driven by a desire to be his own boss, utilized the GI Bill and money borrowed from family and friends to buy a tiny hardware store in Woodmere, a wealthy, growing, all-white Long Island suburb of New York City. The store was not much bigger than some kiosks you can find in shopping malls today. Its length would have fit comfortably between home plate and first base on a baseball diamond. It was wide enough to accommodate narrow shelves on opposite walls and an island of shelves down the middle. But two people could not walk through the door at the same time, nor pass each other in either of the two aisles without turning sideways. It was a start, though, and since discount chains had not yet arrived, a small entrepreneur could eke out a living.

The store opened to ripples of excitement throughout the family. A year later, my parents rented a five-room apartment above a barbershop, just across the street from the hardware store. Besides three of my father's sisters, who had settled in Detroit, my parents were the first of any of their siblings to leave Brooklyn. Woodmere, like our Brooklyn neighborhood, was in transition. The barbershop owner and his wife were Italian immigrants, and they lived in the ground floor apartment behind the barbershop. The two-story brick building was sandwiched between, on one side, a fruit market owned by three brothers, also Italian immigrants, and on the other side, a Methodist church and the parsonage where its pastor lived. Most of the other retail stores along Broadway, the town's lengthy, one-block main street, from the delicatessen to the bicycle shop, were all owned by Jewish immigrants or the children of Jewish immigrants.

There was also a Chinese restaurant. I never knew who owned the restaurant, but we ate there at least once or twice a month, usually on Sunday evenings. My father, who was an atheist but considered himself culturally Jewish, would often scan the other tables and voice his cynicism about "so-called Jews who go to synagogue on Saturday morning and eat pork fried rice on Sunday evening." The era of fast food chains had not yet blossomed, but even if there had been a pair of golden arches on every street corner, my mother, a trained nurse and committed nutritionist, never would have allowed us to eat there.

In the face of competition from two larger hardware stores in town, my father worked long hours. It seemed like he was always working. He kept the store open six days a week, from 8 a.m. to 6 p.m. He ate lunch in the store and had the same telephone number installed for both the store and the apartment. If a call came after hours or on Sunday from a customer who desperately needed a hammer or a dozen nails, or even a single screw, he'd brave my mother's protestations ("Manny, you deserve a day of rest. Those bastards can wait until tomorrow.") and get them what they needed. He would even deliver it, if necessary. To help him, my mother temporarily gave up her nursing career to work alongside him five days a week. At about 8:30 a.m. she'd see Alice and me off to the local elementary school two blocks from the apartment with the daily warning to be careful crossing the street and to "Be sure you hold your sister's hand." Then she'd spend the day in the store. My sister and I walked home from school, arriving in the empty apartment by 3:30 p.m. We would immediately call the store to let my mother know we were home safely. She'd leave the store at about 5 p.m. so she could have dinner on the table by the time my father came home. Tuesday was her "day off" for grocery shopping, the laundry, and other essential errands. When I was old enough, I'd make deliveries for my father after school and during the summer on my bicycle. If I got home from school or from the summer baseball program at the local junior high school early enough to finish the deliveries before the store closed, my reward was to help work the cash register or to cut keys.

Family vacations consisted of a six-day automobile trip each summer to a nearby tourist attraction: Howe Caverns or Niagara Falls in New York, the Pocono Mountains in Pennsylvania, the White Mountains of New Hampshire, or the Green Mountains of Vermont. Our longest trip was to Monticello, Virginia, to see the home of Thomas Jefferson. We would always pack the aging Nash Rambler with great excitement on a Saturday night and leave early Sunday morning, my father at the wheel, my mother in possession of the trusty AAA Triptik, and my sister and I fighting to be sure we each had our fair half of the backseat. Along the way we'd stop at the least expensive AAA-rated motels or guest houses and scour the road for decent-looking restaurants that fit my parents' rigid budget. Usually, we'd return late on a Friday night so my father could open the store on Saturday, the busiest shopping day of the week. If I complained about how short our vacations were—"Other kids' families go away for two weeks"—my mother would coldly respond, "We're not rich like other kids' families." It did not occur to me until I was an adult that my parents never took a vacation without my sister and me until we were in college.

On most Sundays, except during the summer, we visited my grandparents in Brooklyn. On summer Sundays, my mother and

Aunt Ruthie, the librarian, would pack picnic lunches for outings at nearby Brookville Park. Aunt Ruthie and Uncle Sidney had two sons, Victor (who was born in August of 1945 and named for V-J Day) and Eddie. They were respectively about the same ages as my sister and I. We'd play blissfully in the park for most of those afternoons. My Uncle Sidney, a ring-maker on The Bowery in Manhattan, usually supervised our play. Meanwhile, my mother and aunt would talk about family, friends, and politics, and my father would read the Sunday *New York Times*. A special Sunday treat was a trip to Jones Beach, four adults and four growing children squeezed into one car. Occasionally, my father would take me to Ebbets Field to see Jackie Robinson, Pee Wee Reese, and the other "Boys of Summer" who made the Brooklyn Dodgers my childhood passion. As far as I could tell, my father had little interest in sports, and fighting the traffic and crowds was probably the last thing he wanted to do on his one day off. But he had a special affection for the Dodgers because they were perpetual underdogs, and because they'd signed Jackie Robinson as the first African American Major Leaguer of the twentieth century.

In the mid-1950s my father moved to a much bigger store just across the street. Again, he borrowed money from family and friends to renovate the new store. However, he couldn't afford professional movers. So, he commandeered all of the shopping carts from the supermarket that had previously occupied the store, and on a bright Sunday in the spring of 1954, our family and friends, children included, manned the carts and moved all the merchandise, from barrels of nails to kitchen appliances, across the street. It took the entire day and much of the night, but on Monday morning, he was open for business with neatly stocked shelves in a new store larger than his two competitors' stores. About two years later, thanks in part to financial assistance from my grandmother, who had moved in with us after my grandfather died, we left the apartment for a single-family, four-bedroom house three blocks away. It had a screened porch, a large lawn, an attic, a basement, and a garage. It was a huge step up for the family. My father could hardly believe his good fortune. On one Sunday morning not long after we moved, I woke up and came downstairs to find my father strolling the perimeter of the lawn. When I asked him what he was doing, his eyes twinkled as he replied, "Walking my estate."

Our move to Long Island reinforced the subtle message I had absorbed from the divide on my grandparents' block. The town of Woodmere was then a growing suburb about twenty miles from Manhattan, with a population of about 10,000. Its growth was fueled almost entirely by Jewish families on their way up economically. They were fleeing not only their modest beginnings, but also the influx of black people into the city, such as those on Bradford Street. Except for some live-in maids, not a single black person lived in Woodmere or in the towns that surrounded it. However, many black women were visible in the mornings as they walked from the bus stop on Broadway to their jobs as maids in the homes of the *nouveau riche*, as my mother disparagingly referred to most of the town's residents. In the evenings, after fixing dinner for the families of their employers, they returned to the bus stop. These black women knew their place. My father arrived home one evening after closing the store and reported with astonishment that he'd passed a maid on the street and that she'd stepped off the sidewalk when he passed her.

Most of Woodmere's men rode the Long Island Railroad to their offices in Manhattan five days a week, about an hour's commute each way. Meanwhile, their wives pursued social and shopping interests and chauffeured the children to and from school and then to tennis, dance, and music lessons afterward. On weekends from April to October, the men spent their time playing golf at the local private country club, where I had a job as a caddy when I was in high school, thanks to one of my father's customers. The nearest African American families lived in the equally segregated town of Inwood. It was separated from Woodmere by two other all-white towns. Probably no more than four or five miles from us, it may as well have been a continent away. While a few of Inwood's residents were business owners or professionals, the vast majority of its population formed the pool of workers from which families in Woodmere and the adjoining all-white towns drew their domestic help.

The only black employees on Woodmere's main street were two men who worked behind the soda fountain in Sussman's drugstore, next to my father's first store. As a child, I waited expectantly during the lazy, hot summer afternoons for my father to give me fifty cents to get him a lime rickey from next door. Eddie Adams, the younger of the two men, might show me a new card trick or dazzle me with his ability to bend just the first knuckles of his three middle fingers while keeping the lower knuckles stiff. (Try it sometime; it's not easy.) In my preteen years we were "best buddies," but even then that mixed message persisted. My parents talked about what good men they were. Yet Eddie and Wilson, grown men with families, and Juanita, the black woman who cleaned our house and occasionally babysat us, were the only adults besides close family and friends whom I could call by their first names. The distinction between how we addressed Eddie, Wilson, and Juanita and how we addressed white adults never occurred to me as a child, but it was another subtle reminder of the difference in status between blacks and whites.

The unspoken message of my childhood, conveyed by my grandparents' attitude toward the people across the street and by my parents' acceptance of Woodmere's norms, was that black people were different. Those who lived across the street from my grandparents didn't take pride in their homes, or work hard, or place much emphasis on doing well in school. As a child I did not comprehend the fact that they were renting from landlords who had fled the neighborhood and who refused to maintain their properties. Nor was I cognizant of the fact that while my grandfather could get a union job as a skilled laborer in a shoe factory, the best work that the men across the street could hope for were non-union jobs as janitors in the factory. Nor did I perceive anything wrong with the fact that all of the teachers at the local elementary school had my skin color, as did all of the store owners and other financially successful adults I encountered in the neighborhood.

I doubt that any of the adults in our family were conscious of these factors. Certainly, no adult ever tried to discuss any of these issues with me. Of course, I would have been too young to understand such matters, anyway. But these negative racial stereotypes ingrained at an early age took hold, and I was unsettled, nearly fifty years later, by my surprise at finding someone from the even-numbered side of my grandparents' block who had achieved Hector's level of success. It seemed that I had learned the unspoken message quite well. In my head, I knew better, but I was incapable of turning off the default setting in my brain, even if the setting lasted for just a split second. The Woodmere experience—the jobs that people held, the adults we could call by their first names, the fact that the school district's faculty and student body were 100 percent white—simply reinforced the message.

My parents, like other adult members of our family, would have recoiled from any accusation that they held negative racial stereotypes or were complicit in any way with racism. They would have proudly cited their membership in the NAACP, their admiration for leaders like W. E. B. DuBois and Ralph Bunche, and their passionate vocal condemnation of racial segregation in the South. My sister and I accepted their views as articles of faith. When I became a sports fan, I rooted for the New York Knicks because they featured Nat "Sweetwater" Clifton, one of the few black players in the National Basketball Association; I rooted for the Cleveland Browns because they featured African American fullback Marion Motley; and I rooted passionately for the Brooklyn Dodgers and hated, with an equal passion, the colorless New York Yankees—they were one of the last teams to integrate when Elston Howard made their roster in 1955—because of my parents' influence, even before I knew anything about racial discrimination. So passionate was my commitment to the Dodgers that I cried uncontrollably when Bobby Thomson hit the ninth-inning home run in the third game of the 1951 playoffs that enabled the New York Giants to wrest the National League pennant from the Dodgers. But I was relieved that Thomson had hit the home run off reliever Ralph Branca, a white man, rather than off starting pitcher Don Newcombe, a black man.

In 1954, my parents were jubilant at the *Brown v. Board of Education* Supreme Court decision outlawing segregation in public schools. The murder of Emmett Till the following year had my parents' lips dripping with obscenities about evil and inhuman white southerners. In 1957, they expressed fury at Governor Orval Faubus for inciting white anger when nine black children tried to desegregate Central High School in Little Rock. They were equally furious at President Eisenhower for waiting so long before ordering in federal troops to protect the black children. Most charitable contributions my parents could afford went to the NAACP. Later, because of my involvement with the organization at Queens College, their contributions went to James Farmer's Congress of Racial Equality (CORE) or to the Student Nonviolent Coordinating Committee (SNCC) to support sit-ins, freedom rides, and voter registration campaigns in the Deep South. Recordings by African American artists like Paul Robeson and Marian Anderson were among their most cherished possessions. And when Lyndon Johnson assumed the presidency after President Kennedy's assassination, my father spoke with apprehension about having a man with a southern accent in the White House.

Yet, among my father's favorite radio programs was *Beulah*, which depicted a stereotypical black maid serving a white family. It was as much a part of our 7 p.m. dinner every night as the meat, potatoes, and vegetables my mother so carefully balanced on our plates and as the political discussions that animated my parents once they had finished inquiring about our school day. We got our first television in 1951, and Jack Benny's stereotypical black valet, Rochester, quickly became one of the family's favorite television characters. When we moved to 100 percent white and probably 95 percent Jewish Woodmere, my parents expressed no concern that the public schools I would be attending had not a single student or faculty member of color. The kidnapping and killing of Patrice Lumumba in the Congo generated almost as much anger in my house as lynchings in the South did. But no one ever mentioned the locally segregated environment in which we were living.

I recount this background not to condemn my parents, who were activists for social justice long before the civil rights movement and who taught their two children similar principles. They marched for equal rights, outspokenly condemned McCarthyism, worked relentlessly to try to elect the most liberal political candidates, from the Socialist Party of America's Norman Thomas to the American Labor Party's 1952 presidential candidate Vincent Hallinan, and they literally put their limited money where their mouths were. They helped to start the Five Towns Forum, a group that met each month to hear controversial, left-wing speakers, including civil rights leaders and supporters of Fidel Castro's Cuba. They were among the very few white members of their NAACP chapter. They attended chapter meetings in Inwood, and after we moved to my father's "estate," they occasionally hosted meetings at our house. They never gave up their idealism or abandoned the struggle. But as committed as they were, they were oblivious to the ways in which they both perpetuated negative racial stereotypes and were complicit in sustaining the local status quo. They never questioned the fact that the leadership of the Five Towns Forum was all white; nor did they ever examine the realities that all the people they socialized with were white, the African Americans we knew best were servants, and their favorite radio and television programs portrayed African Americans as submissive to white authority.

My parents, Manny and Rosie, had a challenging but rewarding life. They worked hard, struggled to make ends meet, and occasionally endured anti-Semitic incidents. But for the most part, they encountered few immovable barriers on their journey, and they had the support of family, friends, and even business associates as they climbed the ladder toward their version of the American dream. Like millions of other immigrants and first-generation Americans, my parents drew great strength from their cultural backgrounds, support networks, and the expectations of others. Their political views divided everyone into two categories, those with power and money (the bad guys), and those without power or money (the good guys.) But whatever happened in these bad guy—good guy battles, they knew they could build a good life, melt into American society, and establish a legacy upon which their children could build. Perhaps their greatest legacy to their children is this sense of self-assurance. If we don't like aspects of the larger society such as the class divide, we can seek to change them—in fact, we have an obligation to do so—while still building a good life. We are limited only by our own abilities and ambitions. It is this sense of limitlessness that forms the essence of white-skin privilege. Although I was oblivious to it at the time, this sense of possibility has sustained me every day of my life.

In his commencement speech at Howard University in 1965, President Lyndon Johnson defended affirmative action, making reference to the experiences of the "Negro" compared to the experiences of the European immigrants who had been able to pull themselves up by their bootstraps:

> They did not have the heritage of centuries to overcome, and they did not have a cultural tradition which had been twisted and battered by endless years of hatred and hopelessness, nor were they excluded—these others—because of race or color, a feeling whose dark intensity is matched by no other prejudice in our society.

I didn't feel privileged while I was growing up. I doubt my parents did, either. But we had bootstraps, and no chains. As I have come to understand in my life journey, that has made all the difference.

II

My Introduction
To Race And Privilege

George W. Hewlett High School, which opened in 1955, served Woodmere and Hewlett, two of the towns nicknamed the "Golden Ghetto" for the influx of newly wealthy and predominantly Jewish families. My 1959 graduating class was the first to have spent its entire four years in the new high school with its brightly lit classrooms, modern audiovisual equipment, sparkling and spacious gymnasium and outdoor athletic facilities, fully equipped band room and typing lab, and parking lot of sufficient size to accommodate both the faculty's cars and the students' cars. I usually hitchhiked the two miles to school in the morning, and in the evening walked home or to my father's store. Despite my love of sports, I was not much of an athlete, so I became the manager of the basketball and track teams. About 95 percent of my graduating class of 216 students was college-bound, and discussions among seniors focused on which colleges you had applied to and which one was your first choice.

My first choice was Cornell University in Ithaca, New York. The Russians had just launched Sputnik, beating the United States into space, so the competition was on. National pride, as well as economic opportunity, dictated that anyone skilled in math and science must become an engineer or a scientist. My best grades were in math, and I was a member of the Math Team. So I offered no resistance when my guidance counselor suggested a career in engineering and recommended that I apply to Cornell, which had an excellent engineering school. My parents concurred. "It's a secure career," counseled my father. Cornell looked favorably upon applicants from Hewlett High because previous graduates had done well there. With an SAT math score over 700, grades that put me in the top 15 percent of my graduating class, good extracurricular activities, and Cornell's favorable disposition toward our high school, I was accepted into the Cornell University School of Civil Engineering.

My father drove me up to Ithaca in late August. I'd spent the summer earning extra money as part of a work crew scraping and repainting the bleachers at Hewlett High School's football field. My father's membership in the local Exchange Club had also helped me win one of the Club's small annual college scholarships, and I'd won a New York State Regents scholarship. But my summer earnings and my two scholarships would not come close to covering the $3,000 that tuition and room and board cost each year. I'd have to get a job at school, and my parents, at great sacrifice, would still have to make up the difference.

My two years at Cornell did not turn out exactly as I expected. I did not fit in well with my dorm mates, mostly young white men from well-to-do families who could easily finance their educations. I had to work washing dishes in the main cafeteria, and during the second semester's rush period, I did not get into any of the popular fraternities. Worse, in my first semester high above Cayuga's waters, I flunked physics and barely passed calculus. I did better in my second semester, passing everything, although without much margin for error. When I came home after my freshman year, though, I felt that I'd turned a corner. For my sophomore year, I had rented an off-campus apartment with a friend from a working-class family like mine, I had arranged for a job waiting tables at a fraternity house, and I had been accepted for a position as a sports writer at the *Cornell Daily Sun*. With a year of college under my belt, I was confident that I would do better academically. I spent the summer working as a copy boy at the *New York Post* and parking cars on the weekends at a local beach club. In September 1960, I headed back to Cornell full of enthusiasm.

My father again drove me to Ithaca. Our first stop was my new apartment. The student who was to have been my apartment mate, and who had done all of the negotiating with the landlord, had decided not to return to school. I was disappointed, but I expected it would be easy to find someone else to share the apartment. My father waited in the car while I knocked on the landlord's door. When the fifty-something owner opened the door, I introduced myself and told him that my apartment mate was not returning to school, but that I would find a replacement. He looked at me quizzically and then asked, "What did you say your name was?" When he realized I was Jewish, he exploded with anti-Semitic venom and shut the door in my face. I retreated to the car, all the color drained from my face. When I told my father what had happened, he clenched his teeth, but simply said we'd find another place. The other place turned out to be a rooming house just off campus. I shared a room with someone I'd never met and shared a bathroom with five other guys. I hated it. It set the tone for my second—and last—year at Cornell.

One of my advanced physics requirements was an 8 a.m. statics class. I fell behind immediately, started skipping classes, and ultimately earned 33 percent on the final exam. I passed my other classes, but certainly not with flying colors. At the end of that first semester, I was invited out of the School of Civil Engineering and into the Unclassified Division, where a student attempting to transfer from one school at Cornell to another can take classes to determine if he or she can qualify for admission to the desired school. I now had my eye on the School of Liberal Arts. I was marginally more successful, but at the end of the semester, the Dean of the Unclassified Division, who had the ironic last name "Rideout," told me, "You might do better somewhere other than Cornell." Meanwhile, my scholarships had dried up, my parents could not afford to pay another year's expenses for Cornell, and I couldn't work enough hours to make ends meet. It was devastatingly clear that I had come to the end of my Cornell career.

There had been only one bright spot during my two years there: writing about sports for the *Cornell Daily Sun*. During my early teenage years, my passionate interest in baseball had led me to fantasize about being a baseball announcer and following in the footsteps of my favorite Dodgers sportscaster, Vince Scully. Writing for the *Sun* had rekindled my interest in a sports-related career, this time as a sports writer. I applied for and received a summer fellowship from the *Wall Street Journal*. The condition of the fellowship was that the recipient had to find his or her own job with a newspaper, and the *Journal* would pay the recipient's summer salary. Beginning in April 1961, I sent letters of application to over fifty newspapers around the country, from Miami to San Francisco. By early June I'd received letters of rejection from every one of them. Now, with the summer approaching, I had no college to return to and no summer job. A career as a sports writer began to seem as unlikely as a career in civil engineering.

Finally, through a friend of my parents, I got an interview and was offered a job at the *Brooklyn Daily*, a small Coney Island tabloid newspaper I'd never heard of. It claimed a circulation of about 40,000, but that number was probably a gross exaggeration. It was printed five days a week in offices owned by *The Jewish Press*, a weekly English-language newspaper. The company's main source of income, though, was its commercial printing business. The *Brooklyn Daily* had exactly one writer-editor. Arnold Fine, a paunchy, disheveled, bespectacled, thirty-something man, doubled as a substitute linotype operator and an occasional writer for *The Jewish Press*. He would scan the afternoon newspapers—the *New York Post*, the *New York World-Telegram and Sun*, and the *New York Journal American*—for interesting articles, rewrite them, and run them the next morning as if they were breaking news. He also wrote the editorials and the letters to the editor, did the newspaper layout, and occasionally sold advertising. The paper existed because its operating costs were minimal, and because it ran a full complement of horse racing results as well as race analysis provided by a friend of the owner. This made it moderately popular with a certain segment of the horse-playing community.

That summer, Arnie hired two *Wall Street Journal* fellows, me and a young man from the Bronx, also named Mike. He saw us as no-cost help. By the time I received Arnie's job offer, I had, out of necessity, returned to my jobs as a copy boy at the *New York Post* (which did not qualify for the fellowship) and parking cars. So during that summer, I worked at the *New York Post* from 8 a.m. to 4 p.m. and at the *Brooklyn Daily* from 5 p.m. to about 11 p.m., with an hour-long commute at both ends of the day, five days a week. On weekends, I parked cars from 9 a.m. to 6 p.m.

Arnie assigned Mike and me rotating duties. One week, I would rewrite the most interesting news articles from the afternoon papers, and Mike would rewrite the sports articles. The next week, we'd switch. Both of us wrote letters to the editor and signed them with fictitious initials. Arnie continued to write the editorials and do the layout, and when he particularly liked the way we had rewritten a story, we'd get a byline. I enjoyed the work, especially getting bylines, and I came to like and respect Arnie, a man with a young family who did whatever he had to do to make ends meet. I started dating a Coney Island high school girl who was working in the newspaper's business office for the summer. This cut back on my already minimal sleep time but provided benefits to my self-esteem.

One evening, after the other Mike had left for the day, I was in the editorial office finishing up a couple of letters to the editor. Arnie was a few feet away, subbing for an absent linotype operator and casually listening to the police radio for news of any local burglaries, domestic quarrels, or car accidents that might give tomorrow's issue of the *Daily* more originality and local color. Suddenly, he jumped up from the machine and turned toward me, his eyes wide. He hollered, "Mike, there's just been a police shooting on the boardwalk. Go check it out." I grabbed a pad and ran down the steps to my car, a well-used 1954 Plymouth I'd bought with my parents' help at the beginning of the summer. I drove about three blocks down Surf Avenue before encountering a half-dozen police cars. I pulled over, jumped out of my car, crossed the street, and walked up behind a uniformed policeman who seemed to be peering around a corner. As I approached him, I noticed that he had his gun drawn. I backed off quickly and turned to an onlooker. "What's going on?"

"Some guy just walked up behind two cops on the boardwalk and shot them. I think he killed both of them. He's hiding behind a fire hydrant at the end of the street."

Crouched behind my car, I watched two police officers put on bulletproof vests, check their guns, and solemnly nod to each other. One of them motioned to another officer standing on the back of a flatbed truck. Suddenly, the far end of the street leading to the boardwalk was bathed in floodlights. Another solemn nod between the two police officers. Then, in a scene reminiscent of a cowboy shoot-out, they started toward the boardwalk, their guns drawn. When they got within range, they emptied their guns in the direction of the fire hydrant. The police-killer was dead within seconds.

After interviewing a couple of police officers at the scene, I drove to the local police station. When I arrived, an officer ran toward me to ask if I was hurt. He had mistaken rust holes in the side of my car for bullet holes. I assured him I was fine, asked a few questions, and returned to the *Daily*, where I breathlessly briefed Arnie. "Did you see any other reporters there?" he asked.

"I don't think so. It happened so fast, there was no time for anyone else to get there."

"Okay," he said. "Call the *Post* and tell them what you saw. You might get a bylined story out of it. Then, write it for us."

I did as he ordered, and the next day, in addition to the front-page story under a screaming headline in the *Daily*, I had a bylined eyewitness account on page three of the *New York Post*. It was the most excitement I'd ever experienced, and it fueled my attraction to journalism.

I was struggling, though, with what to do about college. My parents suggested taking night classes at Queens College part of the renowned City University of New York. Tuition was free. The only cost besides books was a twenty-four-dollar registration fee each semester. I dismissed their suggestion for most of the summer, feeling it would be a comedown from attending an Ivy League school. However, by the end of the summer, I had resigned myself to having no alternatives. So, buoyed by Arnie's invitation for me to continue working at the *Brooklyn Daily* on a full-time basis, I enrolled in night classes at Queens College in September 1961. It was a life-changing decision, although it took some time for me to recognize its significance.

Early in 1962, the major New York daily newspapers closed down due to a strike of linotype operators. But because the print shop that published the *Brooklyn Daily* and *The Jewish Press* primarily did commercial printing, its employees were covered by a different union contract. They were allowed to keep working. Suddenly, the *Brooklyn Daily* was the only newspaper operating in New York City. Arnie upped the press run to 300,000, hired a *New York Times Magazine* writer named Anthony Austin to run the news section, and appointed me as sports editor. He hired prominent *New York Post* sports columnist Maury Allen to work with me. Suddenly we were a real newspaper reporting real news. It was a heady experience. I had not yet turned twenty, and I was a colleague of Maury Allen.

I came alive overnight. I covered the 1961 NFL championship game between the New York Giants and the Green Bay Packers at Yankee Stadium on a day so cold that my hands were too numb to type the story of the game until hours after it ended. I covered the New York Mets in their first baseball game at the Polo Grounds in April of 1962. Sitting in the press box, I endured the barbs of cigar-chomping Ike Gellis, the *New York Post* sports editor. He was at the game in a nonworking capacity, and he made sure that everyone else in the press box knew that a major part of my job as a copy boy at the *Post* had been to get him coffee. And I covered the Madison Square Garden boxing match between Doug Jones and Cassius Clay, as Muhammad Ali was known then. But after the fight I was too intimidated by Clay's constant recitation, "I am the greatest," to ask him any questions.

During this time I got to know a young rabbi named Meir Kahane, the same Meir Kahane who later founded the Jewish Defense League, moved his family to Israel, became an extremely controversial political leader and member of the Knesset, and ultimately was assassinated for his anti-Arab political beliefs. Rabbi Kahane wrote for *The Jewish Press*, and we shared an office. He was an engaging man in his late twenties whose passion for baseball matched mine. When the newspaper strike hit and the *Brooklyn Daily* expanded, he asked for the opportunity to join Maury Allen and me writing sports, while continuing his primary responsibility to *The Jewish Press*. We saw each other five days a week, went to baseball games together, and became close friends.

We talked about everything. Whether the topic of discussion was the woeful Mets, an article one of us was writing, his wife and young children, his intense religious beliefs, or my future, he would pace the floor and wave his arms, finding release for his nervous energy by constantly lifting and replacing his yarmulke on his head. I had never before witnessed such constant and intense passion in an individual. More important to me, though, was his clarity about the importance of living his beliefs and refusing to shelter himself from whatever demands his beliefs placed on him. Occasionally, he'd be late leaving work on Friday, so he wouldn't be able to make it home before the beginning of the Sabbath at sundown. Rather than break Sabbath law, he would park his car on the shoulder of the busy Belt Parkway and walk the rest of the way home, sometimes five miles or more. The political views he began expressing long after we'd lost contact were abhorrent to me, but for a short time he was one of my best friends. He encouraged me to pursue my passion for sports while helping me to understand the unique opportunities with which I had been presented working at the *Brooklyn Daily* and going to school at Queens College.

My career path now seemed clear. I would be a sports writer. I had begun to love writing and I was pretty good at it, at least according to Arnie Fine, Meir Kahane, and Maury Allen. I'd had unique experiences and made connections in the profession. When the Dodgers had left town in 1957, I had renounced baseball forever. However, the Mets, notwithstanding their bumbling beginning, had rekindled my passion for baseball and sports in general. But I was soon to have two encounters that would change my path dramatically.

I met Dick Schaap, then the sports editor of *Newsweek Magazine* and later a prominent author and sports media personality. I shared with him my passion for sports writing, and he invited me to visit his office at *Newsweek* to talk about my plans. I took him up on his offer. But instead of telling me I had it made and offering me a job at *Newsweek*, he told me I had potential but that I needed to hone my skills in smaller markets, perhaps in the Midwest. I then could work my way back to New York City and its major newspapers. I was crushed. I thought I was too good to start out like anyone else, and the idea of leaving New York City seemed out of the question. I left his office discouraged and depressed.

Not long afterwards, I was walking through the halls of Queens College after a night class. I passed a room where twenty or thirty students were gathered. A young man about my age and stature was standing outside, and I asked him what was going on. "It's a meeting of the Queens College chapter of CORE, you know, the Congress of Racial Equality. Why don't you join us?" I hesitated. It was the spring of 1962, and I'd been reading and watching the reports about sit-ins and freedom rides and the brutality that protesters were encountering. I thought I should do something, but I didn't know what to do, and besides, I was caught up in my writing. I looked in the room and back at the young man. "I think I will." He stuck out his hand and smiled broadly. "Stan Shaw is my name. What's yours?"

By the time I bowed to reality and became a full-time Queens College student in the fall of 1962, the conflict between the courage and passion of young black people throughout the South with their minds "stayed on freedom" and the fear and fury of Southern whites intent on preserving their "southern way of life" had reached fever pitch. The sit-in movement was in full swing, with young men and women being harassed and beaten for simply sitting peacefully at a lunch counter waiting in vain to be served. Freedom riders had been brutally beaten. One of their buses had been burned in Alabama, and they had been arrested in Mississippi. Voter registration drives were underway in several southern communities. Battles over school integration were still going on in many southern towns. In Virginia, resistance to the *Brown* school desegregation decision of 1954 remained strong and had led to the policy of massive resistance in which public schools were closed rather than desegregated. In Prince Edward County, Virginia, public schools had been closed since June of 1959.

Queens College, whose predominantly white student body came mostly from Jewish immigrant and working-class families, had become a hotbed of civil rights activity. Parents of some students had survived the Holocaust and felt a deep, visceral commitment to justice; they had passed this on to their children. For some, the reaction of southern bigots was a reminder of the persecution that they had fled. If this could be happening to Negroes in the South, perhaps it could happen to Jews who got out of line. Other students, including myself, simply could not understand how a desire for basic human rights could generate such brutality. How could other human beings use police dogs, billy clubs, fire hoses, and cattle prods against peacefully protesting human beings who were practicing nonviolence? So, on a small, tree-lined campus in the heart of a bustling, growing, residential part of New York City, the children of these immigrants marched to protest the brutality in the South, conducted fund-raising drives to support the freedom riders and the lunch counter protestors, and arranged lectures and "teach-in" activities on campus to raise student awareness and implore the federal government to do more to support racial justice.

My sports writing gave way to articles in the school newspaper applauding the bravery of the southern protestors, imploring students to join our ranks, and decrying the actions of white southern leaders and the relative inaction of the Kennedy Administration. I became comfortable speaking in front of groups, and by the spring semester of 1963 I had become chair of the campus chapter of CORE. I succeeded Stan, who had quickly become my closest friend and remains so to this day. I felt a sense of belonging. I was among peers who came from the same economic background as I did. Their parents were city workers or police officers or struggling small business owners. Their political views may not have been as radical as those of my parents, but they shared a sense of being part of the political underclass. And while none of us could remotely understand what it meant to be as powerless as a Negro in the South, we shared the kind of connection that binds underdogs to each other.

Although we focused our attention primarily on what was happening in the South, we also began to emerge from the cocoons in which most of us had grown up and to look more critically at our own environment. CORE's faculty advisers, three members of the college's school of education, accelerated the process by challenging us to do more than just protest what was happening hundreds of miles away. If our commitment to justice was real, they told us, we needed to demonstrate that commitment in our own backyards, as well. Within a few miles from our campus was the predominantly black and low-income neighborhood of South Jamaica. Why not, they asked, devote our time and energy to helping the children of South Jamaica overcome some of the barriers they confronted in school? With the help of Dr. Rachel Weddington, one of our three advisers and one of the few African American faculty members at the time, we contacted the New York City Board of Education, which was happy to have our help. Thus was born the Student Help Project (SHP). Queens College students volunteered one afternoon or evening per week to tutor struggling students from the public schools of South Jamaica in reading and math. The Board of Education provided the materials, local public schools and churches provided the space and recruited the students, and Dr. Weddington and our other two faculty advisers, Dr. Sid Simon and Dr. Mickey Brody, both white, provided the training and support we needed.

The response on campus was enormous. Our initial call for volunteers brought applications from over a hundred students. Eventually, the SHP grew so large that it spun off from CORE as an independent project, with Stan as its first chair. As with CORE, I succeeded him as SHP chair. At SHP's height, 500 college student volunteers were tutoring approximately 1,200 elementary and junior high school students. Because the campus was overwhelmingly white, almost all the tutors were white, while virtually all of the youngsters we tutored were black. I spent so much time recruiting volunteers, planning training sessions, and working to locate venues for the tutoring that I did not tutor regularly. When I did, I was struck not only by the eagerness of the children, but also by the differences between their lives and mine. I lived in a comfortable single-family house in a quiet New York City suburb, had gone to public schools with the best facilities and equipment, and had taken vacations with my parents every summer. These children lived in small apartments in densely populated neighborhoods dominated by the noise of buses, subways, and police sirens, went to drab-looking schools with limited equipment, and rarely left the city because their parents did not have the money for such trips. It was my first experience in a predominantly black setting. I felt sorry for the youngsters we were tutoring and proud that we were doing something to help them. We were the "good white folks" nobly working to foster brotherhood and to improve society. We were not conscious of any problem with the leadership of the SHP being entirely white, nor were we conscious of any negative racial stereotyping in our efforts to prepare these "poor black kids" to successfully enter white society. But our consciousness was about to be jolted.

III

STEPPING OUT
OF MY COMFORT ZONE

For me and most of my white friends in 1963, life's journey proceeded on a straight track and a fixed schedule, from public school to college and on to the world of work, marriage, and family. We encountered few detours or delays, and those we did encounter were largely of our own making. Even our civil rights activities on campus were at arm's length from the civil rights activities in the South. But for four years, time stood still for black children in Prince Edward County, Virginia, because of massive resistance to school desegregation by white leaders. My friends and I would soon get a first-hand taste of the price being paid. In the process, we'd learn a lot more about the realities of race in this country.

We were feeling pretty noble about our campus activities, especially the Student Help Project, which was helping black youngsters in New York City who had been victimized by the intersection of race and poverty. Then, early in 1963, came a will-you-walk-the-talk question. Two Queens College students had heard about officials in Prince Edward County closing the public schools rather than desegregating them. The students approached Sid Simon, one of the faculty advisors, and asked what they could do. Dr. Simon posed the question to several of CORE's campus leaders: "Are you prepared to stand up for what you value?"

Among all the civil rights struggles of the 1950s and 1960s, Prince Edward County was unique. In 1951, black high school students had walked out *en masse* to protest the overcrowded and primitive conditions at all-black Robert R. Moton High School in Farmville, the county seat. The Reverend L. Francis Griffin, pastor of Farmville's First Baptist Church, defied the white power structure, as well as the fears of black parents, to support the students. The student walkout led NAACP attorney Thurgood Marshall to include the Prince Edward County School Board as one of the defendants in the *Brown v. Board of Education* case that yielded the Supreme Court's 1954 school desegregation decision. Five years later, in 1959, the Prince Edward County School Board, sticking to the state's massive resistance policy, closed the public schools in defiance of the *Brown* decision. Most white families sent their children to private academies that were established to perpetuate segregation. Black families rejected an offer of segregated academies for their children, and were left without access to county schools. Again, Reverend Griffin's leadership was critical in helping some parents find schools outside of the county, or in recruiting outside groups to work in the summers with the 1,700 remaining black children shut out of school. In 1963, the Reverend's considerable powers of persuasion inspired Attorney General Robert Kennedy's successful plea to the Ford Foundation to financially support the reopening of the schools as "free schools," open to all students. The free schools were due to open in the fall of 1963. Our role would be to get the children ready.

We were full of questions:

"What will we do with the children?" "Where will we teach them?" "What will we teach them?"

"Where will we live?" "What are the people of Prince Edward County like?" "Will it be dangerous?"

"Where will we get the money to do this?" "How can we convince our parents to let us go?"

Despite our anxiety, we did want to go. Ultimately, sixteen Queens College students (ten white females, five white males, and one African American female) and faculty advisor Dr. Rachel Weddington made up the Queens College contingent. We would be joined by a small contingent of teachers from the United Federation of Teachers, the New York City arm of the American Federation of Teachers. During the spring semester of 1963, under the guidance of Drs. Weddington, Simon, Brody, and other faculty supporters, we prepared materials for our summer work. With the help of these same faculty supporters, we tried to allay the fears of our parents. My parents, who hid their fear quite well, called other parents to encourage them to let their sons or daughters go. We raised money from family and friends, and toward the end of the semester, with the help of one mother who had entertainment industry connections, we sponsored a fund-raising concert at Carnegie Hall featuring Dick Gregory, Quincy Jones, and Clark Terry, among others. Mr. Gregory caused some anxiety by arriving about an hour late, but he regaled the packed house with his biting brand of humor well into the evening. We raised $7,000 to cover our living expenses and to purchase a truckload of books for the black children of the county. Press promotion for the concert sparked the interest of *Look* magazine, which assigned a writer and photographer to accompany us to Prince Edward County for the first few days. This was to be the cover story for the July 1963 issue, but it was ultimately bumped by a story about the Vietnam War, and never appeared.

As the summer drew near, we went through intensive training designed to introduce us to the conditions we would be confronting. This included seminars, assigned reading, lesson planning, and role-playing for potentially dangerous situations. We would be living in groups of two, three, or four, with black families who were taking a huge risk by housing us for the summer. We would teach in churches, many of them located in isolated, rural areas of the tobacco-growing county. We would be working with children who, for the most part, had not seen the inside of a school for four years. Some children as old as 10 had never been in school at all, nor read a book, or even held a pencil. In consultation with our faculty advisors, we developed a set of rules to govern our summer behavior. We would not travel alone, or go out at night, or shop in the white part of town, or do anything to call attention to ourselves—as if a group of white students from New York City could blend into Prince Edward County culture. We would not respond to threats or violence from white people, many of whom would view us as outside agitators, and we would not participate in demonstrations. We were warned that although field workers for the Student Nonviolent Coordinating Committee (SNCC) would be training Prince Edward County teenagers in preparation for marches and sit-ins in downtown Farmville, our job was to teach. Only local teenagers were to demonstrate.

Finally, apprehensive but feeling noble and full of excitement, sixteen Queens College students, accompanied by one savvy faculty advisor-mentor, set out early one sunny morning in July 1963 for the ten-hour trip to Prince Edward County. Most of us traveled in cars, including my beat-up Plymouth and Dr. Weddington's Opal, in groups of two or three. Five of the students traveled by bus, and we met them in Richmond for the final hour of the trip southwest. Farmville was a town of about 10,000 that served as the shopping hub for the entire county. Our arrival generated little hostile comment from the white community. As long as we stuck to teaching, an editorial in the *Farmville Herald* advised, we would be tolerated. We experienced some tense moments, but we were not nearly as threatening to the county's way of life as the young people from SNCC were. After all, who could argue with the mission to teach children? In fact, many in the white community felt that our presence helped to relieve them of the onus of having closed the public schools. Although we wanted to demonstrate, we adhered to our rules. We did not want to compromise our mission, or make life even more difficult for our host families, nor to taint the local nature of the demonstrations.

We learned three important lessons that summer. First, we learned that black people welcomed our help, but they didn't need our leadership. For the first time in our experience, white people did not control the situation or dictate action. Reverend Griffin and Dr. Weddington guided our summer activities and helped us enforce our own rules. Most of us had never before been in the minority, but our white arrogance quickly disappeared in the face of the potential dangers we faced. Second, we learned that Jim Crow racism, ranging from economic and political oppression to physical intimidation, had taken a toll on both black people and white people in the South that would leave a legacy for generations. None of us except for Dr. Weddington and Carolyn, the lone African American student among us, had ever felt the searing pain of racism, nor had we grasped how entrenched and far-reaching racial oppression was. Because the oppressors looked like us, some of us began to cringe at our own skin color. We felt the sting of every insult, every threat, and every action designed to keep our newfound friends "in their place." Change now seemed far more complicated and difficult than it had from over 500 miles away in the northeast.

Third, we learned that the movement for integration in the South was not characterized by poor, victimized black people trying to grab a few crumbs from the white man's pie. It was driven by people of enormous strength and courage who were confronting people of high privilege, deep hatred, and consuming fear, and doing so under the kind of life-threatening conditions that might have crushed most people. The black families with whom we stayed had put their livelihoods and their safety at risk by agreeing to house us. Teaching children was one thing, but black people and white people living together was quite another. The power of white people to perpetuate violence and cut off jobs and credit without explanation loomed large. In the face of such threats, these families demonstrated a level of courage that was beyond our comprehension. We could and would leave at the end of the summer. They would remain to face the consequences of our temporary presence, without the protection of whatever national attention our presence had created.

I and Mark Blumberg, a quiet student who had been on the periphery of campus civil rights activities, stayed with Maude Watkins, a gray-haired woman in her fifties. Mrs. Watkins lived with her husband, grown son, and preadolescent granddaughter in a well-kept six-room home across the street from a car repair shop and two blocks from downtown. As in all the black homes we saw, pictures of Jesus Christ and Martin Luther King Jr. were featured in the living room. A porch with room for six chairs faced the shop, and we used it often in the evenings. Both Mrs. Watkins' husband and son had menial factory jobs, while she ran the home. We slept on comfortable couches in the living room and were fawned over by everyone in the family. The other fourteen students and Dr. Weddington had similarly comfortable living situations, most within walking distance of downtown.

Our routine was simple. We were out of the house by 8:30 a.m. to drive to our assigned churches. I was assigned to the St. James African Methodist Episcopal (AME) Church in Prospect. It was a simple old wooden structure desperately in need of paint, situated in a wooded area just off an old country road about ten miles from town. The inside consisted of a chapel and a basement. Four classes met in the basement. I taught a group of about ten teenagers—eight girls and two boys—in one corner. It was summer, and it was hot. But every morning, my ten students, all children of sharecroppers, would be waiting for me when I arrived a few minutes before 9 a.m. We worked mostly on reading comprehension. I tried to plan for a week at a time, but they were so diligent about their assignments that we'd run through the entire week's lessons in three days and spend Thursdays and Fridays talking about current events. They were intensely curious about what our lives were like, why we were there, and what New York was like. Some wanted to join the demonstrations in town, but their parents were afraid to let them. The conversations ended when lunch, which was prepared by local families, arrived at noon. From 1 p.m. to 4 p.m. we organized supervised recreational activities. We were back home by 4:30 p.m. Dinner was at 5:30 p.m., and evenings, for the most part, were spent on the porch or in front of the television. Wednesday was church night, and we usually went as a group to Reverend Griffin's church, although some chose to go to the Beulah AME church across the street, which was pastored by a recently arrived, dynamic young minister named Goodwin ("Goody") Douglas. He was the one who had invited the SNCC organizers to Farmville. Except for Sunday morning church service, weekends belonged to us, and we read, shopped, wrote letters, and spent time talking with each other and with the families with whom we were living.

Just around the corner, Carolyn and Dr. Weddington lived with the Parker family. Because the Parker home was larger than the Watkins' home and had a bigger television, I occasionally watched television over there. One night, a commercial came on for the newest sensation: flesh-colored Band-Aids, replacing the sheet-white Band-Aids that had been standard until then. I'd seen the commercial in previous months in the comfort of my New York home, but I'd never given it a second thought, other than to think how nice it would be to have Band-Aids that didn't advertise your injury. But on that sweltering July evening, I felt an intense discomfort that had nothing to do with the temperature. Those Band-Aids matched my skin, but they were a stark contrast to the darker skin colors of the other Americans sitting in the Parker living room. Nobody said anything, but for me it was a stunning realization of my privilege as a white-skinned American, and of the humiliating invisibility of black Americans, apart from the daily oppression they suffered.

Recently, as I began to write about this "aha" moment in my education about race, I reflected with some satisfaction that things like flesh-colored Band-Aids are no longer an issue. A few days later, I shared this satisfaction with a friend, a white woman who is a social worker. She promptly recounted the story of an African American client who recently had lost a leg in Iraq and was unable to obtain a prosthetic that matched his skin color. "Things haven't changed as much as you think," she declared.

One Saturday, five of us, all white, decided to see the sights in Richmond. Except for our New York license plates, we attracted little attention. We strolled around the capitol grounds and window-shopped downtown, although we had resolved not to do any actual shopping because of the discriminatory hiring practices of virtually all Richmond stores. We were driving back in the late afternoon—we had been warned to be back before the sun went down—when one of the girls with us had to use the restroom. So, we pulled into a gas station, and she got out and went around to the back to use the facilities. She immediately reappeared, clearly agitated.

"What happened?" the other four of us inquired in unison.

"Nothing," she replied. "But it had a 'White women only' sign on it, and we pledged not to use any facilities that Negroes can't use."

"But—" someone stammered.

"But, nothing," she quickly interjected. "We made that pledge, and we're sticking to it."

She remained in some discomfort for the remainder of the trip back to Farmville. But she had a choice. Few lessons about Jim Crow could have been more personal or vivid.

By midsummer, the demonstrations in downtown Farmville were in full bloom. On one Wednesday morning, several teenage demonstrators were arrested. Reverend Griffin, concerned for their safety if they had to remain in jail overnight, decided to act quickly. He sent word for us to urge parents to come to church in Farmville that evening for an important meeting. At 7 p.m., with the church packed, Reverend Griffin began preaching. He was a big man with a booming voice and a deep southern drawl, and he could deliver a powerful message. We listened as he launched into a sermon about living a Christian life, having faith in the Lord, and expecting that the next life would redeem the suffering of this life. As he warmed to the task, he exhorted us to seek fair treatment and equality in this life. His preaching reached a crescendo when he decried the arrest of the teenagers for seeking justice through peaceful protest. People who had initially been anxious were now shouting "Amen!" and "Praise the Lord!" Then, having sufficiently whipped up the emotions of the congregation, Reverend Griffin, still preaching, stepped down from the pulpit and nodded for us to follow him as he strode up the center aisle of the sanctuary. Instantly, the entire church was up and out of their pews, and with Reverend Griffin in the lead, we all marched right out of the church and down the street to the courthouse, singing, "We Shall Overcome," "Oh, Freedom," and "This Little Light of Mine." The teenagers were released unharmed within a few hours, and I, having come from a family of atheists and agnostics, was introduced to the power of the church.

The most dangerous incident we experienced was of our own making. One night, seven of us, including Carolyn, Dr. Weddington, and Reverend "Goody" Douglas, felt the need for some refreshments. Having made a commitment not to shop in any boycotted store in town, we drove out to the Tastee Freez just beyond the town limits. We parked our two cars in the gravel area to one side of the small drive-in and headed for the ordering window. We were in the process of ordering when a car with three white teenagers drove up and parked alongside our cars. A few seconds later, a second car with three more white teenagers pulled up and parked alongside the first one. We'd been warned: don't go out at night, be especially careful when going out in an integrated group, always tell someone else where you're going. But after a month of no real trouble, we'd become complacent.

That night we had violated all three rules, and there we were, out after dark on a country road three miles out of town, with the Tastee Freez and a gas station across the road representing the only visible civilization. We forgot about ice cream and eased slowly toward our cars. Before we got very far, we were surrounded by the white teenagers muttering racial epithets. We froze, and our fear seemed to give the white teenagers courage. One of them kicked the young reverend in his calf. A black man in the company of white girls, he was a natural target. He stood his ground impassively. After what seemed like an eternity but was probably only a few seconds, Dr. Weddington started to stride purposefully toward our cars, and motioned to the rest of us to follow. I don't know whether it was the determination in her walk or the fire in her eyes, but the circle of white teenagers parted, and we fell in right behind her, got into our cars, and headed straight for Reverend Douglas's parsonage on the main street of Farmville. The white teenagers followed. Reverend Douglas immediately called the police station about half a block away, and then Reverend Griffin, who lived about a mile away. Griffin arrived within five minutes. Meanwhile, a police car drove back and forth past Reverend Douglas's house for about ninety minutes, observing the white teenagers as they drove back and forth past the house at the same time. Finally, the police car stopped in front and two officers ambled up the steps to take our statements. They stayed for about five minutes and warned us to stay out of trouble. We never heard anything further about the incident.

None of us slept very well that night, and none of us ever left Farmville again after dark. What strikes me now is the relative ease with which those of us who are white were able to put the incident behind us. We had grown up thinking that policemen were our friends. In times of trouble they were our source of safety and security. In a few weeks, we would return home to that environment and expunge this experience from our minds. But black people in Prince Edward County would continue to face such dangers whenever they crossed the line of "acceptable" behavior. For them, the safety and security we took for granted did not exist. I can't speak for the other white members of our group, but as conscious as I had become of the challenges faced by the black people of Prince Edward County, it never occurred to me that Dr. Weddington and Carolyn confronted similar humiliations wherever they went, North or South. It was years later, after I'd been married to a black woman and had black children, that I came face to face with that reality.

Our plan was to attend the March on Washington on August 28 as part of the Prince Edward County contingent, and then to head home to New York. Our last task of the summer was to clean up Moton High School and make it ready for its opening in September. We knew the school had been padlocked since the last day of the 1958-59 school year, but still we were not prepared for what we found. It seemed not a single person had entered the school in the intervening period. Dust covered our shoes. Rodent droppings were evident. Papers were strewn on desks and trash cans were full, apparently exactly as they'd been left four years earlier. I walked into a classroom and saw a calendar on the teacher's desk opened to the day the school had closed in June 1959. It was a *Twilight Zone* experience.

We headed to D.C. with plans to meet the buses from Prince Edward County at the foot of the Washington Monument on the morning of the twenty-eighth. In the crush of people, it's doubtful we would have found them. However, on the bus ride from Farmville, Reverend Douglas had taught the young people an upbeat version of "We Shall Overcome," and as we approached the monument, it was that unique version of the civil rights anthem that caught our attention and led us to the group and the "Swingin' Rev." We listened together to the music of Pete Seeger, Joan Baez, and Peter, Paul and Mary. Then we marched in a sea of people of all skin colors toward the reflecting pool, and sat in the shadow of the Lincoln Memorial as we listened to speeches by SNCC leader John Lewis, United Auto Workers leader Walter Reuther, Rabbi Joachim Prinz, NAACP leader Roy Wilkins, civil rights icon A. Philip Randolph, and of course, to the "I Have a Dream" speech by Dr. Martin Luther King Jr. Some in the group, including Stan, met with Senator Jacob Javits (R-NY), who commended the work that we'd done. (It is worth noting that moderate, so-called Rockefeller Republicans like then-Senator Javits are virtually extinct in today's Republican Party.)

As we headed for home, our neat vision of the world and our plans for the rest of our lives had been forever altered. We would no longer be so smug about our own virtue. Our arrogance had been permanently muted. On the other hand, our passion had intensified. The sting of racism now had a more personal feel to it, and it became difficult to identify with white people anywhere who were not actively engaged in the struggle. We had gotten a very small taste of the routine economic and physical intimidations used to keep the "southern way of life" in place, of the humiliating deference demanded of black men and women to keep their jobs, and in many cases, their lives. I recognize now that many white southerners were unhappy with the system, but felt powerless to change it. At the time, however, I was incapable of understanding that distinction. We had begun to recognize the privilege we enjoyed because of our skin color, and to understand that the legacy of racism would not be wiped out in a generation or two; the struggle would likely go on well beyond our lifetimes.

As we reflected on Dr. King's assertions that "there will be neither rest nor tranquility in America until the Negro is granted his citizenship rights," and that "the whirlwinds of revolt will continue to shake the foundations of our nation until the bright day of justice emerges," we had a new appreciation for the courage of a people who had learned to survive under intensely oppressive conditions and who were unwilling to accept those conditions any longer. At the same time, we were sobered by the fact that we'd left behind nine- and ten-year-old children who could not read, write, or count, and teenagers who had seen their high school years evaporate and their futures stolen from them. The price they paid for the inhuman behavior of their white neighbors is incalculable. In many cases, their children have also paid a price, seared by the indelible scars their parents bear from the childhood experiences that irreversibly detoured their lives. It is testimony to their uncommon strength that so many have been able to navigate those detours so successfully.

We returned to campus in September 1963, energized and excited. The peaceful gathering of more than 250,000 people for the March on Washington and the speeches from the steps of the Lincoln Memorial had been the inspiring culmination of a life-changing summer. In a matter of weeks, however, we were once again confronted with the ferocity of hate and the violence it spawned. On September 15, the Sixteenth Street Baptist

Church in Birmingham, Alabama, was bombed. Four teenage girls attending Sunday School classes were killed by 122 sticks of dynamite planted outside the church basement. Nonviolent demonstrations by African Americans in Birmingham ensued and were met by local authorities with police dogs, fire hoses streaming high-pressure water that could tear the bark off a tree, electric cattle prods, and police billy clubs. We were horrified, but from several hundred miles away, we didn't know what we could do.

Several of us had registered for Sid Simon's Education I class that semester. Sid, as he liked to be called, had a particularly sunny disposition under almost any circumstances and a strong interest in the lives of his students. He often invited students to weekend cookouts with his family on the beach near his Lido Beach home. His Monday morning classes usually began with a discussion of whether our weekend activities had been purposeful. But one Monday morning, after the weekend television newscasts had been filled with pictures of police violence against young demonstrators, the smile and warm "good morning" were missing when Sid entered the classroom. He strode purposefully to the front, picked up a heavy book from the desk, raised it high above his head, paused for an instant as he looked at our puzzled expressions, and then, with all the force he could muster, slammed it down on the desk. He gave us time to gather ourselves, and then he simply said, "That's the sound of a police billy club on a child's head. Now, what are you going to do about it?"

During that semester he taught us seven criteria by which to measure the true depth of our commitment to our principles, criteria we could use to gauge whether our expressed belief in freedom and justice was truly an immutable and enduring value or whether it vanished when it meant disrupting our lives. The first three criteria related to choice:

Was your belief chosen from among alternatives?

Was it chosen after careful consideration of the consequences of each alternative?

And was it freely chosen, without peer pressure or other forms of pressure?

These did not seem difficult criteria to meet. We believed in freedom and justice for all. The alternatives, allowing injustice to continue to flourish, or accepting the gradualism advocated by many in the South, were unacceptable. We understood the consequences of each of the alternatives, and after careful consideration, we freely chose to believe that freedom and justice for all our citizens were essential elements of the kind of society in which we wanted to live.

The fourth and fifth criteria did not unduly challenge us either:

Do you prize and cherish your choice?

Are you willing to publicly affirm your choice?

Most of us clearly prized and cherished the ideals of freedom and justice for all, and we were certainly willing to publicly affirm this belief. We did so when we marched, when we wrote letters to the editor, and when we engaged in fund-raising activities.

The sixth and seventh criteria, however, demanded more from us and challenged the depth of our commitment:

Do you act upon your choice?

Do you act upon your choice repeatedly, over time, making it a pattern in your life?

Certainly, we had acted on our choice when we started the Student Help Project in South Jamaica and when we spent six weeks in Prince Edward County. But Sid was telling us that this wasn't enough. If our commitment to freedom and justice was truly a deeply held value, we had to act repeatedly over time, incorporating our commitment into our everyday activities. It was not enough to shout our beliefs from the rooftops or even to act on our commitment occasionally. We had to be willing to step out of our comfort zone on a regular basis to back up our words. At its core, it was an issue of moral integrity.

Sid's demonstration of the sound of a police-wielded billy club on a child's head shook us out of any sense of self-satisfaction we might have felt after our summer in Prince Edward County.

We intensified our activities as we sought to generate wider and stronger support for the civil rights movement among students, and to raise their awareness of the persistent double standard with which our society viewed the value of a human life.

Then came the November 22 assassination of President Kennedy in Dallas, Texas. It was an event so stunning and bewildering in its magnitude that it temporarily immobilized us. We had been disappointed by JFK's moderate attitude toward civil rights, particularly his lukewarm endorsement of the March on Washington, but he had seemed to rise to the occasion when circumstances demanded it. Despite our disappointment, we had remained inspired by his inaugural speech in which he had urged us, "Ask not what your country can do for you, ask what you can do for your country." As we watched a tearful Walter Cronkite report that President Kennedy had died, and Lyndon Johnson somberly take the oath of office while a blood-stained Jacqueline Kennedy looked on, Stan and I looked at each other. Was this the end of the civil rights movement? Were the sacrifices that had been made, the beatings that had been endured, and the lives that had been lost by black people throughout the South all in vain? Would massive resistance win the day? The weeks following the assassination were consumed with soul-searching discussions about the future of the civil rights movement and the future of our own activities. Gradually, though, encouraged by President Johnson's apparent embrace of the goals of the civil rights movement, we resumed our activities. Our Prince Edward County experience strengthened our resolve, and for many of us, gave the struggle a more personal meaning. We knew and now counted as friends some of the people who were being so grievously devalued and mistreated. Abandoning the struggle was not an option.

In the spring of 1964, we met with a group of Queens College students who were planning to spend the summer registering black voters in Mississippi. They had volunteered for the SNCC-inspired Mississippi Freedom Summer, and they were anxious to hear from others who'd been in the South. We shared our Prince Edward County experiences and what we'd learned from them. One of the students was Andy Goodman. Less than two months later, Andy, Michael Schwerner, a social worker from New York City whose wife was a Queens College student, and James Chaney, a young black man from Mississippi, were brutally murdered near Philadelphia, Mississippi, with the complicity of at least two law enforcement officials. They had been visiting the site of a burned-out black church, and in midafternoon they had been arrested for allegedly speeding. They were released and ordered to leave town at about 10 p.m., but then were ambushed, beaten, and shot by several carloads of Ku Klux Klan members. The deaths of Goodman and Schwerner, unlike the countless deaths of black people engaged in similar work, sparked a firestorm across the country. During the five weeks from the time they disappeared on June 21 to the discovery of their bodies buried in an earthen dam, the newspapers were filled with stories about the search for their bodies, a search which ironically turned up the bodies of several black men who'd been missing for varying lengths of time. Although some southern leaders insisted that the disappearance was a trick to gain sympathy, President Johnson expressed his outrage, as did many prominent political figures across the country. The FBI presence in Mississippi increased dramatically. And while the perpetrators were acquitted of the murders by a jury of their peers, several were eventually prosecuted and convicted in federal court of violating the civil rights of the three men, and they served prison terms.

I'd been scared initially about going to Prince Edward County. I had worried about being verbally assaulted, threatened, even physically beaten. But any thought of not coming back alive had been buried beneath layers of privilege and self-protective denial. They wouldn't dare kill a white student from the North, I reasoned, knowing instinctively the national firestorm it would ignite. I'd allowed myself to feel the same way about the students going to Mississippi. Now these layers of denial had been ripped open. What were they feeling when their car was stopped? Did they try to reason with the murderers as they were being tortured?

When did they know they were about to die? What had their last few minutes been like? What if I'd been there?

Because Andy had been a Queens College student, we organized fund-raising activities to support Mississippi Freedom Summer and publicly demanded that President Johnson send federal troops to Mississippi to protect civil rights workers. To publicize our efforts, seven Queens College students launched a five-day hunger strike that drew the attention of the *New York Times* and local television stations. I was one of the seven, along with Gary Ackerman, editor of a student newspaper (and since 1984 a member of Congress from New York), and Ron Pollack, newly elected student body president (and now head of Families USA, one of the foremost consumer advocates for access to quality health care for all Americans). My mother encouraged our protests and brought us food when we decided to end the fast. My father, uncomfortable expressing his pride directly, looked me up and down when my mother and I returned from the church basement where we'd stayed for the fast. "My God, he's got no ass," he laughed. The tone of his voice made it clear he was proud of what I was doing.

In subsequent months we organized a Freedom Week teach-in on campus, staged a march to the New York City World's Fair to protest city and state spending priorities, and stepped up efforts to expand our tutoring project in South Jamaica. We hosted a fund-raising visit from Aaron Henry, head of the Mississippi Freedom Democratic Party, and I felt particularly proud that he stayed at our house during his visit. My parents organized a fund-raising event at my old high school in support of our activities. Hundreds of people, almost all white, packed the auditorium for the event, which was headlined by well-known actor Ossie Davis. Both I and Andy Goodman's devastated father spoke at the event. In my brief speech I declared, "As long as conditions in the South remain as they are, as long as black people in the South cannot vote, cannot be served at a lunch counter, and are not free to pursue their dreams and aspirations, the memory of Goodman, Schwerner, and Chaney will live on." The morning after the event, I awoke to find that the windshield of my car had been shattered, an act of vandalism perhaps associated with my activities. Rather than deter me, it stiffened my resolve.

These and hundreds of other activities in communities across the country were precipitated by the deaths of the two young white men. The lynching of thousands of black men and women, the deaths of four girls in the Birmingham church bombing, and the murder of Emmett Till, Mississippi NAACP President Medgar Evers, and countless other black people in the South had yielded little more than a tepid peep from a complacent nation. The killing of two white men had evoked a collective national scream. The message was not subtle. Even among well-meaning, sincere, and justice-conscious white people, a black life was important, but a white life was absolutely precious.

Notwithstanding the searing anger that drove us in the following months, and the fear that the anger masked—it could have been any one of us buried in that earthen dam—it was not until fourteen years later that I really understood how deeply I'd been affected, how time had stood still for me. In September 1978, I and two of our children, Ian and Regina, drove from our home in Charleston, West Virginia, to drop Regina off for her senior year in high school at Boggs Academy, near Augusta, Georgia. After I made sure that she was settled, I headed with Ian, not quite six years old, from Augusta to New Orleans to visit my sister and brother-in-law. The trip through Georgia and Alabama on a sunny, late summer day was uneventful. But as we approached Mississippi, I began to feel tense. It seemed like a lifetime since the murders of the three young men, but the thought of driving through Mississippi with a black child terrified me. What if we were stopped by the state police? What if some Klan member saw us and decided to teach us a lesson? I told myself I was being irrational, that attitudes certainly had changed. Such things didn't happen anymore. But I couldn't stop my stomach from doing flip-flops or my hands from sliding on the steering wheel, wet with sweat.

We stopped at a busy service station in west Alabama, and I insisted that Ian go to the bathroom despite his protestations that he didn't have to go. I was determined not to stop for any reason once we crossed the state line. When he asked if we could stop to get something to eat, I told him no. I wanted to get through Mississippi during daylight. When we crossed into Mississippi, I directed him to keep his head down so he wouldn't be easily visible. When he asked why, with a scared and puzzled look, I curtly answered that I'd tell him later. From the moment we crossed from Alabama into Mississippi to the moment we crossed from Mississippi into Louisiana, I drove not a single mile over the speed limit, and I kept the car firmly anchored in the right lane of Interstate 20. It was not until we were several miles into Louisiana that I took a deep breath and began to feel my stomach settle down. I tried to explain to Ian that some people didn't like the idea of a white man and a black child together, to which he innocently responded, "But you're my daddy." I had no response for him.

IV

A Winding Road
In "Almost Heaven"

Because of my two lost years at Cornell, I was in college on the six-year plan and expected to graduate in May 1965. Most of my friends, Stan Shaw and Ron Pollack among them, were planning to graduate at the same time. Ron was going on to law school at New York University, but Stan and I, shaped by Rachel Weddington and Sid Simon, felt called to teaching. Prior to graduation, both of us were hired for the fall of 1965 by the South Huntington, Long Island, School District to teach in an expanded junior high school special education program. We'd be teaching in different schools, but in the same district and the same program. We were excited about working together, and teaching youngsters who needed special help seemed a logical extension of our college activities. We began our lesson planning even before graduation.

But as graduation time approached, I realized I needed six additional credits to graduate. I had misunderstood the foreign language requirement and was one Spanish course short. I had also flunked or withdrawn from the mandated art appreciation course four times. The content was not beyond my capacity, but the course, offered in the late afternoon, consisted primarily of a lecturer showing a series of slides in a darkened auditorium while explaining the significance of each. I attended fairly regularly for the first few weeks each time I took the course, but when the lights went down, my eyes closed and I would make up for many lost hours of sleep. So, in the summer of 1965, with my teaching job hanging in the balance, I had to take and pass an advanced Spanish class and an art appreciation class. Gone was the sense of excitement and purpose brought on by our campus activities and the Prince Edward County experience. Instead, I was confronted by two classes in which I had little interest. I struggled through that summer, reading Spanish short stories, one challenging word after another, and, with apologies to art aficionados, trying to keep my eyes open through every mind-numbing art appreciation lecture. Less than a month before I was to begin teaching, I passed both final exams. Finally, I had a BA degree with a major in political science and a minor in education. "It's about time," my father chided me with just the hint of a smile.

College had been a unique experience. We'd been visible, vocal, and vigorous in our civil rights activities. We had engaged thousands of fellow students in these activities. And we had been recognized for our achievements by the local B'nai B'rith, which honored Stan and me with its human relations award. We'd had lighter moments, as well. Stan and I frequently double-dated or shot pool in his basement, sometimes joined by his two younger brothers. Occasionally, we'd spend time listening to music at Ron's house, frequently interrupted by his German immigrant father, who loved to stick his head into Ron's room with his stock question as a prelude to a joke he thought was funny: "Have you heard this one?" Because my parents lived further away from Queens College, we spent less time at my house. But the time we did spend there was usually filled with discussions of the latest incident in the civil rights struggle or the latest political event. Our years at Queens College had changed our lives, and we were eager for the challenges ahead. Long forgotten was my reluctance to attend Queens College or my vision of a sports writing career.

But, as with my failed attempt at civil engineering and my aborted pursuit of a sports writing career, teaching did not turn out quite as I had expected. One experience late that summer set the tone for the year. Several days before school started, Stan and

I drove out to South Huntington to familiarize ourselves with the schools in which we'd be teaching. Workmen were renovating the cafeteria in my school, and as we walked past, one of them shouted at us, "No students allowed until school opens." At five-foot-six, 140 pounds and sporting a crew cut, I knew I was young-looking. Nonetheless, I'd been a "big man" on campus. Now I was being mistaken for a junior high school student. I was devastated.

My first adult job became a nightmare. I could not control my class of seventh- and eighth-grade slow learners (all white). I imagined that to them, I didn't look much older than they were. When they tested me by talking in class or not following directions, I tried to reason with them. But they needed structure and discipline, neither of which I felt confident enough to provide. Furthermore, I was bored teaching English and social studies at simplified levels, and they sensed my boredom, which made them more unruly. Stan had considerably more success in the classroom than I did. At the end of that first year, he got married (I was his best man) and moved west to teach and attend graduate school at the University of Northern Colorado. Although I visited him and Wilma once in Boulder, we soon lost touch (in that pre-computer age) and did not reconnect until a rare coincidence brought us back together nearly a decade later. Today, he is a professor emeritus of special education at the University of Connecticut, where he has taught undergraduate and graduate students for more than thirty-five years, authored several textbooks, and become a nationally recognized leader in the field of teaching children with disabilities.

I left South Huntington and took a job teaching American history to slow learners (again all white) at Yorktown Heights High School in Westchester County, New York. I thought that perhaps high school students would be easier to teach. I rented an apartment in the charming village of Crompond, which featured its own lake, got a summer job mentoring an all-black group of disadvantaged youngsters from Harlem, and prepared for a fresh start. The summer was rewarding. The other mentors and I played ball with the youngsters, tutored them in English and social studies, and took them to places most of them had never been, such as the Bronx Zoo, the Museum of Natural History, and a Broadway show. They were excited by their new experiences, and I was excited by their excitement. By the end of the summer I felt we had made a real difference in their lives, and I was feeling newly energized as the school term began.

But the fresh start quickly disintegrated into another nightmarish experience. Again, I couldn't control my classes, and I was bored. Furthermore, unlike the youngsters in South Huntington, who had low IQ scores, I felt these youngsters were bright, but had been tracked into slow-learner classes largely because they had behavioral problems. They needed the hand of a strong disciplinarian who could also raise their self-esteem and their expectations for themselves. I tried to treat them with respect, but I was not a strong disciplinarian, and though I tried to hide my boredom, these youngsters perceived my lack of enthusiasm. Complicating the situation, I did not get along well with my two colleagues in the department, a woman who'd been teaching special education at the same school for over twenty-five years and a middle-aged man returning to teaching after a mediocre corporate career. I found her rigid and condescending, and he seemed insecure and disinterested. I'm sure they both considered me arrogant and incompetent, which may not have been far from the truth.

I searched desperately for ways to recapture the excitement and fulfillment of my college days and of the summer that had just ended. Touting my journalism experience, I persuaded the principal, a kind man who coincidentally had grown up in Woodmere prior to the influx of Brooklyn transplants, to appoint me as faculty advisor to the senior yearbook staff. I became friendly with a young social studies teacher who invited me to co-teach his honors current events class during my free period. Several of the students in the class were on the yearbook staff. I taught them Sid Simon's seven criteria for a value, and we discussed and debated contemporary issues from civil rights to the Vietnam

War. I began to look forward to this daily diversion from the grind of my regular teaching responsibilities. A month later, I became friendly with a French teacher who was the faculty advisor to the drama club. He lived about a block from my apartment in Crompond, and we spent evenings at his apartment listening to music and watching television. On occasional Saturdays, we'd make the hour-long drive into New York City to see a Broadway play. He invited me to help him direct the senior play, which offered me another diversion from the job for which I actually was being paid.

A couple of these diversions led to an experience that helped me recapture some of the excitement I sought. Two girls on the yearbook staff, who also were in the honors class and on the debate team, asked me if I'd support an invitation to Pete Seeger to give a concert at Yorktown High School. The legendary folk singer, a hero to me because of his willingness, at considerable personal sacrifice, to lend his voice to the cause of social justice, lived in nearby Beacon, New York. With some of his most prominent protest songs spinning in my head ("Little Boxes," "If I Had a Hammer"), I enthusiastically agreed. The board of education approved the request, Pete accepted the invitation, and the concert was set for February 1967.

To my surprise, the impending concert created a firestorm of protest. Calls to the school principal and letters to the editor of the local newspaper charged that Pete was a communist sympathizer and would be a dangerous influence on malleable young minds. Demands to cancel the concert swirled about, and a few veteran teachers pilloried me verbally as a thoughtless young radical who had created a controversy that could cost them salary increases. The protests became so intense that the board of education called a special meeting to hear all views. It lasted into the wee hours of the morning. I and several other faculty members spoke in support of the invitation as a free speech issue and as a way of exposing students to controversial thought so they could learn to think for themselves. We were vastly outnumbered by those who demanded that the invitation be withdrawn and that the teacher allegedly responsible for the invitation—me—be fired. Following six hours of often heated debate, the board, to my great relief, reaffirmed its approval of the invitation. On the night of the concert, despite heavy rain and a small band of water-logged protestors, the auditorium was packed. One of the girls who had issued the invitation came on stage to introduce Pete. Pete, who had called the girls regularly during the controversy to offer moral support, ambled onto the stage to thunderous applause, banjo and twelve-string guitar in hand. Without a word, he tuned his guitar and then launched into a moving rendition of "America the Beautiful." The response was electric, as was the entire concert. In the afterglow of that evening, I recalled Sid Simon's seven criteria for a value and felt proud that I'd supported and encouraged the students.

However, I had been stamped in the minds of a few conservative community activists as a left-wing activist and a danger to the students. Race was not the issue; it was primarily the fear of communism, a remnant of the McCarthy era of the 1950s. The controversy became ludicrous when a letter to the editor of the local newspaper charged that the yearbook staff's choice of a red cover for the yearbook confirmed that I had succeeded in turning the students into unwitting communist fellow travelers. Senator Joe McCarthy had died ten years earlier, in 1957, and McCarthyism had faded as an issue. But the fear it had engendered in decent people had not fully disappeared. Today, I shudder at the bizarre charges some have made that President Obama is foreign-born and a Muslim and is leading us into socialism. They are a stark reminder of the McCarthy era and the dangers that still lurk.

The controversy whetted my appetite for something other than teaching. At a subsequent party, I ran into Steve Kramer, another former Queens College student who had become a VISTA (Volunteers in Service to America) volunteer in the anti-poverty program in southern West Virginia's coal fields. He suggested I join him in organizing poor, predominantly white people in Appalachia who he claimed were as exploited and oppressed as black people in the South. I took him up on an offer to visit him in Beckley, West Virginia, over the Christmas holidays. Among the other VISTA volunteers I met were David Beismeyer, a big, outgoing Wisconsin farm boy who later married one of Harry Belafonte's daughters and remained in West Virginia, and a slim, contemplative, somewhat Machiavellian young man from California, Gibbs Kinderman. Gibbs had masterminded a strategy a few months earlier to wrest control of the Raleigh County Community Action Association from the Raleigh County Board of Education and put it in the hands of the poor people in the county. After the takeover, he had been named the association's executive director.

While I was visiting, Gibbs mentioned a tutoring program for which they were seeking funds from the U.S. Office of Economic Opportunity. Because of my background at Queens College, he asked if I'd be interested in running the program once funding was secured. I gave a vague answer without any expectation of ever returning to the county. Living conditions in the rural areas of the county, where running water and central heating were frequently unaffordable luxuries, seemed even worse than those I'd encountered in Prince Edward County. Most VISTA volunteers ignored such inconveniences in order to live in the communities they were organizing. I was interested in the struggle, but not at the expense of creature comforts I took for granted. I returned to Yorktown High School and put West Virginia out of mind.

On the evening of March 15, 1967, my phone rang. It was Gibbs Kinderman. They had received funds for the tutoring program, and he wanted to know when I could start. I stammered, stalling for time while I formulated my refusal. "You know I have a teaching job, and I can't just pack up and leave." But he would not take no for an answer, and by the time we hung up, I'd agreed to be there by April 15. As with my enrollment in Queens College, the direction of my life was about to change in ways I would only come to appreciate much later.

The next day, I sheepishly informed an angry principal who had vigorously defended me through the Pete Seeger and yearbook cover controversies of my departure. I was putting him in the difficult position of finding a replacement for the final two months of the semester, and I could not blame him for his anger. But I was stunned when my special education students were visibly upset. I did not feel I'd succeeded in relating to them or motivating them, but they apparently had sensed my desire to treat them with respect, and justifiably felt that I was abandoning them. My two special education colleagues seemed only to care that it would mean more work for them. My honors students and the yearbook staff, as well as friends on the faculty, were disappointed but supportive of what I was setting out to do. However, for the first time, my parents were not supportive of my plans. My father reacted with disgust. "You have a good job. How can you just throw it away on some wild goose chase?" My mother was concerned. "Where will you live? What will you do? It's so far away."

But the die had been cast. So, with decidedly mixed feelings, on April 14, 1967, my Volkswagen bug (I'd bought the bug when I'd returned from Prince Edward County) packed so tightly there was no room for passengers, I said my goodbyes and set out for Beckley. I was twenty-five and there was no precedent in my family for what I was doing. Except for that summer in Prince Edward County, I'd never lived anywhere but in the state of New York, nor in an environment that was not predominantly white and Jewish. My mother had always lived in the New York City area, as had my father since coming to this country at the age of thirteen. My Aunt Ruthie asked me with genuine incredulousness, "Why would anyone want to live anywhere but New York?" It was a question I asked myself several times during my first few weeks in West Virginia.

The civil rights struggle had largely bypassed West Virginia. Originally part of Virginia, it had split with the rest of the Commonwealth over secession and was rewarded with statehood in 1863. Black and white families generally lived in separate communities, though without any evident hostility. Often they lived in adjoining coal camps or company towns. The men worked together in the mines where the darkness and the coal dust made one man's skin color virtually indistinguishable from that of another and where shared dangers created common bonds among the men. Unlike many unions, the United Mine Workers of America, organized under the leadership of the legendary John L. Lewis in the 1920s and1930s in bitter and violent wars with the coal companies, could not afford to exclude any miners. Thus, the men not only worked together underground, they had reason to come together above ground in pursuit of better pay and safer working conditions. Although skin color was a determining factor in who got promoted underground, who held political power above ground, and who achieved higher social status, the separate facilities that characterized the Jim Crow South had never been as much in evidence in the Mountain State. For these reasons and because the mountainous terrain and poor road system made it difficult to get in or out of the state or to get around within the state, civil rights organizers had ignored it. They had more significant challenges further south.

In contrast to the living rooms of Prince Edward County's black families, where pictures of Jesus Christ and Martin Luther King Jr. hung side by side, in the living rooms of West Virginia's poor families, both black and white, pictures of Jesus Christ and the late President Kennedy hung side by side. Kennedy had become a local hero when, during his 1960 primary battle against Hubert Humphrey, he uncovered for the nation the stark face of abject poverty in Appalachia and promised to do something about it when elected President. Ultimately, it was Lyndon Johnson, riding the wave of national sentiment following Kennedy's assassination, who redeemed the promise by steering both the Economic Opportunity Act and the Appalachian Regional Development Act through the Congress in 1965.

I hugged my parents and left Woodmere on Friday evening after a sumptuous dinner of roast beef and potato pancakes, my favorite meal, and of course the requisite peas and carrots to balance it. About halfway through the trip, I'd stopped at a rest area in Virginia for a brief nap before tackling Route 60, the two-lane road that would lead me into the Appalachian Mountains and through some of the range's more modest hills and valleys into West Virginia. Then, I'd picked up Route 19-21, which led me through southeastern West Virginia into Beckley. Today, Interstates 64, 77, and 79 have made access easier and more direct and helped to energize the tourist trade in the parts of the state that fit the labels "Almost Heaven" or "Wild and Wonderful." In 1967, they were but dreams in the eyes of highway planners. I arrived in Beckley at about 1 p.m. on Saturday, April 15, 1967, weary after nearly sixteen hours on the road.

The monthly board of directors meeting of the Raleigh County Community Action Association (RCCAA) had just begun in the second-floor courtroom of the county courthouse when I entered. Gibbs was sitting at a table in front of the judge's podium. He nodded as I entered and stood just inside the door, surveying the packed courtroom. Black people were sitting side by side with white people. People dressed in their Sunday best were sitting next to people in denim overalls. Everyone was listening intently as Gibbs spoke about RCCAA programs—a summer youth employment program, plans for a health clinic and a free bus system, and Head Start—and answered questions. I was lost in thought when I heard my name as Gibbs introduced me to the crowd as the new director of the community education program. There was polite applause, and as people left the two-hour meeting, several shook my hand and welcomed me to the county. Gibbs asked me to meet him at his house at 5 p.m. "We're going to a ramps festival tonight."

"What," I asked, "is a ramps festival?"

"You'll see," Gibbs responded with a sly smile.

I had a couple of hours to kill, so I decided to explore the town. Beckley was an old coal-mining town that had evolved into the shopping hub for much of southern West Virginia. It was a town of approximately 10,000 during the week, but the population probably doubled on busy Saturdays as people from Wyoming, Fayette, and other nearby counties came to town for their regular shopping trips. By mid-morning on many

Saturdays, traffic was gridlocked as people headed for the variety of mom-and-pop stores that sold everything from new and second-hand furniture and clothing to groceries and meals with all the fixings for a buck ninety-five. Several store owners lived above their stores. Sitting in the center of the hustle and bustle was the county courthouse, a large old brick structure in need of a power-washing. After a brief walk around the two-square-block downtown, I drove down South Kanawha Street, a main access road into town, passing the local commuter college, the small frame house in which Gibbs and his wife lived, and the Town & Country Motel and Restaurant, where I would eat many meals over the next two years. I headed back toward town on South Fayette Street, which ran approximately parallel to South Kanawha Street, passing several churches and an elementary school. On my left, the cross streets were not paved. Must be the black community, I thought. I turned left onto Barber Street and instantly recognized the old frame house on the left where Dave Beismeyer lived and where I had stayed when I visited Beckley earlier. I recalled waking up that first morning and looking out the window at the sun shining brightly. It had been December and there was snow on the ground, but under the electric blanket I had felt as warm and toasty as the sun looked outside. So, I had thrown off the electric blanket—and frozen like a statue in a semiprone position as Dave watched me and chuckled. I had forgotten that the house had no central heating, and the bright sun masked a temperature of about twenty degrees, inside and outside.

I shivered at the memory of my rude introduction to a different world. Further up Barber Street was a series of aging frame houses of varying sizes. Chickens wandered around the dusty yards, mingling easily with dogs, cats, and children playing happily. Some people, all black, were sitting on their front porches. A few looked at me quizzically and waved. I waved back.

At 5 p.m., I knocked on the Kindermans' door and was greeted by Gibbs' wife, Kathy. She was the daughter of Arthur Schlesinger, Jr., the prominent historian and former aide to

President Kennedy. She'd been a VISTA volunteer in Raleigh County, and she and Gibbs had been married for about a year. By 5:30 p.m. we were in Gibbs' Scout, heading out of Beckley on the two-lane country road to Arnett, about fifteen miles away. Gibbs pointed out a number of sights foreign to my experience. I'd never seen, even in pictures, a burning slag pile (abandoned coal waste that has ignited and smolders continuously, giving off toxic fumes), a coal tipple (processing plant), or a strip mine site. He noted the homes of some allies and told me briefly about ramps, early-spring wild onions that grow in the mountains of West Virginia, among other places. The small green plant had helped the early settlers to survive, and its importance spawned a tradition of ramps festivals during spring harvest time. What sets it apart from other foods is its pungent odor, an odor that some compare to that of jet fuel. For the festivals, bushels of ramps are boiled in water with cider vinegar for fifteen to twenty minutes and then drained. Then bacon grease is heated in a cast-iron skillet, and the boiled ramps are flash fried for a minute and served. "There's only one defense," laughed Gibbs as we turned onto a dirt road and arrived at a clearing where a crowd of people were milling about in front of an old wooden building. "Eat some right away. You won't smell a thing. Otherwise, you'll die from the aroma."

He pulled the Scout into a vacant spot in front of the building, which served as a community center, and was immediately surrounded by well-wishers. He introduced me around, and I answered several questions about where I was from, what I had done, and whether I knew anything about ramps. This was an all-white crowd, and I didn't know what to expect, so I stayed away from my civil rights activities and stuck to describing my tutoring and teaching experience. I could smell the ramps, but we were outside on a cool evening, so the smell wasn't overpowering. I relaxed. This won't be so bad, I thought. Finally, someone said, "Mike, let's get you some ramps." Inside, the ramps were boiling and frying. I inhaled and nearly gagged. Someone handed me a plate and laughed. "Eat 'em quick." I did. Gibbs was right.

Once you've eaten some, you don't smell them anymore. It was a memorable introduction to West Virginia.

I stayed with Dave on Barber Street that evening. On Sunday morning I checked the newspaper for available rentals, and headed out to look for an apartment. I drove first to Raleigh, down in the bottom at the foot of South Fayette Street. An old railroad town, it was a collection of wooden buildings. Many of them were abandoned, and most of them looked like a strong wind would flatten them. A few people were walking on the dirt road leading in and out of the bottom. They were all black and looked as fragile as the buildings surrounding them. I spotted the "For Rent" sign on a two-story apartment building that seemed to lean ever so slightly to the right. I turned around at the first opportunity and drove back up toward town. My second stop was at a well-kept, two-story red brick house on Stanley Street, just under the water tower off South Kanawha Street. It had a small front lawn and a driveway leading to a detached garage in the back. I knocked on the door. A plain-looking white woman probably in her thirties answered it and eyed me closely without saying a word. I asked her about the apartment, and she handed me a key. "Out back over the garage."

I walked up the driveway, climbed the creaky wooden steps on the side of the garage, unlocked the door, and walked into the living room of a three-room apartment. An old tan leather couch sat against the double windows on my left overlooking the driveway and a matching leather armchair faced me. Both sat on a well-worn, dark brown rug. One of the pillows that formed the seat of the couch had a slit in it that had been covered with duct tape. The bedroom on my right was barely large enough for the double bed and the dresser it contained. I took three steps through the living room and found a small bathroom with a bathtub but no shower on the left, and a small kitchen on the right with a refrigerator, stove, single sink, and a table and two chairs.

"Fifty dollars a month in advance and a month's deposit," the woman said when I returned the key. I wrote her a check for a hundred dollars. She gave me back the key, and warned, "No parties, no drinking, no pets, and no loud noise."

The following morning, I met Gibbs at the RCCAA office in Glen White, a small town about five miles outside of Beckley. The office was located off a two-lane country road behind a general store in what was once Glen White Elementary School. A large, unpaved parking area separated the general store from the whitewashed frame building. Inside, on creaky wooden floors, were two large rooms that had once been classrooms, and an office that used to be the principal's office. The two large rooms were bustling with activity.

Gibbs introduced me around and provided a brief overview of recent events. "The Board of Education ran the Community Action Association for the first year. Last fall, we packed the annual meeting, voted out the board's handpicked directors, and elected our own local folks. You know, 'maximum feasible participation' of the poor. Now we have to prove we can make this work." Head Start and the Neighborhood Youth Corps were already operating. There were plans for a community health center, a revamped Neighborhood Youth Corps, a housing rehabilitation project, and a bus transportation program. But the community education project, said Gibbs, was key.

We were to organize and train low-income parents to tutor children in their communities, thereby helping the children. More importantly, this would expose parents more directly to deficiencies in the school system, particularly deficiencies in rural areas. Our larger agenda was to parlay the new awareness of parents into organizing them to demand a role in the decision-making process for the use of Title I funds under the Elementary and Secondary Education Act (ESEA). Title I was designed specifically to improve educational outcomes for disadvantaged children, and it required parent involvement in the decisions on how to distribute the funds. This requirement was routinely ignored by the school system, which operated like a small fiefdom. If we could organize parents, Gibbs reasoned, they would demand greater involvement in the process. The result would be a more equitable distribution of Title I funds and greater transparency and accountability in how the money was spent. Poverty and powerlessness knew no color in the mountains, Gibbs assured me, so black parents and white parents would have no trouble coming together to fight the common enemy.

For those of us who believe government has an important role to play in fostering social justice, the latter part of the 1960s was an extraordinary time. The federal government had made commitments to wipe out poverty, provide equal educational opportunities to all children, end racial discrimination in public places, promote equal employment opportunity, guarantee voting rights to all, open the doors to a new wave of immigrants, and provide health insurance to all senior citizens. One of President Johnson's singular accomplishments was the anti-poverty program. The Economic Opportunity Act of 1965, which authorized the program, created strategies for every age group. For young children there was Head Start; for adolescents, the Neighborhood Youth Corps and Job Corps; for adults, job training and health care programs; for communities, Community Action Agencies, which incorporated most of the strategies under a single, local administrative structure and gave local people the opportunity to create and operate programs to address specific local issues.

For committed individuals who wanted to be part of the promised change, there was VISTA, a domestic version of the Peace Corps, established by President Kennedy prior to his assassination. Undergirding all these strategies was a commitment to the "maximum feasible participation of the poor," which embodied the notion that the poor know best what they need to climb the economic ladder. This latter notion was not a high priority in Raleigh County until the Appalachian Volunteers (AVs), a group of VISTA volunteers operating in the Appalachian Mountains of Kentucky, Tennessee, Virginia, and West Virginia, determined, under Gibbs' leadership, to make real the program's promise.

Though I relished the task ahead, I felt woefully unprepared for the responsibility Gibbs had thrust in my lap. This was not just organizing a tutoring program and getting parents involved in their children's education; this involved confronting the most established and entrenched institution in the county, the school system, to show that maximum feasible participation of the poor could work. I'd helped organize the SHP tutoring program, the Prince Edward County project, the march on the World's Fair, Freedom Week, and the hunger strike. But I'd never done any organizing on this scale with this much at stake. Furthermore, I was suffering from culture shock. I'd never lived anywhere but the New York City area, except for my two years at Cornell and six weeks in Prince Edward County. And those instances didn't really count, since a significant portion of Cornell's student body was from the New York City area, and the Prince Edward County experience had been brief and temporary.

Here, the food was different—ramps, chili and slaw on hot dogs, and chitterlings had never been on any menu I'd seen. The setting was different—two-lane winding and hilly country roads, mountains all around us, vast areas of barren land, sparse population, burning slag heaps. The power dynamics were different—the political power structure was more entrenched and less responsive to local needs than any I'd ever known, except in Prince Edward County. The people were different. They had accents I had difficulty understanding, their economic struggles and health deficiencies were beyond anything I'd ever seen, and their race relations puzzled me. And they had an insularity I could not comprehend coupled with an outward warmth and friendliness foreign to most New Yorkers. And I was lonely.

For the first week or two, I was convinced I'd made a serious mistake. I could never fit in here, I was ill-prepared for the job, and people would never accept me. And I struggled with the concept of poor white people who were as oppressed and powerless as poor black people. I kept my bags packed for a potential quick getaway. But there was no place to go. I'd given up my teaching job, and the abruptness of my departure, not to mention the quality of my performance, would make it difficult to get another job. I'd gone against my parents' wishes, particularly my father's wishes, in giving up a secure job for "some wild goose chase," and I was too proud to admit my mistake to them. I had no money. I saw no options. I was on my own.

So, after a few days of feeling sorry for myself, I dove right in. Despite my initial unease, it was an exciting time. People who'd been powerless were confronting those who had kept them powerless. The powerless came in all colors—black, white and brown—but skin color didn't seem to matter. I spent hours in their living rooms talking about what we wanted to do, seeking their advice and guidance, and getting their commitment to be involved. I shared my experiences in setting up a tutoring program at Queens College and teaching children in Prince Edward County. I sugarcoated my teaching experience. I explained the details of the Title I program and the right of poor people to have a voice in how the money was spent. I played with their children. They listened, asked questions, watched me closely, and sized me up. Among the people I visited was Chester Workman in Richmond District, the most rural, remote, and least diverse magisterial district in the county. Chester, a barrel-chested coal miner with four kids and a take-no-prisoners attitude who commuted two hours to his job, had been elected chairman of the board of the RCCAA after the takeover. He did not hide his skepticism about the community-organizing ability of this young-looking Yankee.

My immediate tasks were to develop an advisory committee of parents, to find venues for tutoring in local churches or community buildings in each of the county's eight magisterial districts, to prepare materials for tutoring, and to train parents to tutor. We would use the training sessions to help parents understand the inequitable distribution of funds, the consequences for their children, and how to change the system. It became clear during my visits around the county that I would have to rely heavily on people who were highly respected in their communities and who recognized the power dynamics of the county, although for the most part they had little formal education and had felt powerless, until now, to effect change. In some ways, there was little difference between the powerful and the powerless. Both came from coal-mining backgrounds, had not strayed far from the county, and were suspicious of outsiders like me. Those who held power were usually better educated, less scrupulous, and more manipulative, and they had used these characteristics to gain and sustain power and to pass it on to succeeding generations. The primary seat of power was the school system, the largest single employer in the county. Through the school system, those in power controlled non-mining employment opportunities, local elections, the allocation of resources, and even the disciplining of children. It was best not to anger the school superintendent. The AVs, in particular Gibbs, Dave, and Steve, had won people over by making good on their promise to take control of the RCCAA. I benefited from the fact that I'd been brought in by Gibbs, but I still had to prove myself.

The people I came to rely on most heavily were a diverse group: a black disabled coal miner suffering from black lung disease; two white disabled coal miners who had been severely injured in the mines and their respective wives, both strong individuals in their own right; and two black women who took a backseat to nobody. None of them had much formal education, but all of them were street-smart from the challenging lives they'd led. They could read a person like a book, and they possessed a steely determination that life would be better for their children than it had been for them.

We set as our initial goal the formation of a Title I Parent Advisory Committee to meet regularly with C. G. Peregoy, director of the Title I program. A retired county school superintendent, Peregoy was not a physically imposing figure; he was small, bent over, and wrinkled, with a gravelly voice. But until his retirement, he had been lord and master of the county school system. He was not used to having his authority challenged, and he initially refused our request for a meeting. But when I drafted a letter signed by a number of parents quoting the section in Title I of the ESEA that mandated a representative Citizens Advisory Committee, he agreed to meet.

With the summer came the arrival of summer VISTA volunteers, as well as volunteers committed to two years of service. Among the latter group were Rick and Rita Bank, a young, recently married white couple from New York City. Perhaps due to our New York backgrounds, our moderately radical politics, our personalities, or a combination of all three, we quickly became fast friends. They rented an apartment on Johnstown Road, just a block from my Stanley Street apartment. Rick and I would jog in the evenings, and Rita, a math teacher by training, became a key member of the community education team. I'd often have dinner at their apartment while trying to avoid Milton, their ugly dachshund who was insistent on corralling table scraps and was distinctly more friendly to me than I was to him. Rick, dark-haired, muscular and compact, had recently graduated from law school and was itching to use his training to promote social justice. He would later play a key role in successful efforts to enact the Federal Coal Mine Health and Safety Act of 1969, which provides cash benefits to those disabled by black lung disease and to their widows. After their time in Beckley, they moved to Charleston, the state capital, where Rick practiced law for a short time before becoming instrumental in Arnold Miller's successful 1972 campaign to replace Tony Boyle as head of the United Mine Workers (UMW). When Arnold asked Rick to become his chief of staff at UMW headquarters, he and Rita moved to Washington, D.C. Not long after they moved, Rita enrolled in the Catholic University Law School, and she has gone on to become one of the most prominent domestic affairs attorneys in D.C.

But in the summer of 1967, she was a math teacher, and she gravitated immediately toward the community education project. An attractive, dark-haired young woman with a disarming and outgoing personality, she was an immediate hit with our core group and with the youngsters we were tutoring. She assumed primary responsibility for the tutoring program, while I focused largely on organizing parents and planning for the meetings with Peregoy. We planned meticulously, deciding what issues to raise, who would speak on which issue, and how to respond to Peregoy's likely noncommittal responses. Making progress in guiding Title I expenditures toward the truly low-income seemed almost as difficult as trying to push an elephant forward. But slowly, more money was directed away from the Beckley schools that served the children of more prosperous families and toward rural schools, where children of most of the poorest families lived. More importantly, the parents learned that their voices could be heard, and they gradually began to feel empowered. Once previously powerless people had gotten a sense of empowerment, the effect was irreversible. A genie had been let out of the bottle, and Raleigh County would never be the same. Today, while some deride the anti-poverty program as a failure, this sense of empowerment, in addition to programs like Head Start and Job Corps, stands as a lasting legacy.

The project was going well. A recreation program during that first summer attracted hundreds of children. Children at one of the summer locations spray-painted my car, and my multicolored Volkswagen attracted attention throughout the county. With money I saved from my spartan living style, I bought Christmas presents for about a hundred children and had a joyful time delivering them on Christmas Eve. A significant number of the children were doing better in school. Parents were more engaged with their children's education and were beginning to challenge unfair school policies. School administrators who were used to doling out money at their own discretion and principals who were used to total autonomy in their schools came under scrutiny and were forced to modify their decision-making processes. Teachers who manifested their negative stereotypes of children from poor families by the disparate ways they treated the children and meted out discipline were forced to modify their approaches. An Office of Economic Opportunity (OEO) team sent to evaluate the program concluded that we were achieving our objectives.

Despite the success, I sensed doubt that in a crunch I would be able to stand up to the school powers. Perhaps it was partly projection on my part. I didn't like personal conflict, and my calm demeanor, even when meeting with Peregoy, conveyed that reluctance. The opportunity to test my mettle came unexpectedly in Richmond District, where Chester Workman had been a local agitator for years before becoming RCCAA's board chair. The residents of Richmond District, the most isolated place I'd ever been, were all white. Many subsisted on farming, and I'd actually attended Richmond District meetings in a converted chicken coop. Richmond District was also where I'd been introduced to grits one morning after spending the night at a local farmer's home.

Although the district was perhaps ten miles from Beckley as the crow flies, crossing the mountains through a series of 180-degree switchbacks took an hour. People seemed to like it that way. Dick Yannantuono, a tall, lanky VISTA volunteer from Westchester County, New York, who had become a close friend and later roomed with me in my garage apartment, told of trying to get people from Richmond District to attend a public hearing about an I-64 on/off ramp proposed for the district. Access to the Interstate would cut driving time to Beckley from an hour to ten or fifteen minutes and open the area to economic development. With our urban orientation we could not imagine any opposition from Richmond District residents. Dick had approached an elderly man who was sitting in a rocking chair on his porch, puffing on a pipe. "Can you make it to the hearing tonight?"

"What hearing's that, son?" the man drawled.

"It's about having an on/off ramp from the new Interstate right here. You'd be able to get to Beckley in just ten minutes."

"Well, I don't know. I kinda like to take my time 'bout goin' to Beckley."

"No, you don't understand. You can drive as slow as you want. It's just that you don't have to go over the mountains. You would have a straight shot to Beckley."

"Well, like I said, son, I kinda like to take my time 'bout goin' to Beckley."

That man reflected the sentiment of many Richmond District residents. They certainly were not prosperous, but they liked their lifestyle and saw no reason to change. One consequence of the isolation was that the local high school principal, a round-faced, bespectacled, middle-aged man named Redden, was arguably the most powerful person in the district because he employed the most people locally. Furthermore, the school received a significant amount of federal money through the county, largely because of the poverty of the student population. This gave him even more power. He didn't like Chester, because the RCCAA was a potential threat to his authority. And unlike many of his neighbors, Chester was not financially dependent on Redden, so he did not defer to his authority. But two of Chester's children were students at the high school, and they sometimes paid a price for their father's independence.

The particular incident that brought me to Richmond District was the suspension of one of Chester's children for fighting with another student. It seemed like a typical, relatively harmless teen altercation. It ended quickly, and nobody was hurt. The other student, who according to most eyewitnesses was equally at fault, received no punishment. Since Chester's children were part of our tutoring program, his wife, Margaret, asked me to accompany her to speak with Redden. I was reluctant to get involved, especially because I didn't know exactly what had happened. But Dick strongly suggested that I go, and I trusted his judgment. As I negotiated the Pluto Road through the mountains, I pondered how to handle the situation. Should I simply provide moral support and remain silent? Should I speak up if I thought Margaret was not holding her own with Redden? Would Redden even allow me into the meeting? I met Margaret at the school. Redden greeted us warily and ushered us into his office.

"Now, what can I do for you, Margaret?"

"I want to know why Buster was suspended and the other child wasn't."

"Now, Margaret. You know we can't tolerate fighting in school. Buster got out of hand, and I had to punish him."

"But what about the other boy?"

"Well, that's simply none of your affair, Margaret," Redden replied.

I did not have a favorable impression of Redden, and his patronizing attitude annoyed me. "Excuse me," I interjected. "The issue here is fairness. Both boys were equally responsible, so they should be treated equally."

"I don't think this is any of your business, son," Mr. Redden responded icily.

"I think fairness is everybody's business."

"This is between Mrs. Workman and me. I believe you should wait outside." He waved toward the door.

"I don't plan to leave until we get an answer to Mrs. Workman's question and Buster Workman gets treated fairly."

Redden clearly did not expect such a challenge from me. Frankly, I surprised myself with my assertiveness. The discussion got louder and more heated, with Mr. Redden insisting that I leave and me refusing to leave until the matter was resolved. The noise carried beyond the thin walls of the office, and unbeknownst to Margaret or to me, a small crowd of Redden supporters, teachers and a few neighbors, had gathered outside the office. Unaware of the potential danger lurking just beyond the door, I refused to be intimidated. If we left his office without a fair resolution, I threatened, he would be hearing from federal authorities about the dictatorial way he ran the school. I had no idea if I could make good on such a threat, but I'd worry about that later.

Suddenly, the door burst open and in stormed Chester, shotgun in hand. He looked at Margaret and me. "Buster told me you were over here. Come on now, let's go," he ordered. Margaret and I followed him out the door and through the angry crowd. When we got to his house, he turned to me, still fuming. "Now, Mike, I appreciate what you were trying to do, but you stirred up a hornet's nest in there."

"Chester," Margaret cut in. "I was real proud of Mike. I never heard anyone talk to Mr. Redden like that."

"I know," Chester replied, calming down. "But you and Mike could have been killed. Those folks don't mess around." He paused. "Why don't you stay for dinner, Mike?"

Word of the confrontation with Redden quickly spread. Later that evening, I saw Dick. He patted me on the shoulder: "I heard you really gave it to Redden today." Chester had been concerned for our safety, but he clearly was proud, and surprised, at what had occurred. "Mike really stood up for us," he told people with an air of admiration. It didn't hurt that Buster's suspension was lifted the next day. I'd passed my own test of personal courage, and at the same time, earned a new level of respect among colleagues and friends. Even Mr. Peregoy, who had undoubtedly heard about the incident from Redden, seemed to tread more lightly in my presence.

V

NAVIGATING
THE RACIAL MINEFIELD

The spring of 1968 was traumatic, nationally and locally. In April, Martin Luther King, Jr., was shot and killed in Memphis, Tennessee. The murder stirred no visible unrest in Beckley, but people both black and white were shaken by the violence of the act and by the loss of leadership. Dr. King had embarked on the Poor People's Campaign, and we anticipated being a part of it. I heard about the Memphis tragedy on the radio while driving to a meeting about our next encounter with Peregoy. Peregoy's name never came up as we somberly contemplated the potential impact of the murder.

Two months later, Bobby Kennedy was the victim of another crazed gunman. I was visiting New York when I heard the news. People in West Virginia were even more shaken this time, not only because this was the second assassination of a cherished leader in less than three months, but because the Kennedy name was so revered in West Virginia. I arrived back in Beckley to find people glum and discouraged. Kennedy had inspired the powerless; he was the leader who would make the government care about them. A part of their spirit seemed to die with him. For others the impact was more practical. "The War on Poverty is dead without him," lamented several colleagues. "All the money will go to the Vietnam War."

To complicate matters in Raleigh County, about this time Gibbs decided he'd had enough of administrative work. He'd obtained federal government grant funds for a range of projects, including the Mountaineer Family Health Project, the first comprehensive health care program for low-income citizens of Raleigh County, and a bus project that offered inexpensive transportation to shopping and health care destinations for rural county residents. He'd revitalized Head Start and the Neighborhood Youth Corps, and he'd initiated two major grassroots campaigns, one to achieve benefits for victims of black lung disease, in which Rick Bank was playing a leading role, and another to halt the destructive practice of strip mining, in which Dick Yannantuono was playing a leading role. Perhaps most importantly, he had established a precedent for empowering poor people to run the organization. So, with the concurrence of Chester and the board of directors, he handed the reins to Al Harrah, a local white man who'd been his deputy and whose administrative skills seemed more suited to everyday program management. There was some grumbling that a black man should succeed Gibbs, but no specific candidate emerged, and the grumbling died out. Gibbs remained in Raleigh County for a short while, but eventually moved to Pocahontas County, West Virginia, where he was instrumental in founding a public radio station, and where he still lives and works.

Morale was low as we tried to make sense of the two assassinations while maintaining momentum under new leadership. The OEO also was concerned. It had invested a substantial amount of money in the RCCAA, more than four million dollars in the past two years, and held up the RCCAA as a model program for rural America. Now, needing reassurance that a change in administrative leadership would not have an adverse impact, the OEO sent a consultant to Beckley to evaluate the situation. Al was relying on me as an informal second-in-command and asked me to pick up the consultant from the Beckley airport.

I arrived early and watched as she stepped off the plane and walked purposefully toward the one-room terminal. Tall, thin, and elegant, skin the color of polished mahogany, and dressed in a business suit, Tempie was easy to distinguish from the small group of deplaning passengers. We began working the day after she arrived, reviewing organization records and accomplishments and analyzing possible challenges. The plan was for her to remain for most of the summer as OEO's eyes and ears. I was her guide, taking her along when I traveled the county, introducing her to project personnel and explaining program goals, and shepherding her to meetings with Peregoy and others. She was initially reticent, trying to establish a professional image in the eyes of the three white males—Al, Chester, and me—with whom she interacted most closely. Eventually, though, she began to loosen up and talk to me about herself.

She was married, though not happily, to her high school sweetheart, a career military man stationed overseas, and she was the mother of two girls aged six and four. They were staying with her parents in Clinton, North Carolina, for the summer. As we compared life experiences, I began to understand how different our paths had been. Her family's journey was typical of many black families in the American South. Her grandfathers had been neither tailors nor shoemakers. They had been born into slavery somewhere in the Carolinas, descended from generations of enslaved people. Despite the fact that her forefathers had toiled to build our nation's economic infrastructure long before my ancestors set foot on American soil, their abilities and ambitions had never been enough to lift them out of the chains in which they had arrived. Tempie's parents, instead of being able to treasure a heritage of independence and opportunity and pass that on to their children, could only look back on a history of captivity and oppression while confronting the daily indignities of Jim Crow racism.

What Tempie and her family experienced in daily life, most of us had only read about in high school textbooks, if that. Her parents were not allowed to vote, or shop in many stores in town, or be employed in any of them. Only at their peril could they look a white person in the eye. Tempie and her brother Don had to sit in the balcony at the movies, couldn't use the municipal swimming pool in the sweltering summer heat, were barred from sitting at local lunch counters, and were taught to fear police officers rather than rely on them for protection. Perhaps most egregiously, they had to walk past gleaming whites-only schools to get to their aging segregated school. They read from textbooks that had been trashed by white schools because they were either outdated or in bad condition, their pages marked with racist epithets or torn out completely. And they had to make do with makeshift equipment for science labs and athletics.

We learned little in school about the economic repression that characterized Jim Crow racism in the South, but Tempie's parents faced it with brutal regularity. Actually, they had tried to escape early on. They had saved some money and moved north to Washington, D.C., after getting married. But her father was seriously injured in a logging accident, and with no union to protect him and no benefits from the company, they were forced to return to North Carolina and their support network of family and friends. Though she was educated and intelligent, Tempie's mother could only find work as a servant for a white family. She became the family's primary source of income. Tempie's father was unable to work steadily. He mowed lawns occasionally and kept hogs in the backyard that he had slaughtered each year for meat for the family.

Tempie and Don were taught to work hard and to play by the rules, but they were white people's rules, rules designed to dictate limits rather than to give full flower to their abilities and ambitions. They could pick cotton, as they had done as youngsters. They could aspire to be servants, factory workers, or sharecroppers, and be thankful to the white bosses for their jobs. In contrast to my military deferments for college and teaching, Don saw no alternative after high school but to enlist in the Marines. He served two tours in Vietnam. Tempie, thanks to a fierce determination instilled in her by her mother, was able to surmount the odds, obtain financial aid, and, despite having two children, enroll in North Carolina Central College (now University), an HBCU (historically black college [or] university). She had been fortunate enough to meet a mentor who helped to connect her to opportunities like the consulting job in Raleigh County.

The civil rights struggles of the 1950s and 1960s ostensibly put an end to the outrages endured by Tempie, her family, and millions of others. Gone, thanks to the Supreme Court, was the flawed concept of "separate but equal." In its place, theoretically protected by congressional legislation, was a new day in which anyone with ability and ambition, irrespective of skin color, could succeed.

If only it were so simple. The wounds were too deep, the abuses too pervasive, the burdens too daunting, the attitudes too ingrained, the institutions too entrenched to be overcome by a few Supreme Court decisions and some modest pieces of congressional legislation. The strength my parents drew from their cultural backgrounds, their wide support networks, and the expectations of others was unavailable to Tempie's parents. The legacy of limitless possibilities that my parents passed on to me was inaccessible to Tempie, through no fault of her own or of her parents.

Despite my involvement in civil rights activities, Tempie was the first black person I was really getting to know. She provided me with a much more intimate understanding of racism in America. In Prince Edward County I'd been little more than an observer of racism—a close observer for sure, but one who would leave it behind at the end of the summer. As I drew closer to Tempie, racism became increasingly personal. I couldn't walk in her shoes, but I was beginning to feel the pain and anger in a way that had never before been accessible to me. One night, I asked if she wanted to go out for a late-night snack. She was hesitant. "Won't there be trouble if we're seen together in a social setting?"

Naively, I answered: "Don't worry. This isn't the Deep South. Nobody will care that we're together."

A new phase of my education about navigating the nation's racial minefield was about to begin, driven by my desire to impress a woman who was becoming special to me. We headed out to the only place that was open late at night, a rest stop on the

West Virginia Turnpike, the mostly two-lane mountain road that ran along the outskirts of Beckley on its way from Charleston to Bluefield. With its twists and turns, and only one lane in each direction for most of its length, it was a turnpike in name only. Danger lurked around every curve. Nonetheless, it was an important north/south route for truckers, tourists, and in-state travelers.

The Glass House was located at the halfway point of the turnpike. Like most rest stops, it had a small gift shop, vending machines, a restaurant area, and three U-shaped counters for those who wanted to make their stops as brief as possible. We arrived at nearly 10 p.m., and the gift shop, restaurant area, and two of the three counters were closed. We sat at the open counter. There were twelve stools, four on each of three sides. The fourth side was open and led into the kitchen. One server, a young white woman, was on duty, and three men occupied stools on the left side. We sat together at the top of the U, facing the kitchen—and waited. And waited.

At first, engrossed in conversation, we didn't notice that we were being ignored. But when the waitress appeared for the second or third time to pour coffee for the three men and then turned back to the kitchen without looking in our direction, we began to suspect something was amiss. When she appeared again, I said in a loud, but polite voice, "Excuse me, but we're ready to order."

"I'll get to you when I can," was her curt reply as she headed back toward the kitchen.

"Maybe we should leave," whispered Tempie.

"No," I replied crisply. I did not intend to allow this young snip of a waitress to embarrass me. When the waitress reappeared to clear the three places the men had now vacated, I cleared my throat and declared, "We're ready to order, and we've been waiting twenty minutes."

"Can't you see I'm busy?" she said sharply, again without looking at us.

"There's nobody here. There's no reason for you not to take our order."

Tempie tugged on my arm. "C'mon, let's go. I don't want any trouble."

"No." I tightened my jaw. "She's not going to drive us away."

I turned back toward the waitress. "Where's the manager," I demanded.

"He's not here."

"Well, who's in charge?" I asked loudly.

"Ain't nobody here but me and the boy in the kitchen," she replied without looking in our direction.

Tempie tugged on my arm again. "Let's get out of here."

I pulled away. "We came here to eat, and we don't have to take this." In truth, I didn't know what to do, and I was embarrassed and frustrated at how impotent I felt. If we simply walked out, it would feel like the waitress had won. If we stayed, it was clear that we would probably sit there all night and not be served. When the waitress finished cleaning up the counter, she turned back toward the kitchen. In a rage fueled by feeling utterly helpless, I pushed a water glass that had been sitting near me, probably left by a previous customer, off of the counter. It shattered near her feet. She screamed in shock.

Tempie grabbed my arm and this time literally pulled me away from the counter and toward the door. "You damn fool," she muttered. "Now we're getting out of here."

The waitress's ankle was bleeding, nicked by a flying piece of glass. She shouted, "He cut me. That nigger-lovin' Yankee cut me."

As we headed hurriedly out of the Glass House and toward the car, I stammered, "I just couldn't help it. It made me so angry."

To which Tempie replied, "When you experience it every day, you learn to cope with it and not sink to their level."

She was right, of course. I've done a lot of learning since then. The clear lesson of that night, however, was that I had never experienced what it meant to be black, and I'd not been strong enough to cope with the feeling of powerlessness that had enveloped me. I'd never experienced such a feeling, not even in Prince Edward County. Tempie had endured this behavior from white people regularly during her twenty-six years, and she knew how to handle it with dignity and grace while avoiding the inherent dangers. She explained to me in several subsequent conversations that I could have gotten both of us killed. At the very least, I had assaulted the waitress and could be criminally liable. Moreover, I had handed the waitress a victory. She hadn't served us, and I'd confirmed the stereotypes she probably held of arrogant Yankee troublemakers and "uppity n—s." What I had achieved was very temporary and inadequate relief from my rage. Weeks later, I was still angry, as much at myself for losing control as at the waitress. As Tempie pointed out, now I had some very cursory knowledge of what it felt like to be black.

Fortunately, we did not encounter the police that night. It was a different story several weeks later. We were in the living room of my garage apartment at about 10 p.m. when we heard heavy footsteps on the stairway outside. A hard knock on the door was followed by, "This is the police. Open up!" I opened the door and was confronted by four of Beckley's finest. They were large men with their holstered guns in prominent view. They pushed their way inside, and one of them pointed at Tempie, who was sitting stiffly on the couch with her jaw clenched. "What's she doing here?"

"She's my friend," I stammered. "We were just talking."

"Right." he sneered. "Get her out of here and back where she belongs, or we'll arrest both of you for cohabitation."

"But we were just talking," I protested.

He put his hand on his gun. "I could arrest both of you now, but I'll give you five minutes to get her out of here."

I nodded helplessly. When the police left, I drove Tempie to where she'd been staying, a friend's house in a predominantly black neighborhood just outside Beckley. We exchanged barely a half-dozen words. For the remainder of the summer, we met socially only in black neighborhoods. I never brought her back to my apartment.

In September, Tempie, seeking a trial separation from her husband, rented a house in Bethesda, Maryland, just outside Washington, D.C., with her two children. Regina was almost seven, and Arnya was four. I'd make the six-hour drive from Beckley every other weekend. Dick often accompanied me to share the driving and to visit friends in D.C. I'd arrive late on a Friday night. The girls would usually be asleep. On Saturday we'd all go out together, to Rock Creek Park, or the zoo, or to buy fresh clams on the Potomac River waterfront. On Sunday, we might ride bicycles or simply relax. After a late-afternoon dinner, I'd kiss Tempie and the girls goodbye and head back to Beckley.

As Tempie and I grew closer, we confronted challenges beyond those presented by the police and racist white people. We were often the object of stares when we went out in public. Tempie seemed to feel each stare acutely. For her the greatest challenge came from black men. I presumed their stares represented a combination of anger for a white man "stealing" one of their women and anguish at the historical image of white men taking advantage of black women. I ignored them. Tempie could not. To her, the stares seemed to communicate contempt for her because she had abandoned black men. Several black male colleagues in the consulting firm she had joined also told her she was making a mistake. "Stick with your own kind," they counseled. Tempie struggled with the guilt such comments produced. Years later, after we were married, she said to me in a particularly tender moment one night, "Michael, I wish you were black." I didn't pursue the comment out of fear that it would lead to a conversation I didn't want to have.

In the spring of 1969 we decided to try living together for a year, as a prelude to seriously contemplating marriage. The girls and I had become best buddies. They were too young to see skin color differences in any meaningful sense. Tempie and I loved each other, but we also needed each other. I needed female companionship, and I'd fallen in love with Regina and Arnya and couldn't imagine not having them in my life. Tempie was looking for a way out of her marriage and for help managing her children and her career. The immediate issue was where we would live. It was complicated by the fact that in September 1968, shortly after Tempie had left Beckley, Al Harrah had stepped aside, and I'd been asked to succeed him as executive director. I felt a commitment to the people involved with the organization, and I wanted Tempie and the children to move to Beckley. She would not hear of it, even though I promised it would only be for a year. She wanted to stay in the D.C. area. She had a good job and the girls were getting settled. Eventually, we decided to move to Charleston, West Virginia's capital city, and I reiterated my one-year commitment. At that point we would decide whether to get married and where to live. For the year we were in Charleston, the plan was that I would commute daily to Beckley, and Tempie would stay home to be available for the girls. I rented a circa-1930s, three-bedroom brick house with a front porch and an adjoining vacant lot on which the girls could play. It was located in the historic East End of Charleston, where the rich and powerful had lived generations earlier, and it was still predominantly, though not exclusively, a white neighborhood. But the rich and powerful had long since moved across the Kanawha River into South Hills, and the current East End residents were mostly middle-class families. The house was a block from the Capitol. I moved my stuff from the Beckley apartment, and in late August 1969, with the help of my sister, her husband, and Dick, we packed Tempie's belongings in a U-Haul truck and Dick drove them to Charleston. The rest of us followed, Tempie, the girls, and I in one car and my sister and her husband in another.

Our best laid plans didn't last long. By October the hour-long commute to Beckley had grown tiresome, and after much soul-searching, I resigned as RCCAA's executive director. I decided I could make ends meet for a year as a consultant to other anti-poverty programs. Tempie, despite her desire to be a stay-at-home mom, began looking for a job because she was reluctant to be dependent on anyone. And in a spontaneous moment, we decided to get married. We set the wedding for February 1970. It was just three years after the Supreme Court had ruled, in *Loving v. Virginia,* that bans on interracial marriage were unconstitutional.

Not everyone greeted our decision with joy. Dick loved Tempie and the girls, but when I told him of our decision, he asked incredulously, "Why would you do that? It just means trouble." A college classmate who had been part of the Prince Edward County group asked with disbelief, "Are you crazy? Somebody will kill you. The country's not ready for this yet." Among our black Raleigh County friends, one cautioned that I was not prepared for the challenges. Another wondered if I'd lost my mind. This just did not happen in Raleigh County, where Jim Crow had not been a significant fact of life, but where black people still knew their place. Our white friends just didn't understand. One couple just looked at me quizzically. A woman with whom I'd worked closely wondered aloud why someone would do such a thing. Chester, to whom I'd grown closer since the Redden incident, thought I was a "damn fool." One elderly woman actually asked a friend if our children would have zebra stripes or leopard spots. Only Rick and Rita Bank welcomed our marriage with open arms. "This marriage can't and won't fail," Rick assured me.

And then, there were the family reactions. My mother was pleased. My father's only question was whether I was sure I wanted the responsibility of raising two small children. My mother's sisters, with whom our family had always been close, had no objections either. But several of my father's eight siblings had difficulty understanding why "such a nice Jewish boy" would do such a strange thing. My mother recounted that one of my father's sisters, when told that Tempie was not Jewish, said that was fine, "As long as she's not a 'schvartzer'" (a disparaging Yiddish word for a Negro). She then almost worked herself into apoplexy trying to apologize after my mother told her that Tempie was indeed black. This same aunt saw Tempie for the first time some five years later, at my father's funeral. When they met, she hugged Tempie with a warmth that gave the impression they'd been best friends for years. It took a while, but family finally trumped prejudice.

Except for her mother, Tempie's family seemed to have no problem with the impending marriage, although they were a bit reserved at first. However, after meeting me on a trip to D.C., Tempie's mother warned her daughter that I was a "white devil." She announced she would not come to the wedding, and Tempie's pain over this as the wedding day approached was palpable. She faithfully endured a telephone call to her mother at least once a week, and the call the week before the wedding was especially painful. But for reasons we never knew, her mother unexpectedly arrived the day before the wedding with Tempie's godparents. She displayed no hostility or resistance and had a terrific time at the wedding, even consuming some alcohol, which, judging from her reaction, was not something she had done very often. She and I went on to become fast friends, and the "white devil" label never came up again.

But her initial reaction was instructive. She had grown up in segregated North Carolina during the height of Jim Crow racism and the Ku Klux Klan. She had done what was necessary to survive. That included spending virtually her entire working life as a loyal domestic worker for a white family in Clinton. She had never in my presence, and to the best of my knowledge rarely in Tempie's presence, uttered a negative word about the family whose children she raised, whose house she cleaned, whose food she cooked, and whose dirty clothes she washed. She had done all this often with the needs of her own two children coming after the needs of her employer's children.

I have little doubt that her white employers thought they treated her with kindness and generosity. They frequently sent leftover food home with "Miss Lillie." They usually let her off a bit early on Thanksgiving and Christmas so that after serving them, she could spend at least part of these holidays with her own family. They saved their children's clothes to hand down to

Tempie and her brother, drove Miss Lillie home in bad weather, and were flexible if Tempie or her brother was sick. As Miss Lillie got older and more frail, and unable to work regularly, they became even more flexible. When Miss Lillie died, the woman of the house came to the funeral and was extremely gracious. She even commented how close her family felt to Miss Lillie. But it seems clear that Miss Lillie's initial reaction to me came a lot closer to how she truly felt about her station in life, and about the white people who persevered day and night to keep her right there.

Tempie possessed none of her mother's deferential manner. Her scorn for the white family that had consumed so much of her mother's time and energy at the expense of her and her brother showed itself often. The incident I remember best occurred when we were about to leave Clinton for the six-hour drive back to Charleston after a visit of several days. Miss Lillie emerged from the back bedroom with a bag of hand-me-down clothing from her employer's granddaughters. They were intended for Regina and Arnya. Tempie took them without protest, not wishing to provoke an argument with her mother. But they went straight to the Salvation Army when we got home. Tempie had no intention of ever letting her children wear hand-me-downs from that family.

That childhood pain of holidays and Saturdays alone because her mother was taking care of a white family, the embarrassment of wearing clothes handed down from the children of that family, the sting of being humiliated by that family's condescending attitudes, had stayed with her. It infused every aspect of growing up black in the segregated South: the burden Tempie's mother had to carry, the dismissive way her father was treated after his logging accident, the taunts of white children riding by in their school bus while she and her friends trudged to school in the blistering heat or the pouring rain, the brand-new school she couldn't go to, the stores in town she couldn't shop in, the many things white kids had that she could not have. This was a pain with which I could sympathize, but never empathize. And so began my journey through the minefield of race relations in the United States.

VI

FINDING A PLACE FOR US

I wanted to bottle the feelings of our wedding night: the ecstasy, warmth, invincibility, anticipation about the future. Gone were the misgivings of friends and family, the hostility of Tempie's mother, the subtle reservations of my father, the questions about when we'd leave Charleston and where we'd go. We were just another newly married couple basking in the company of family and friends, celebrating a milestone in our lives at a raucous and fun-filled party.

We had decided to get married in late February. Only briefly had we discussed the challenges we would confront as an interracial couple—where we would live, how that would affect our social lives and employment options, and how we would raise the children. I believed we could handle the challenges, and I was anxious to get married. Tempie seemed to take strength from my optimism, even though she may have thought me naïve. For the location we chose a Baptist church in Beckley pastored by a black minister who'd been involved with some of our community action programs. We hoped that would appeal to Tempie's mother. To marry us, we chose a community action colleague from another county, a white Presbyterian preacher who was quietly questioning his belief in God. That, we hoped, would appeal to my mother. The compromise reflected our own different religious upbringings, as well.

We invited virtually everyone we knew in Raleigh County to the ceremony on Saturday at 2 p.m., to be followed immediately by wedding cake and punch in the church basement. The real bash for family and close friends would be that evening at the mountaintop home of Jeff and Beverly Monroe in nearby Fayette County. Jeff was also a Presbyterian minister, and he had been the head of the Governor's Office of Economic Opportunity in Charleston during most of my time in Beckley. I had come to know him well. By the time Tempie and I moved to Charleston, he'd become head of the Tech Foundation, the development and outreach arm of the West Virginia Institute of Technology in Montgomery, West Virginia, about thirty miles southeast of Charleston. He'd bought an abandoned country club on top of a mountain near Montgomery and converted it into his home. By February I had abandoned my lame efforts at consulting and accepted Jeff's invitation to join him at the Tech Foundation. When I told him of our marriage plans, he insisted on hosting the wedding night party.

The days leading up to the wedding were typically tense. Tempie had decided to make the girls' dresses for the ceremony. She was proud of her sewing ability, and it would save money. In the wee hours of Saturday morning, she was still putting the finishing touches on the dresses. We had agreed to write our own vows, and I was still working on mine as Tempie put her old Singer sewing machine through its final paces. On Thursday morning, in an astounding change of heart, Tempie's mother arrived. She commandeered the kitchen and took over household chores. Although her arrival threw us a bit off our stride, it eliminated a key source of tension for Tempie.

On Saturday, I left for Beckley at 11 a.m. with my best man, my sister's then-husband, Bob. We'd rented rooms at the Town and Country Motel in which to change clothes before and after the ceremony. Tempie and the girls were to follow shortly thereafter. I arrived at the church in full dress at about 1:30 p.m., but as 2 p.m. approached, there was no sign of Tempie. By 2:15 p.m., the people in the packed church were getting restless. By 2:25 p.m., I was imagining the embarrassment of being left at the altar. Finally, at 2:30 p.m., the car with Tempie and the girls pulled up. Tempie breathlessly explained that they'd had trouble fitting the girls' dresses. Oh, and by the way, she'd lost the paper on which she'd written the vows, so could she share my copy? The ceremony, though, went off without a hitch. As I stood at the altar watching Tempie walk up the aisle in her flowing white dress, surrounded by family and good friends, I felt there was nothing we couldn't do. Together, we would change the world.

The feeling continued uninterrupted into the night. There was a seated dinner prepared largely by Beverly Monroe and other friends, in what had been the banquet room of the country club. Liquor flowed in the adjacent room, which had been the club's bar, and where Jeff, who had a substantial capacity for alcohol, had mixed several punches spiked with vodka, gin, and grain alcohol. After dinner, a band led by Jeff's teenage son played dance music, from the big band sounds of the 1940s to Elvis Presley, the Platters, Chubby Checker, and the Beatles, into the wee hours of the morning. They began and ended the night with our wedding song, Dionne Warwick's rendition of the *West Side Story* classic, "There's a Place for Us."

I'd never before experienced a more racially or economically diverse group gathered for a party. Mingling and dancing together as if this were an everyday event in the hills of West Virginia were Tempie's family and friends, my family and friends, and our mutual friends from Beckley. The latter included community organizers like Gibbs, David, Steve, Dick, and Rick and Rita, and all of the local leaders with whom we'd worked. The middle-aged, white Raleigh County woman who worked for the Community Action Association and who'd wondered earlier why anyone would get married to someone of a different race had knitted us a wall hanging with the inscription, "Smile on your brother." One of Tempie's new colleagues on a job she had just taken, a black man named LaVonda Tucker whose wife, Ruth, was white, took charge of Tempie's mother for the evening. He plied her with glasses of Jeff's punch, which tasted like fruit juice but packed a hidden wallop. When he thought she'd had enough, which wasn't much, he settled her gently into an easy chair in a quiet room where she promptly fell fast asleep. Until the day she passed away, she denied having had any alcohol. She was just tired, she insisted.

The girls, full of themselves like typical eight—and five-year-olds on such an occasion, had sneaked some of Jeff's punch and were also out cold by 9 p.m. in one of the bedrooms.

My Uncle Sam was the only one of my father's eight siblings to attend the wedding. For him, family trumped everything. "If Michael loves her," he said to my mother in his thick Yiddish accent, "that's good enough for me." He and Aunt Shirley were in their late sixties at the time. They had lived all their working lives in a predominantly white environment in Brooklyn, and had retired to a similar environment in Florida a few years earlier. They danced well into the night, surrounded by surely the most integrated group of people they'd ever encountered. Later, Uncle Sam could have us laughing uproariously by recounting their experience driving back to the hotel, my father at the helm, slightly inebriated and in a totally unfamiliar environment, driving off of the mountain on the narrow, winding road, without street lights in the late night. "You know," he'd conclude with a twinkle, "if the snow had not melted, we might still be dancing." Fortunately, a late winter thaw had saved the day. I never forgot his support.

Rick and Rita had agreed to keep the girls for a week while Tempie and I honeymooned in Freeport in the Bahamas. Sometime after midnight, Rick and I carried the girls to the car, and then they all headed off the mountain. Tempie and I had a 10 a.m. Sunday flight from Charleston to Miami, where we would connect to a Freeport flight. We left the party after 2 a.m., arrived home about an hour later, set the alarm for 8 a.m., and fell asleep in each other's arms.

When I awoke the next morning, I rolled over and looked at the clock. I shook Tempie gently. "Hey, Babe," I whispered. "What time was our flight?"

"I think it's ten." She yawned without opening her eyes. "Why?"

"Because it's ten-thirty now."

After several frantic calls to the airlines, we were able to rearrange our flight reservations to arrive in Freeport late that night. We were still flying high from the bliss of the night before, and we were looking forward to the future, certain in the knowledge that there was a special "place for us."

We returned home a week later to face the more mundane realities of life. I had meant it when I promised Tempie that we'd only stay in Charleston for a year. But looking back now, I realize I had been deceiving both of us. I had grown to love West Virginia—the beauty of the mountains and the challenge of guiding my Volkswagen around the twisting, roller-coaster roads, the pace of life where people took time to know you and to exchange daily pleasantries, and the people, both local folks and outsiders, whose warmth could envelop you. Furthermore, I was sensitive to the charge that so-called "poverty warriors" came to the mountains for a year or two, stirred things up, and then headed back home to their comfortable environments. Too often, they disrupted carefully balanced power relationships and left in their wake chaos along with heightened and unrealistic expectations. I saw a number of young VISTA volunteers do just that, but I wanted to finish what I'd started. Living in Charleston, I had told myself, would allow me to run the program and maintain key relationships in Raleigh County. I soon recognized my self-deception. Within a couple of months I'd given up the reins of the RCCAA and the daily, hour-long commute to Raleigh County.

Charleston's appeal, however, was growing. The children were adjusting nicely. Although Regina was a bit more headstrong than Arnya, both girls accepted me as their father and only occasionally referred to their biological father, who called infrequently from North Carolina to talk with them. They had made friends with girls their ages and seemed happy in school. Rick and Rita were frequent Sunday visitors for steaks on the grill. Both Tempie and I had new jobs and were beginning to find our rhythm. We were also pleasantly surprised by the relative lack of hostility to our marriage. There were a few "n—r-lover" epithets shouted occasionally from passing cars, but most white people we encountered either seemed genuinely indifferent, or they bent over backwards trying to demonstrate their lack of prejudice by giving us better-than-average service in stores and restaurants. Most black people welcomed us with open arms, inviting us into their homes and fussing over the girls. We also met several other interracial couples. A couple of black men who worked with Tempie, including Tucker, were married to white women. There were also some interracial couples associated with nearby West Virginia State College, an HBCU. The presence of the college, the state capitol, and major chemical plants created a diverse and cosmopolitan environment.

Our job situation was a decisive factor. Jeff Monroe had reached out to me shortly after we'd moved to Charleston. His new job involved community outreach and fund-raising for West Virginia Tech, one of the leading smaller colleges in West Virginia. Jeff, a good old boy from southwest Virginia with a preacher's gift for gab and connections throughout the state, was the perfect choice for the job. He asked me to join him as head of the Community Service Center, which he'd created inside the Tech Foundation to address community needs. His not-so-hidden agenda was to organize the unincorporated thirty-mile strip between Charleston and Montgomery, where West Virginia Tech was located, into a single incorporated municipality. Jeff reasoned (correctly, as our research later showed) that with municipal tax revenues, the area could be one of the richest municipalities in the state with vastly improved public services (sewage treatment, storm drainage, garbage pickup, recreational and health facilities) for the thousands of people living in the local hollows. He wanted me to build grassroots support for the idea. Thus was born the "skinny city" concept.

As Jeff and I launched the skinny city concept with the tacit approval of West Virginia Tech's president and the assistance of several professors, I was reminded of a Sunday afternoon I'd spent with Gibbs in his living room about six months after I arrived in Beckley. Kathy was away, and Gibbs had asked me to come by. When I arrived he brought out a huge watermelon, a bottle of gin, and a couple of knives. We cut holes in the watermelon, poured gin into the holes, and put the watermelon in the refrigerator to marinate. Gibbs then produced a map of West

Virginia. Calmly, he laid out his vision for repeating the success of the Raleigh County community-organizing experience in several other key counties and, thus, "taking over the state." Once the watermelon was ready, we ingested it as we detailed plans for achieving his vision. By early evening we were in an advanced state of inebriation, and our plans reflected our condition. Not surprisingly, Gibbs' vision never made it out of his living room. Our skinny city plans proved equally unrealistic.

Nonetheless, for nearly two years, from November 1969 to September 1971, we worked on the concept. With grant funds from the U.S. Department of Housing and Urban Development, we did the research necessary to demonstrate the financial efficacy of the idea, to identify appropriate boundaries for the new municipality, and to determine the most effective legal processes for incorporating the area. I organized a community advisory committee to build grassroots support for the idea. We generated significant local support, substantial interest from "good government" people both locally and nationally, and considerable media coverage. However, we had two powerful opponents: the Republican governor, whose support would be needed to pass incorporation legislation but who saw the project as anti-business, and the large chemical and coal companies located in the unincorporated area that wanted to avoid paying municipal taxes. The skinny city idea, idealistic and economically feasible though it may have been, had about as much chance of becoming reality as did our gin-induced plans for taking over the state. It died a premature death two years after we began, victimized by political and business muscle that shut off funds and quieted public interest. Perhaps, as a friend of mine often says, it was an idea ahead of its time. Today, the concept of regional government is accepted in many places as a way to achieve economies of scale in providing public services to a wider and more diverse population.

While Jeff and I were pursuing "skinny city," Tempie had found a job as a recruiter for the Charleston Opportunities Industrialization Center (OIC), a local branch of a national job training and placement program headquartered in Philadelphia, Pennsylvania. It had been founded by Reverend Leon Sullivan, a large, imposing man with a booming voice and consummate leadership skills. Reverend Sullivan was a Charleston native and later became a prime mover in applying corporate pressure to end apartheid through principles he developed for corporations doing business in South Africa. Despite the fact that my mother and all three of her sisters were professionals, I had grown up with the distinctly old-school notion that it was a husband's responsibility to be the breadwinner and the wife's responsibility to remain at home with the children. In fact, I took pride in earning what I thought was enough money to support our entire family. So, I did not encourage Tempie to seek work. But her fear of dependency, as well as her more realistic view of our financial needs, drove her. The job with OIC proved enjoyable and fulfilling, and it enabled us to live a bit better than from paycheck to paycheck. Tempie met people at work who would become lifelong friends, including Beverly Jones, a single mother whose son Billy was about Regina's age, and the aforementioned LaVonda Tucker, who usually went simply by the name Tucker.

Sadly, Tucker died of an asthmatic attack in the 1990s. Beverly, now Beverly Martin, lives in the D.C. area and remains a close friend. Billy died prematurely from heart problems in 2010, but Beverly's second son, Jamal, is one of my son Ian's closest friends. I took both of them on several summer trips when they were adolescents.

As is often the case, events surrounding children accelerated the process of settling in. Arnya was five years old when we moved to Charleston, not quite old enough for the first grade, so we enrolled her in a daycare center three blocks from our house. She was one of two black children out of a total of about fifty children. Tempie dropped her off at 9 a.m. in the morning and picked her up at 3 p.m. so they could both be home when Regina, then nearly eight years old and a third-grader, returned from school. One day at about noon, Tempie, who was not yet working, was in the kitchen when she heard the front door open. "I'm home,

Mommy," came the small voice. Tempie rushed into the front hall to find Arnya staring up at her with a sly smile. "How did you get home?" she demanded. "I walked," came the proud reply. She had left the center and walked home, crossing two busy streets in the process. Tempie immediately called the center to demand an explanation, only to discover that the teachers hadn't noticed Arnya missing. Tempie fumed: "As long as black children aren't causing any trouble, they don't pay any attention to them." There was no way to know for sure whether racism or incompetence or both had been at play. What we did know was that the center had put our little girl's life in danger by allowing her to walk away. We would never send her back there.

Shortly before Arnya's solo trip home, we had read an article about a group of low-income African American parents who, dissatisfied with Charleston's official Head Start program and unsuccessful in getting it changed, were seeking to start their own parent-run preschool program. We decided to investigate it as an option for Arnya. It didn't take us long to become totally immersed in the effort, helping to raise money through raffles and selling fried chicken dinners out of parents' homes, designing promotional flyers to recruit children, and working with sympathetic professional educators, several of them white, on a curriculum development committee. Soon, I became editor of the newsletter. Arnya thrived in the program, and we all developed new friendships. With Tempie's job at the OIC and our involvement in the Triangle Community School, as the preschool came to be called, we began to develop deep roots in Charleston's black community.

Toward the end of the first year, rather than leaving Charleston, we began looking for a house to buy. The house we were living in was not for sale, so we found an appealing house at an affordable price on Carney Road, a little cul-de-sac across the Kanawha River in South Hills, a more upscale, predominantly white area. It was modest, with a front entrance into a finished basement on the ground floor and another front entrance into the living room one flight up. A kitchen lay directly behind the living room, and a bedroom and bathroom were to the right of the kitchen. Beyond the kitchen, a large wooden deck led into the woods, and at the side of the house there was a decent-sized piece of sloping land on which the girls could play. Another flight up were two bedrooms separated by a bathroom. Tempie and I took the larger bedroom, and the girls shared the other one. It was perfect for us. The price was under $25,000, and we borrowed the down payment of $5,000 from my parents. It was the first home either of us had owned, and we were awestruck. On the day we officially became the owners, we invited Rick and Rita and two other VISTA volunteers we knew from Mingo County, West Virginia, Bill and Claudia Schechter, to share a champagne toast with us on the floor of our empty living room. We weren't moving for another couple of days, but we couldn't wait to celebrate.

Beyond being awestruck, however, we were somewhat apprehensive. The cul-de-sac had four other houses, all owned by white families. Despite the relative lack of hostility we'd experienced so far, we worried about our reception. We didn't expect a warm greeting; we agreed that we'd be happy to be ignored. But would there be antagonism about our moving next door? Should we be concerned about harassment—or worse? Could we bring our African American friends to the house? We had talked about these things, but not in great detail. I think both Tempie and I hoped that ignoring the problem would make it go away. As the movers unloaded the truck, though, I began to worry that we'd been horribly blind. In the east end of Charleston there were a few other black families. But up here, we were alone. What would we do if neighbors petitioned us to leave? Or worse, if our home was vandalized? Or even worse, if the girls were mistreated? My midday nightmare was interrupted by a knock on the door. A young woman introduced herself as Mary Hoyer, our neighbor across the street. She and her husband Gene had two young children, and she hoped our children could play together. She handed us a plate of cookies she had baked to welcome us to the neighborhood. As profusely as Tempie and I thanked her, I still don't think she ever knew how important that gesture was in easing our adjustment to Carney Road.

Shortly after we moved in, I confronted a vivid example of my white privilege. Urban renewal had come to Clinton, North Carolina, where Tempie's parents lived. The old frame houses on Maple Street were going to be torn down. The residents, all black, were offered opportunities to buy newly constructed homes several blocks away on paved streets with sidewalks. These houses fit Pete Seeger's description as "little boxes," but they were a dramatic improvement on the old ones. They were more spacious, with central heating and air conditioning, modern kitchen appliances, and small lawns. They were affordably priced at $15,000, but Tempie's parents could not come close to affording that price. So we scraped together money for a down payment and made the mortgage payments ourselves. I was struck by the contrast. When we had needed money for a down payment on our house, we borrowed it from my parents. But Tempie's parents needed money from us to purchase their house. After we divorced, Tempie continued to make the mortgage payments for her parents, thus limiting her ability to save money. This was a clear example of how our history of economic oppression of African Americans has a legacy that keeps on taking.

This legacy of oppression surfaced in several other ways early in our marriage. In 1972, we left the girls with Tempie's parents so we could return to the Bahamas for a vacation, this time in Nassau. We arrived back at the Raleigh-Durham Airport late one night, retrieved our car from the parking lot, and headed to Clinton ninety minutes southwest. As we approached the town of Smithville, we saw red lights in the distance. When we got closer, we saw that the lights illuminated a huge billboard. When we got still closer, we could read the billboard: "This is Klan country. Fight integration and communism. Impeach Earl Warren. Welcome to Smithville." Tempie and I looked at each other, and I slowed down as we got closer to town. The one traffic light in town turned red as we approached it. I cursed under my breath as I came to a stop. Across the street stood a group of about a half-dozen white teenage boys. They were too busy smoking and laughing to notice us, and in the dark night, they would have had a difficult time making out the skin color of the car's occupants. Nonetheless, we were frightened. Much had changed in the South in the previous decade, but we were not anxious to test the extent of that change. Tempie slid down in the passenger seat in order to be less visible and admonished me, "Don't drive a single mile over the speed limit until we get to Mama's house." Normally an incurably fast driver, I obeyed her with precision.

I've never forgotten that sign. As a white man alone, I can drive through Smithville and walk its streets unnoticed unless I open my mouth to reveal my Yankee accent. However, since experiencing that sign with Tempie, I've never been back there, although I've been to North Carolina countless times. I presume the sign is long since gone, and Smithville may now be a wonderfully open-minded town. But I still remember the fear and anger I felt that night, and it's difficult to imagine ever feeling comfortable there. It is another legacy of an era not quite consigned to history.

On another occasion early in our marriage, we were returning from our Easter visit to my in-laws. As usual, we left for home after a Sunday afternoon dinner. We were on Interstate 85 between Durham and Greensboro when I saw the flashing red and blue lights of a state trooper in my rearview mirror. I didn't think I'd been speeding, but I wasn't sure because I'd been talking with Tempie and joking with the girls. I cursed under my breath at my inattention and pulled over. The trooper, tall, young, and white, had his hand on his gun holster as he approached and ordered me out of the car. "What's wrong, officer?" I had learned to be especially polite to the police since I'd been married.

"Are you going to get out of this car or am I going to have to pull you out?" He unbuttoned his holster. I did not look at Tempie or the girls. I opened the door and got out. "What's wrong, officer," I asked, the fear—make that terror—resonating in my voice. "Your license and registration," the trooper ordered. I took them out of my wallet and handed them to him. He glanced at them. "Come with me," he commanded. I glanced back at Tempie as I followed the trooper's order. Her eyes were wide as she watched me and tried to calm the girls at the same time.

Sitting in the police car, I tried to imagine what the problem was and what Tempie would do if I were arrested. Visions of "Mississippi justice" flashed through my head. Meanwhile, the officer was radioing headquarters to check on the license plate of the car. Finally, after about fifteen minutes that seemed like fifteen hours, the trooper got out of the car, motioned me out of the backseat, handed me my license and registration, and said, "You're free to go." I stammered, "Can you tell me what this was all about, please?" Without looking at me, he said, "There was a bank robbery by a colored man and woman, and they were driving a blue Buick. We were just checking you out." I started to protest, thought better of it, and headed back to the car. I've heard of cases of mistaken identity, but we were not "a colored man and woman," we were driving a green Chevy Impala, and we had two children with us. But we were a mixed-race couple in a place where it was frowned upon, and I presume we were victims of the trooper's desire to put us in our place, to let us know that the multiracial composition of our family was not acceptable to him.

These early experiences—the confrontations in Beckley with the waitress and with the police, encountering the Smithville sign, the incident with the state trooper—were humiliating and reminded me of my feeling in Prince Edward County that white people could not be trusted. I trusted my family—most of them, at least—and my friends, and some other white people I knew well. But when I was with Tempie, I found myself looking at police officers with suspicion and being wary of strangers on the street. I approached sales clerks with misgiving. In restaurants I often wondered whether we were getting slower or less courteous service than white patrons. When we traveled, I'd leave Tempie and the children in the car while I checked on room availability at motels, and we looked closely at restaurants to determine whether the location and look were congenial or might foreshadow trouble.

In Clinton, when I ventured out of the black community, I felt like I was in enemy territory, even when I was alone and the white people I encountered couldn't possibly know who I was. I learned to instinctively recognize the stores in which my black family was not welcome by their atmosphere, by the look of the sales people and customers, and by the quality of the products on display. I knew my place and felt similarly unwelcome. Even in stores where my family could shop, I would feel uncomfortable if there were too many white people around. On one visit to Clinton, I took Regina and Arnya, then nine and seven, to the five-and-ten store. I was holding the hands of both girls as we walked down the toy aisle searching for the special toy I had promised each of them. We passed two white women walking in the opposite direction. When they got past us, one of them said, "Isn't it so nice that he's brought the maid's children with him?" The girls were too absorbed by the toys to pay attention. I felt humiliated, though. I started to tell them these were my children, but I stopped. What good would it do?

In Clinton's black community, on the other hand, I was welcomed, even protected. I quickly became one of the family and hung out with Tempie's aunts, uncles, and cousins. I felt much safer there than I did downtown or in any part of the white community. On one visit, Tempie's brother Don was home as well. A kind and generous man, he'd had some traumatic experiences in Vietnam, had returned home on a stretcher, and recovered physically. But for years he was plagued with nightmares and a drinking problem. With steely determination, he conquered both. On this Saturday night, we decided to go to the American Legion club, a weekend hangout for many young blacks, a place where they felt safe from the whims of local police. Tempie wondered out loud whether my presence might cause trouble. Don never hesitated. "If there's trouble, they'll have to deal with me. This is my brother, man, and nobody messes with my family." We had no trouble that night. I have often wondered whether my family of origin would have had my back so openly and clearly. I was beginning to find my place.

VII

EMBRACING OUR PLACE

I embraced fatherhood. Tempie and I attended every back-to-school night and PTA meeting. We talked with the girls about the importance of doing well in school and sat through more school band and choir recitals than I care to remember. We chauffeured them to piano lessons. I took the girls and Beverly's son, Billy, to the movies and to the games of the Charleston Charlies, the local minor league baseball team. We hosted sleepovers for the girls and became the go-to house for their friends. For a time we virtually adopted Regina's best friend, Brenda, whose single mother worked nights as a singer at a local club. We went on a vacation trip for at least a week every summer, to Niagara Falls and Toronto, Six Flags Amusement Park in Cincinnati, Disney World in Florida, Williamsburg, and Puerto Rico. We visited Tempie's parents for Easter, my parents for Thanksgiving, and hosted out-of-town family for Christmas. Christmas was a fun-filled time, especially the shopping: train sets, children's cooking items, games, dolls with dark skin, books, three-speed bicycles that Rick and I tried to assemble one Christmas Eve in between gulps of eggnog. I loved the girls and reveled in being their father. There was one missing ingredient, though—a child of our own. Since our honeymoon, we had been trying to get pregnant without success. After a year of disappointment, we resigned ourselves to failure.

In the summer of 1971, on our way home from a Niagara Falls vacation, we stopped in Boston to visit Dick Yannantuono, my former Beckley roommate, who had recently moved there. We toured Harvard University and spoke with an admissions officer in the Graduate School of Education. She encouraged both of us to apply for the Master's Program in Education. Although we had been on Carney Road for only a year, it was clear that skinny city would soon be a casualty of political and business pressures and that a transition was approaching. A visit to the Harvard Book Store clinched it. We would apply. Tempie followed through as soon as we returned home, but I procrastinated.

Then in October I was offered a job working for Charleston's newly elected mayor. Skinny city had indeed died, and Jeff had arranged an interview for me with Don Richardson, Charleston's new city manager and a close friend of Jeff's. I agreed to the interview at Jeff's insistence, even though we were planning to move. John Hutchinson was, at thirty-seven, the youngest mayor ever elected to lead the state's capital city, and only its second Democratic mayor of the twentieth century. A good-looking, dynamic white man with an attractive, strong-willed wife whose father had once been the state's attorney general, John had left his insurance business to run on a progressive platform. He advocated ending the allegedly discriminatory relocation practices of the Urban Renewal Authority in the Triangle, a black community just west of the downtown area and the site of the preschool program in which we'd become so involved. He opposed a planned interstate highway through the heart of the Triangle. He promised to bring more federal grant money into the city to improve poor neighborhoods.

Of Charleston's 70,000 residents, fewer than 10 percent were black. But the planned destruction of the Triangle community had spawned vocal protests. When the phlegmatic incumbent mayor remained silent, John took advantage of the controversy by appealing to the consciences of many white residents and their desire to maintain racial harmony. He'd eked out a narrow victory. His wife's political lineage had also helped. The creation of a Mayor's Office of Federal-State Programs was an important step toward fulfilling his promises.

Busy with a new family, a job thirty miles away, and helping to get the Triangle Community School off the ground, I had ignored the campaign and knew nobody in Charleston's political community. After a few brief pleasantries, Don ushered me upstairs to see the mayor. I hadn't expected to talk directly with him. It doesn't matter, I told myself; I'm not going to work for a politician, and besides, we're moving to Boston. But as I sat in his office answering questions about my Beckley experiences and my views on urban renewal and interstate highway construction, I found myself drawn to the man. He was a compelling figure, tall and erect, congenial, with a hearty laugh that seemed to rise from the pit of his stomach. However, he could turn serious in an instant, and his probing questions focused on my understanding of and commitment to carrying out his campaign promises. After an hour of intense conversation, the mayor stood up and declared, "I think you're my man, Mike. Now, before we seal the deal, is there anything in your background that you haven't told me that might embarrass the administration?"

I hesitated. Should I tell him? I was sure he'd change his mind. He'd say how sorry he was, how he didn't have a racist bone in his body, but that Charleston was just not ready for this yet. He'd claim that it would be a distraction that would interfere with my ability to work effectively with all sectors of the community. Then he'd shake my hand and wish me luck as he ushered me out of his office. So what? I really didn't want the job anyway, I reasoned. "Well, Mr. Mayor, I'm married to a black woman." He waved his arm dismissively. "I know that. I couldn't care less." Then he pointed his finger at me and concluded: "But if you have any parking tickets you haven't paid,"—I did—"pay them before you start work. There'll be no special favors in my administration." Moving to Boston lost its luster for me. With Tempie's reluctant concurrence, I accepted the job, although she still expected me to submit the Harvard application. To her chagrin the deadline passed, and the application remained unfinished. I told myself that she would not be accepted, and her frustration would pass.

In the spring of 1972, Tempie announced startling news: she was pregnant. Joy reigned in the Wenger household for about a week—and then the letter from Harvard arrived. Tempie had been accepted. She was determined to go, and who could blame her? Acceptance at Harvard is a striking accomplishment for anyone, but for a southern black woman in 1972, a master's degree in education from Harvard meant she could write her own career ticket. I was immensely proud of her, but my agenda had changed. I liked my new job; I didn't want to move. At the same time, I desperately wanted to be an integral part of the pregnancy, to watch her stomach grow, feel the baby kicking, take care of her as the pregnancy progressed. We argued about it several times, and as her deadline for replying to Harvard approached, the tension in the household thickened. "If you leave," I said to her one day, "I'm afraid our marriage will be over." "Our marriage will be fine," she replied. "We can see each other a couple of weekends a month. And, besides, we wouldn't have this problem if you'd applied like we agreed." On the day before the deadline, Tempie informed me that she would not go. Selfishly, I was thrilled. She handled the situation with grace, but it created a divide between us that I believe never fully healed. She would make occasional references to her disappointment in the ensuing years of our marriage, and I never was able to purge the guilt I felt at costing her that opportunity.

The pregnancy proceeded without incident and with much excitement. The girls could hardly wait to be able to take care of the baby, and we included them in discussing possible names. From the library we got a book of Hebrew names and a book of African names; we were determined that the baby's name would reflect its unique heritage. We all went through names, looking for combinations with meaning and a harmonious sound. As the mid-December due date approached, my mother made plans to spend two weeks with us to help take care of the baby. She arrived the day before the due date, but the next several days passed without a hint of approaching labor. Finally, my mother could stand it no longer. On December 23, she took Tempie downtown, and they walked, and walked, and walked. That night, Tempie's water broke. It was a snowy night. As I backed the car out of our cul-de-sac at about 11 p.m. to head for the hospital, a naked man appeared in my rear view mirror, waving his arms. I was stunned into immobility. Tempie snapped me out of it with a crisp, "Drive, Michael." When we got to the hospital, I called my mother and warned her to lock the doors and windows. Then I called the police. I later found out that the police picked him up shortly afterward and that he'd been spaced out on drugs.

Tempie was in labor for the remainder of the night. At 6:21 a.m. on December 24, 1972, Ian Kimani Wenger—the name means merciful sailor—was born, 50 percent Eastern European, 37.5 percent African American, and 12.5 percent Native American. He was the spitting image of my father. "Mini-Manny," I christened him. My father arrived a day later, and a picture of him holding Ian confirms my assessment. Ian's eyes and the shape of his mouth were pure Wenger, but his olive skin and his hair texture clearly reflected his mixed heritage. Tempie and Ian came home on December 26. With Ian in her arms, Tempie carefully navigated the slippery, snowy steps up to our house while I gripped her arm in case she lost her footing. Waiting expectantly at the top of the steps were my parents, and between them, eleven-year-old Regina and eight-year-old Arnya. A new phase in our lives was about to begin.

Meanwhile, I was growing to love my job as head of Charleston's Office of Federal-State Programs. Because of my community organizing experience, I quickly became John's go-to guy on neighborhood problems. I worked with community organizations in both black and white neighborhoods in preparing federal funding proposals to build community centers, lay storm sewers in the hill sections, rehabilitate housing, and develop job training programs. At first, community leaders were suspicious. I had not been in Charleston very long, had not been involved in the Hutchinson campaign, and had a Yankee accent. But as federal funds began flowing into the city, my credibility rose. Having an African American spouse eased my acceptance in black neighborhoods and did not seem to be a problem in white communities.

About a year after I took the job, I confronted an issue for which there were no good options. John had been elected with strong union support, but he did not get along well with Miles Stanley, head of the state AFL-CIO. In the flush of a rare Democratic victory in the mayor's office, Stanley tried to force a public employees union on the city. John resisted, citing state law and his responsibility to represent the people without third-party interference. The conflict quickly became a political power struggle, and two things were clear. First, there would be no compromise between these two strong-willed men. A city workers' strike seemed inevitable. Second, since the prime organizing targets were sanitation and street workers, who were overwhelmingly black, the strike would become a racial issue. I felt trapped. On the one hand, despite his resistance to a union, the mayor was fulfilling his promises to the black community. Even before the strike threat, he had raised salaries and improved working conditions in the sanitation and street departments. On the other hand, most of our Charleston friends were black, although not city workers, and I'd learned from my parents that crossing a picket line bought you a ticket straight to hell. I suggested possible compromises to the mayor, driven more by my own need to find a solution than by his. He was immovable. Finally, in a telephone conversation before a critical city council meeting, he told me I could either be with him or take a walk. With Tempie's support, I stayed, telling myself that this was just a power grab by Stanley and that John had the best interests of the workers and of the city at heart.

My decision filled me with dread. Telling my parents I would cross a picket line was the first challenge. This was not a typical strike, I told them. It was not about good versus evil; there were shades of gray. There was a long silence on the other end of the phone line. Then there was the risk of losing our friends. Rick and Rita, like me, believed that a public employees union was the workers' right, and they felt that John's position was indefensible. So did most other progressive people I knew. I was surprised, though, when our black friends, many of them long-time residents of Charleston, did not automatically support the strike. They were not happy about the gathering storm, but the history of being ignored by city fathers was fresh in their minds. John listened to them, he was fulfilling his campaign promises, and the door to city hall was open. A philosophical commitment to labor unions was less important to them than having immediate community needs met.

Perhaps most challenging for me was the need to confront my own principles, especially after John threatened to fire striking workers for illegally walking off the job. The strike leaders retaliated by bringing in Ralph Abernathy, Martin Luther King Jr.'s longtime ally and successor as head of the Southern Christian Leadership Conference, for a downtown rally in support of the strikers. I wanted to attend, but that surely would have meant my job. Tempie and I sat at home that evening as I consoled myself with opiates like, "I have a family to support," "I can do more good for the community by keeping my job," "John is keeping his campaign promises," and "The strike is just a power grab by the union." But I could not avoid the conclusion that life was much more complicated than I'd imagined.

Few people expected the young mayor to be able to hold out against union-organizing efforts in a state where unions dominated. Surely, after some brave rhetoric, he'd cave in when the heat became too intense. After all, they reasoned, he almost certainly had political ambitions beyond being mayor. And yet, besieged by frightened politicians, harassed by union organizers, threatened by striking workers, branded a racist by some, and beset by citizens who simply wanted their trash collected, he prevailed, through a combination of ingenuity and grit. He replaced striking workers with unemployed residents, also predominantly black. He rode with police as they provided protection against threats of violence to the new workers and their families. He made trash collection less labor-intensive by issuing plastic garbage bags free to all city residents and requiring that trash be bagged and placed in front of the house on collection days. His attorneys vigorously and successfully defended his action in court. And he refused to break, even when Democratic presidential candidate George McGovern declined to campaign in Charleston in the fall of 1972 because of the strike. Eventually, as the city prevailed in court battles, as the trash was picked up efficiently, and as John's resolve remained unyielding, the strike leaders disappeared from public view, the issue gradually faded, and John was twice reelected as mayor by margins of four to one, each time garnering overwhelming support from the black community.

The only time this issue came up again for me was several months later, when my parents visited us in Charleston. As was his style, the mayor invited Tempie and me and my parents to his house one evening for drinks with him and his wife. He answered the doorbell himself, shook hands with my father, and stuck out his hand to my mother. She backed up a step, put her hands on her hips, looked up from her four-foot-eight vantage point directly into John's eyes, and declared, "I wanted to meet the man who made my son cross a picket line." Without missing a beat, he let out his trademark hearty laugh, invited us all in, and charmed my parents over the next two hours as he plied us all with liquor.

Not long after the strike faded and political tempers cooled, John asked me to take over the reins of the Charleston Urban Renewal Authority on an acting basis. I was charged with making good on his promise to end the alleged racial discrimination in relocation activities. During the previous administration, the seven-member authority composed solely of white businessmen appointed by the mayor for staggered terms had developed a plan for bulldozing the houses in the Triangle. They planned to relocate the black residents, many of whom owned their homes, to the far end of the city or beyond, and to utilize a planned exit off the Interstate as a magnet for commercial development on the cleared land. They called it removing "a blot on the downtown." Others called it, more accurately, "planned black removal."

John's opposition to the plan had won him overwhelming black support in the election. However, it was not until the third year of his first term that he had a sufficient number of appointments to the Urban Renewal Authority to wrest effective control from the incumbents. By that time, relocation activities were well underway amid charges that the Authority was harassing black homeowners to get them to sell, low-balling them on appraisals of their properties, and threatening to condemn their properties if they didn't take the "fair market" offer. Some families had already sold their homes and moved; others were holding out hope that John could save their community.

On the day his appointments gave him effective control, I was appointed acting director of the Urban Renewal Authority. But John's appointments to the authority concerned me. He'd appointed one African American community activist, but among his other choices were a prominent attorney and four wealthy business leaders, all white men, none with a reputation for sensitivity to the black community. Many Triangle residents felt betrayed. Once again, however, my preconceived notions were wrong. The new members of the authority worked assiduously to understand the issues and bent over backwards to be fair and inclusive. They supported my effort to hire black people to administer the relocation program, made history by inviting community leaders from the Triangle to meet with them, and ordered reappraisals of properties. When some downtown business interests who had supported the previous plan challenged our revised plans for revitalizing the Triangle community and providing new housing for the displaced residents, John's appointees were immoveable. Because of their credibility with the downtown business community, they were able to allay the business community's unfounded fears in ways that others could not. Six months later, a new executive director was hired, and I returned to my original position at city hall. From there I watched with satisfaction and pride as new affordable housing units sprang up in the Triangle alongside a new inner-city shopping mall and were made available for purchase by many of the community's longtime residents. Unfortunately, our success with interstate construction along the border of the Triangle community was limited to noise and air pollution abatement measures, largely because the plans were already too far along by the time John took office.

During the five years I worked for city government, we brought in more federal money than the city had ever seen, and I could see the tangible impact in poor neighborhoods, both black and white: new community centers in Kanawha City and North Charleston, new housing in the Triangle, sewer construction on Wertz Avenue, a swimming pool in Coal Branch Heights, and playground facilities for children in several neighborhoods. One of my colleagues at city hall called it the time of Camelot for Charleston. That's how it felt. We were transforming the city, and I was at the center of the action. Some of my assumptions about good and evil and haves and have-nots were being ripped apart. John and his wife and other members of Charleston's white establishment didn't care that I had a black wife. Black members of the community did not automatically support a strike of black workers. The white businessmen John appointed to the Urban Renewal Authority did not march in lockstep with the business community. Particularly as a result of my urban renewal experience, in addressing racism I began to see ignorance as a more significant problem than evil intent. Living in their cocoons of privilege, much as I had before Prince Edward County and Beckley and Tempie, the new members of the Urban Renewal Authority had been ignorant of the challenges faced by Triangle residents. When they saw and heard about these challenges for themselves, they moved quickly to try to address them in an equitable manner.

As my professional journey proceeded, so did my personal journey as a father. It was framed by an unexpected encounter on a return flight from Washington, D.C., just a few months after Ian was born. As I boarded the plane, I noticed an acquaintance, a lawyer for one of Kanawha Valley's utility companies. Normally an erect, distinguished, cheerful man, he was slouched in his seat, head back, mouth tightly drawn, eyes staring into space. I asked him, "Is anything wrong? You look like you just lost your best friend." He nodded slowly. "Worse. My son got married last weekend, and I was just thinking how little time we'd spent together while he was growing up. Now there's no more time. Don't let it happen to you." I nodded and moved on to my seat. I've never forgotten the sorrowful look on his face and the pain in his voice.

While his admonition applies to all parents, parents of African American children bear a unique responsibility. They have to steer their children through a minefield of challenges that transcend normal childhood torments. As we grow up, most of us are plagued by doubts and insecurities. We suffer through the intrigue of shifting friendships and anguish over our appearance, and we feel buffeted by peer pressure. During our teenage years, concerns about doing well in school and finding a career pile on, adding to our already considerable stress. But if your skin is white, you do not have to cope with a host of additional burdens: the subconscious racism of low expectations, social exclusion because of your skin color, the scrutiny of always being on trial for your race, the frustration of being labeled based on the errant behavior of others who share your skin color. Parents of African American children often are on edge about what difficulties their children may encounter on any particular day. Did a teacher ignore your daughter for the umpteenth time when she raised her hand, calling on a white student instead? Was your daughter excluded from a party to which most of her white classmates were invited? As the only black student in the class, was your son queried about how black people feel about Martin Luther King Jr., or Vietnam, or protest marches? Was he followed by a sales clerk while browsing through a clothing store, or stopped by a police officer for no apparent reason while driving home in your late model car?

Tempie had warned me that our children would have to work twice as hard and be twice as strong to get as far as an average white child. Intellectually, I knew the truth of her warning. I knew our children would travel a tougher road, encounter more pitfalls, and endure greater stress than most white children. But intellectual knowledge did not prepare me to deal effectively with the day-to-day encounters that are a normal part of a black child's life. At times I found myself so concerned that our children would develop a victim mentality and become discouraged by the barriers they encountered that I'd dismiss incidents they described that in retrospect may indeed have had racist overtones. At other times I found myself frustrated and angry about incidents that may not have been about skin color. After all, as much as I love them, our children, like all children, were not always saints, and their perceptions were not always accurate. But since actual intentions were often in doubt, Tempie and I frequently confronted the question, "Is it or isn't it racism?" and didn't always get it right. We unknowingly overlooked some incidents motivated by a conscious racist attitude, and we were mistaken in believing that racism was at the root of some other incidents.

This is one of the great frustrations, I discovered, of living black in a desegregated society. You cannot always know if a particular incident is motivated by racism. Sometimes, blatant and intentional racism is clear; it must be labeled for what it is and dealt with promptly and forcefully. But in my experience, much racist behavior is subtle and unintentional, often arising out of ignorance. In such cases, a more measured response may be appropriate. On other occasions, race may not be a factor at all, but you can't be sure. After a while, though, it hardly matters. The accumulation of incidents that seem to have racial overtones, especially when they affect your children, can simply overwhelm you, making you wary of virtually every white person and prepared to believe the worst in all situations. In fact, whether an incident arises from racist intent or not, the ramifications are often the same.

Arnya was six when she began the first grade in the same school as her sister, who was entering the fourth grade. The school was approximately 80 percent white and 20 percent black. During a school open house about a month into the school year, we met Arnya's first grade teacher, a young, pleasant white woman in her first year of teaching. She assured us that Arnya was extremely well-behaved in class, describing her as "my favorite student." Tempie thanked her and then asked whether Arnya's performance in reading and arithmetic matched her behavior. The teacher seemed taken aback. From her reaction, both Tempie and I concluded that she had not paid much attention to Arnya's school work. Was it a case of a young teacher feeling overwhelmed by a too-large class of rambunctious six-year-olds, or was it that she did not expect much from Arnya and was simply relieved that she did not fit some stereotype of how black children usually behave?

The issue of teacher expectations is critical. Research indicates that a student will perform better if the teacher expects more from him or her, rather than less. Throughout our children's elementary and secondary school years, Tempie and I engaged in constant struggles with teachers and guidance counselors, almost all white, over what we perceived to be limited expectations for our children. Too often, teachers seemed perfectly happy for our children to simply sit in the back of the room and not cause trouble. When we went to parent-teacher meetings, a common first comment was how well-behaved our children were. When we asked about their performance, the response was frequently similar to the surprise of Arnya's first-grade teacher. Since we are both college-educated and all three of our children are well above average in intelligence, we could only conclude that this obsession with our children's behavior and the seeming indifference to our children's academic performance reflected stereotyping that labeled most black children as unruly and incapable of high academic achievement.

Regina had a similar, though more blatant, experience. Midway through the seventh grade, she was advised by her guidance counselor not to pursue her interest in science because she "didn't have the intellectual gifts to succeed." A vocational program would suit her better, she was told. She was not among the school's highest achievers from the standpoint of grades, but she worked hard and had shown a particular aptitude in science. As a seventh grader, she had no idea what she wanted to do, but we had made it clear, as we did to all three children, that a complete education included at least one college degree. Even at the age of twelve, Regina expected no less of herself. Now, a person in authority was telling her she didn't have what it took to fulfill her own expectations. With that simple assertion, the guidance counselor deflated her self-esteem as quickly as you deflate a balloon by sticking a needle in it. The next day, when I appeared with Tempie at the counselor's office and announced that I was Regina's father, the face of this sixty-something white woman was a study in disbelief. In no uncertain terms, we informed her that Regina would not be tracked into a vocational program and we expected the school and all its personnel to encourage and support Regina, not label her because of her skin color. The guidance counselor, of course, denied any racial motivation, and her attitude toward Regina was markedly different from that day forward.

Regina did not burn up the corridors of academe, but she continued to work hard, aided by the prodding and encouragement of her parents. Since graduating from North Carolina A&T University with a BS degree in agricultural science, she has carved out a highly successful career as a health inspector and quality control manager for several major food service corporations. Had we not gone to the school that day and then undertaken a concerted effort to counteract the damage done by an ignorant guidance counselor, her career path might have been quite different. Even today, millions of capable black children continue to be discouraged and demoralized by the often subconscious racism of low expectations. In fact, years later in the Washington, D.C., area a guidance counselor attempted to place Ian, an excellent student, in a vocational track program, and again Tempie and I had to confront this professional woman's ignorance. To this day, many black parents with whom I speak confirm similar experiences.

Partly because of the children, our personal lives took place almost entirely in the black community. Tempie and I had hung out with a mixed group of friends in Beckley. We were community organizers, and nobody cared what color your skin was. But in Charleston it was different, at least socially. Through our work with the Triangle Community School, we met and became close to several working-class black families. Their children and our children played together, and we became regulars at their Saturday evening parties, drinking moderately, dancing vigorously, and listening to the music of Ray Charles and Dionne Warwick as we shed the pressures of the week. Through Tempie's job at OIC, we became close with several families in the middle-class black community. They were teachers, social workers, and government managers. We became regulars at their fraternity and sorority formal dances, where we danced, ate and drank, and talked about Charleston politics, sports, and our children.

Not long after Ian was born, we moved to a bigger house with a finished basement, and we began having parties there. Rarely was there a white face besides mine and those of spouses in other interracial marriages. On one occasion, we had coincidentally scheduled a party when track star Wilma Rudolph was in town to promote the Track and Field Hall of Fame, an initiative that the mayor was pushing. Tempie invited her to dinner and to join us at the party. She quickly became the evening's center of attention. Our social lives outside the black community consisted of occasional parties at the mayor's house and intermittent receptions related to my job. My skin color still was white, but I felt like I had become a part of the black community. The ultimate compliment came one night when a friend said to me: "Michael, your skin may be white, but in your heart you're black."

Our lives felt full and satisfying to me. We had a comfortable routine and fulfilling jobs, the girls were doing well and they doted over baby Ian, and our relationship felt strong. We had challenges, but they seemed no different from the challenges of other families: stretching our resources to cover our desires, making sure the children studied and stayed out of trouble, trying to balance careers and family. Tempie had engaged a young woman named Veronica to take care of Ian during the day. I usually dropped the girls off at school, and Veronica picked them up. Although both Tempie and I had occasional evening meetings, we almost always ate dinner as a family. Despite the occasional incident at school, skin color seemed to be a non-issue in our relationship. Tempie even did some modeling for Mountain Artisans, a women's sewing cooperative with which Rita Bank, Claudia Schechter, and some other friends were involved. The cooperative helped rural women, almost all white, market patchwork women's wear to high-end fashion outlets in major cities. In part because of our jobs—I was still with the mayor and Tempie had become manager of a public housing project in the Triangle—we were featured in a 1973 *Charleston Gazette* newspaper article about influential families in Charleston, with Tempie modeling a Mountain Artisans creation.

Shortly thereafter, the routine of our lives was interrupted. I could not resist a cause. My discomforting experience during the city workers' strike made me all the more ready to energize my social justice gene. Frustrated with what I considered poor leadership and encouraged by Tempie, I had run for and been elected president of the Piedmont Elementary School PTA, where both Regina and Arnya were students. Piedmont was a new, experimental school in downtown Charleston, just three blocks from where we'd lived when we came to Charleston. It had no internal walls separating classrooms, only moveable room dividers. The youngsters moved around more freely, the curriculum reflected the progressive nature of the school, the teachers were supposedly the best-qualified, and parental involvement was encouraged. Although it was outside our attendance district, we were allowed to enroll the girls in the school since we were willing to transport them there. Part of my frustration was that the school's PTA leadership had been unwilling to challenge the principal, a tall, strait-laced white woman of about fifty, who I felt was too rigid and too insensitive to the black children and to the few black teachers in the school. As PTA president, I thought

I'd be in a stronger position to challenge her, as well as to confront insensitive teachers and guidance counselors. I completely misjudged her. In fact, the principal and I became close allies in what turned out to be the most controversial episode of our lives in Charleston.

In early 1974, the Kanawha County Board of Education adopted a new set of English and social studies textbooks. One member of the five-person board, who had been elected with strong support from fundamentalist activists in rural areas of the county, dissented because the books allegedly taught moral relativism and immorality. But the real objection soon became clear. The anthologies contained the "anti-American" writings of such African American writers as James Baldwin, Langston Hughes, Ralph Ellison, and Richard Wright, and raised difficult issues such as war and peace, racial prejudice, poverty, and environmental degradation. The books encouraged youngsters to think, to question, and to reason. Those who believed there was only one set of correct answers to complex issues were terrified that their children would be exposed to viewpoints at variance with their own beliefs. In response to the protests that erupted, the board of education scheduled a special meeting to review its earlier decision. The controversy quickly attracted national headlines. Walter Cronkite described the controversy on his evening newscast, all three major television networks aired live reports from the county, Phil Donahue devoted an entire show to the issue, and the *Today Show* did a segment on which I appeared. "Book-burners" from as far away as Texas invaded the county, charging that the school board members who endorsed the books were "Godless communists" and provoking venomous divisiveness in the community.

At first, I tried to maintain distance from the controversy because of my position with the mayor, who had no jurisdiction over the elected board of education. But one morning about a week before the scheduled special board meeting, Piedmont's principal stunned me with a telephone call. As PTA president at the newest and most progressive school in the county, she entreated, I had an obligation to speak at the meeting, not only on behalf of the vast majority of students and parents, but also on behalf of faculty and staff who were being vilified as unpatriotic for being willing to teach from these books. I could not refuse. With some trepidation I told John what I was planning to do. His response was what I'd hoped it would be: "Do what you think is right." By that time I was a fairly accomplished public speaker, but I felt this was my most important speech since the fund-raising event my parents had organized following the deaths of Andy Goodman, Michael Schwerner, and James Chaney. I spent hours polishing what was to be a five-minute speech. It turned out to be well worth it. My speech implored the board to allow our children to learn to think critically by exposing them to different points of view on controversial issues. It set the tone for book proponents. The board established a citizens' review committee to review the books, and they invited me to serve. For weeks, textbooks covered our dining room table as we were tasked with reviewing and analyzing them page by page. Finally, upon the committee's recommendation, the board reaffirmed its decision to purchase the books.

Unfortunately, it was a pyrrhic victory. The controversy had unnerved many teachers, and in the classroom they avoided controversial themes in the books. The book-burners might have lost the battle, but they won the war. Little would change. The virtual exclusion of black writers from our English curriculum and of black leaders from our American history curriculum would continue. The myths that most enslaved people had been happy and rarely sought freedom, that there were no black inventors of consequence other than George Washington Carver, that black intellectuals and artists were rare, would remain intact. The resulting unspoken message was that black people were not equal to white people.

My appearance on the *Today Show*, though, had a totally unrelated and unexpected result. I arrived back home from the studio at about 8:30 a.m. to find a message that Stan Shaw had called. Apart from my visit to Colorado shortly after Stan's marriage, we had not been in touch since our year teaching together in South Huntington. In the interim, Stan had earned a Ph.D. and was now at the University of Connecticut training prospective teachers of students with disabilities. I immediately called back. "There I was," he said, "absent-mindedly watching the *Today Show* while getting ready for class, and who shows up on the screen but you. I screamed so loudly for Wilma that she thought I was having a heart attack." Thirty-eight years later, Stan and I have maintained our close friendship without further interruption, and we see each other as often as our schedules allow. In fact, we recently co-authored a chapter about our memories of that summer in Prince Edward County for a book about the larger story of Prince Edward's public schools closing.

My leadership role in the Kanawha County book controversy made me even better known in the community. On the negative side, it was the only time during our years in Charleston that we received telephone threats. In the week following the speech, we received about a half-dozen phone calls labeling me as a "n—r-lover," among other things, and promising that both Tempie and I and our children would pay. The threats never materialized, but they scared us, and they were a sobering reminder of our potential vulnerability. Tempie was more unnerved than I, perhaps because she received most of the calls and because the threats brought back childhood memories of intimidation. As a result of my role in the controversy, we identified even more with the black community. White colleagues wondered why I had spoken up so forcefully and asked if I was worried about the potential dangers. Friends in the black community, on the other hand, wondered if I'd consider running for the board of education or for higher elective office. Although I had begun to nurture aspirations for political office, I couldn't muster enough chutzpah to say yes. But the bottom line was that because of our children, and notwithstanding my prominent position in the community's white power structure, our social life was rooted almost totally in the black community. We shared common bonds: the recognition that we were outsiders in a white, often inhospitable world, and the knowledge that our children had to be prepared to confront similar daunting challenges as they grew to adulthood.

As Regina approached her teenage years, we began to encounter the usual bumps that accompany adolescence. She is a strong-willed adult, and she was a strong-willed child. After some struggles with discipline, when Regina was thirteen she decided that she wanted to live with her biological father, who had remarried and was living in Goldsboro, North Carolina. Both girls spent a week or two each summer with him, but Tempie didn't think he was reliable. Somehow, it felt like we had failed Regina. We resisted, but her determination made it clear we had to let her go. So in 1975, the year she was to enter high school, Regina headed for Goldsboro. She came home on holidays and for the summers, but that didn't ease the emptiness we felt. Toward the end of her junior year in high school, tragedy struck. Her father dropped dead of a heart attack. We let her remain in Goldsboro until the end of her junior year, and then, despite her pleading to remain in Goldsboro for her senior year, we enrolled her in Boggs Academy near Augusta, Georgia. Her graduation from Boggs featured a moving speech by Dr. Benjamin Mays, long-time president of Morehouse College. Amid great fanfare, she headed off to North Carolina A&T in September 1979.

Meanwhile, Arnya had her heart set on being a cheerleader. She had a cheerleader's figure, she was athletic, and she practiced hard. But we lived in predominantly white South Hills, and George Washington High School had never had a black cheerleader. Arnya tried out for the squad as a sophomore, and according to a friend who watched the tryouts, she was among the most impressive. Nevertheless, she was not selected by the returning squad members. It was one of those times when I didn't know what to say. I felt in my gut that racial bias was a factor, but I couldn't prove it. And I felt if I allowed her to believe it, she would be discouraged and bitter. So, I attributed the rejection to cliquishness among the cheerleaders and encouraged her to keep practicing, to be so good they would have no choice but to select her the following year. She did exactly that, and as a junior, she became the first black cheerleader in school history. As Tempie had warned, Arnya had had to be head and shoulders better than the other girls to have a chance of being selected. Yet, although she was too good to be kept off the squad, other squad members would "forget" to tell her about parties and other social events. This is not an uncommon price for black children to pay when they are in a predominantly white environment.

I had not forgotten my plane-mate's admonition: "Don't let it happen to you." I left work to attend every football and basketball game at which the cheerleaders performed. As soon as Ian was ready, I put a baseball glove on him and started tossing a ball to him. When he was ready for T-ball, I volunteered to coach his team. When he wanted to play touch football at the age of six, I didn't miss a game or a practice. When I went jogging on the high school track, I took him with me. Except when I was traveling, I was home every night for dinner. I recognize my good fortune to have had jobs that allowed me to be available. But even the black parents I knew with considerably less flexibility spent quality time with their children, demanded more of them in school, and held a tight rein on their outside activities. They knew the need to prepare their children for the challenges ahead. And I was learning.

VIII

Confronting The Challenges And Tensions

We were gearing up for John's 1975 reelection campaign when in mid-February I received a frantic call from my mother. My father had been hospitalized with severe abdominal pain. She and my father had been vacationing near Fort Lauderdale, Florida, at the time. Tests revealed colon cancer that had metastasized to his liver, and the prognosis was bleak. Over the next three weeks, I flew to Florida twice, the first time alone and the second time with Tempie and Ian, who was then two years old. The girls remained behind with friends. During the second trip, my father passed away. He was sixty-seven. The loss caught me off guard. I agonized over not having told him more frequently how much I loved and respected him. I worried about how my mother would do without him, and I was heartbroken that Ian would never know him. For a time, working at city hall—or anywhere, for that matter—lost its allure. My absence from John's reelection campaign to help wind up my father's affairs left me feeling disconnected.

I reflected on his influence on my life and on my career. He'd shown me how to work hard and how to live a life of principle, he had always loved his children unconditionally and been proud of what we were doing, he had made sacrifices for Alice and me that we were never aware of as children, and he'd been a stalwart supporter of my marriage to Tempie despite his doubts. Career-wise, I'd had early designs on a career as a sports writer and had spent most of my college life as a civil rights activist. But coming out of college, I saw myself, largely because of my father's influence, as a teacher. He saw teaching as both a noble undertaking and a secure career. He was initially skeptical about my West Virginia adventure, but he'd followed my activities in Beckley and then as an advocate for skinny city with pride. He was dubious about my venture into Charleston politics, but he lauded my involvement in the textbook crisis, and on his visits to Charleston, he came to like John Hutchinson. He might have had a harder time with my next employer, who epitomized the political and economic class he saw as the enemy of working-class people.

In 1972, John D. Rockefeller IV had run unsuccessfully for governor against incumbent Republican Governor Arch Moore. The great-grandson of John D. Rockefeller and a Democrat in a family of Republicans, "Jay" had come to West Virginia as a VISTA volunteer shortly before I arrived, and he had attracted attention because of his famous lineage. In 1968, after two years with VISTA, he was elected to the state legislature and primed himself for the governorship in 1972. But he ran into the potent Arch Moore political machine, which hung the label "carpetbagger" on him and won handily. Contrary to speculation that he would leave the state, Jay accepted the presidency of West Virginia Wesleyan College in Buckhannon, West Virginia. With him went Charleston city manager Don Richardson to help run the college. Clearly, Jay intended to seek the governorship again in 1976, when Governor Moore would be term-limited, and Don would play a key role in the campaign.

Meanwhile, John Hutchinson's popularity in Charleston had soared to record levels. He easily won reelection in the 1975 municipal election, garnering 80 percent of the vote and carrying every precinct in the city. Early in 1976, he announced he was running for governor in the Democratic primary—against Jay. He never had a chance. He had but a fraction of Jay's resources and strong union opposition due to the city workers' strike, and he could not overcome the charge that in a largely rural state he'd be partial to Charleston's more urban interests. Jay got more than 50 percent of the vote, and John finished fourth among the four major candidates, garnering only about 5 percent of the vote. I supported and campaigned for John in my free time, and following the primary I settled back into my job at city hall. Don, who would become Jay's chief of staff, had hinted at a job for me in the Rockefeller administration, but I presumed that my support for John in the primary would doom that possibility.

However, at about 11:30 a.m. on a mid-December day following the general election, which Jay won easily over the Republican nominee, my phone buzzed. "He says it's Jay Rockefeller," my secretary informed me sarcastically. I picked up the phone. "Mike, this is Jay. Can you come over to the transition office in about an hour?" At 12:30 p.m. I was sitting in the outer office of transition headquarters two blocks from city hall. Jay ushered me into his office, motioned me to a folding chair in front of his desk, and settled his six-foot-six-inch frame back into the comfortable executive chair behind his desk. "Mike," he said between bites of his sandwich, "I want you to run the Governor's Office of Federal-State Relations." I had thought the call might mean a job offer, and I'd quickly formulated some questions to ask about responsibilities, salary, and so on. But the abruptness of his request caught me off guard. "Uh, well, sure, I think I'd like to do that." Thus began my career in the Rockefeller administration. Arch Moore had once said, "It will be a cold day in hell when Jay Rockefeller is governor of West Virginia." And on inauguration day, the temperature was near zero, close to a record for a January day. But few cared. We braved the temperature to watch Jay take his oath of office at a midday outdoor ceremony on the Capitol grounds. And in the evening, dressed in our finest formal clothing, Tempie and I danced the night away.

Working for Governor John D. Rockefeller IV was an important step in my education about not being too quick to judge people. He was from one of this nation's quintessential establishment families, a family I viewed with suspicion and with which I had little in common. But I had been learning that people could not easily be pigeonholed. I knew, liked, and respected Sharon Percy Rockefeller, Jay's wife and the daughter of Republican Senator Charles Percy. We'd met through our work with Mountain Artisans, the patchwork sewing cooperative on whose board we both served, she as chair and I as treasurer. Jay and I shared a lively interest in sports. Both Jay and Sharon had warm and outgoing personalities. And, soon after I took the job, Ian and young Charles Rockefeller, who attended the same day care center, became best friends. In fact, because Ian was at the Governor's Mansion playing with Charles on the December afternoon in 1977 when the governor was scheduled to light the state Christmas tree, Jay included him in the family picture of the tree-lighting ceremony. The picture ran on the front pages of most of the state's newspapers and appeared on the local evening news of all three television networks.

During Jay's first four-year term, I held four separate positions. Don Richardson had alerted me during the transition that in July 1977 my office would be subsumed into the newly created Office of Economic and Community Development (OECD), which was to be led by Don Moyer. Moyer had developed a comprehensive state economic development plan that Jay had touted during the 1972 campaign. His prospective return to the state was heralded with much fanfare during the 1976 campaign. When he returned and the reorganization was implemented, I became the chief of the Community Development Division within OECD. But although I'd known Moyer from his previous work in West Virginia, and looked forward to the opportunity to be part of the purported economic rebound he promised, we did not get along in this new arrangement. Because of the enormous public pressure Moyer was under to lead us out of the economic doldrums, he became a micromanager with a rigid agenda and a heightened sense of insecurity. It seemed to me that he was threatened by my relationship with Jay and with Don Richardson and that he looked for opportunities to criticize my work. He even claimed that the picture of Ian in the tree-lighting ceremony with the governor's family undermined his authority. The last straw came when Jay asked me in late 1977 to take charge of a floundering flood relief program for southern West Virginia. We rescued the program, but Moyer felt further undermined and made no secret of his displeasure.

In March 1978, I accepted an invitation from Leon Ginsberg, the commissioner of the Welfare Department, to become his deputy commissioner for operations. Although I had no experience with the welfare bureaucracy, I wanted to escape Moyer. An added attraction was that the new deputy commissioner for evaluation would be Sally Richardson, Don Richardson's wife and by then a good friend. We had adjoining offices and worked well with each other and with Leon, whose management style was to set goals, give people free rein, and hold them accountable. We began making progress in shaking up the bureaucracy; Sally was installing a management by objectives system and I was promoting greater diversity and local office autonomy. Then, in June 1979, I received an urgent call from Jay. Ten minutes later, I was in his office and he was asking me to become the commissioner of the Department of Employment Security, a position I held for the remainder of his first term.

While in state government, I confronted several racial issues. Two brief encounters stand out. Shortly after the announcement of my appointment as the head of the Governor's Office of Federal-State Relations, I received a call at home from a black man who was in charge of personnel for the office. "Mike, I know you're a fair man, but I need to know what your intentions are with the governor's reorganization plans. I've got a family to take care of, and if I'm going to be out of a job, I need to know now, because it's going to take me a lot longer to find a new job." He was not talking about his qualifications, which were stellar. His legitimate concern was that his skin color would be a disadvantage in seeking work outside of government in Charleston. The other four high-level managers in the office were white men, and none of them called me, although all were equally at risk in Jay's promised reorganization. I assured the caller that I knew his ability and had no intention of dismissing him. But the call was disturbing. It raised my awareness of a source of stress for African Americans that was foreign to me, and it alerted me to stresses my children might face in the future.

Midway through my tenure at the Welfare Department, the position of director of training became vacant. It was one of the positions in my authority that held the most responsibility, and there were a number of people qualified for and interested in it. One of them was an African American man who'd been with the department for nearly twenty years but had felt stymied in his efforts to advance. He came to my office one afternoon. "I want to apply for the position, Mike, but I know the routine. I'll be the most experienced applicant, I'll have a good interview, and the position will go to someone else, who just happens to be white. Maybe you'll be different, but I need you to tell me now if I have a legitimate chance at the job, because I can't put myself through these charades any longer." I assured him that the process would be fair and objective. When word got out that he was applying for the position, I had a visit from another high-ranking career official. "He's a good man," he told me, "but I don't think people will want to work for him. It would be better to leave him where he is." I was speechless. This was a man I had respected and thought to be fair-minded. I dismissed his warning. The man in question got the job and he performed admirably. But this incident reinforced my consciousness of the challenges African Americans faced; they were challenges my children would likely face. No incidents like this arose at the Department of Employment Security, largely because there was so little diversity in the department when I arrived. I sought, with Jay's support, to correct that situation, partially through my leadership of a task force that developed an affirmative action plan for state government.

As my career progressed, however, Tempie and I began to struggle. Our marriage was becoming increasingly routinized and boring. We got up in the morning, got ourselves and the children ready for the day, spent eight to ten hours at work, came home for dinner, spent the evening watching television, helping the children with their homework, or occasionally attending a meeting, then went to sleep, and started all over the next morning. I was comfortable with the routine, happy with my job, and oblivious to the trouble brewing. But Tempie, like many career women, bore heavier burdens. She had a responsible job—she was now the head of residential management for the Charleston Job Corps Center—and she ran the household, burdens to which I was not sensitive. Exacerbating the pressures she felt at home were unfounded rumors that she had risen in her career because of me. In truth, she had risen solely due to her talent and hard work. Nevertheless, people would stop her to say how lucky she was to be married to me, implying that my position or perhaps my white skin was responsible for her success. The ultimate discomfort occurred when she'd be introduced as Mike Wenger's wife rather than as Tempie Wenger. It was not clear if racism, sexism, or both played a role in the way she was viewed, but it hardly mattered. She chafed at not being seen as an independent individual. I offered little solace, thoughtlessly dismissing her complaints as petty.

We began to argue about discipline. Having grown up in a family where spanking was rarely used as a disciplinary tool, I was dismayed by Tempie's belief that corporal punishment was an important tool for raising well-behaved children. It was a belief learned in a family in which misbehavior resulted in an order from her mother to get a switch. At first I felt uncomfortable interfering with the pattern of discipline Tempie had established with the girls. As I became more comfortable in my role as father, I expressed my dismay, but our discussions neither convinced Tempie to change her approach nor helped me to understand the origins of it.

Money was another subject of conflict, especially regarding expenditures for the children. I felt that they didn't need designer clothes that they would outgrow in a matter of months. But Tempie had grown up with much less than I had, and she was determined that her children would have the best of everything. We nearly maxed out our credit cards, and at one point we agreed,

I thought, to temporarily stop charging purchases. Tempie had understood the conversation differently, and when the next bill came, I exploded. On another occasion I accused her of trying to dress the children as though we were the Rockefellers. She exploded.

As the tension increased, Tempie decided to pursue a master's degree in Social Work Management at West Virginia University. A portion of the degree could be completed remotely, but she would need to spend a semester on the Morgantown campus, a three-hour drive from Charleston. I was hesitant, because I was beginning to see the marriage slipping away. But after the Harvard debacle, I felt I couldn't object. Her six-month stint in Morgantown came shortly after Jay was inaugurated in 1977. She spent another several months on an internship in Mingo County, in the southwestern part of the state. Veronica, the young woman whom Tempie had engaged to take care of Ian, came to live with us. This relieved me of much of the pressure, and Tempie returned home every weekend. But the tension grew. In mid-1978, Tempie received a job offer from a Washington, D.C., consulting firm with which some of our friends from community organizing days were involved. She wanted the job, but I had just recently moved to the Welfare Department and didn't want to leave Charleston. So Tempie left, and though we didn't acknowledge it, we were happy with this trial separation. Regina was entering her senior year at Boggs Academy in Georgia, but by mutual agreement, Arnya, who had just turned fourteen, and Ian, then five and a half, remained in Charleston with me. Tempie needed time without child-rearing responsibilities to become established in a new location, and I did not want to give up the children. She returned to Charleston every other weekend, and on occasion, Arnya, Ian, and I would drive to D.C. for the weekend. But it was not an ideal arrangement. Both children, although they wanted to stay in Charleston, missed their mother. I essentially set my own schedule at both the Welfare and Employment Security departments, so I usually could accommodate whatever needs

Arnya and Ian had, at least those I recognized. But I could not replace their mother.

By early 1979, Tempie and I had decided that we could not sustain a long-distance relationship. We were barely communicating. Ian missed his mother and often sat quietly on the side of his bed with a sad face. Arnya was angry and becoming increasingly difficult. In May of that year I described my situation to Jay, and told him I had to leave Charleston to try to save my marriage. "I understand, Mike," he said. "Just tell me how I can be helpful." Two weeks later, I was about to sign a consulting agreement with the Appalachian Regional Commission in Washington, D.C., when the call came from Jay asking me to take over the Department of Employment Security. The incumbent had contracted for the installation of a new computerized system to improve the efficiency of the department's response to unemployment compensation claims. However, he failed to maintain a backup, and when the new system developed major glitches, chaos reigned. During the previous winter, when the weather had been particularly brutal and unemployment had increased significantly, the system had locked up. The only way many eligible recipients could get unemployment compensation benefits was to call the local office and complain about not having received a check. It was an economic nightmare for the unemployed, a bureaucratic nightmare for stressed-out Employment Security employees, and a political nightmare for Jay. With reelection just eighteen months away, he needed to make a change.

"Mike, I need you to do Employment Security," he insisted.

"But Governor," I replied, "two weeks ago I told you I needed to leave Charleston to save my marriage, and you promised to help."

"I know," he responded, leaning forward in his chair and peering directly into my eyes. "But then I was talking to you as a friend. Now, I'm talking to you as governor."

"How much time do I have to decide?" He looked at his watch. "It's 11:15 a.m. I'll need your answer in twenty-four hours."

Confused, I called Tempie. She told me, "Do whatever you think is best." I consulted my Welfare Department colleague, Sally Richardson, who cautioned, "You don't say no to a Rockefeller." I weighed this new opportunity against my commitment to our marriage and the well-being of Arnya, who now wanted to leave Charleston, and Ian, who didn't want to leave.

At 11:15 a.m. the next morning I was still unsure what to do. The phone rang. It was the governor. "I'll do it," I stammered. It was effectively the end of my marriage. On a weekend in July when Tempie returned to Charleston, we decided that divorce was the best option. We were more sad than angry. The children cried and were angry. In September Regina left for college in North Carolina, and Arnya left to live with Tempie. Ian remained with me in Charleston. But their reactions gave us pause. We did not immediately pursue a formal divorce and continued with the visits every other weekend as if nothing had happened.

West Virginia's Department of Employment Security was a unique challenge. With an entrenched bureaucracy of 800 employees, mostly white, and fifty offices throughout the state, it had long been reputed to be a repository for patronage hirings. Prior to Jay's election as governor, Clement Bassett had been the commissioner for many years, through both Democratic and Republican administrations. Jay's first appointee, a young black woman, had apparently not been sufficiently deferential for some members of the state legislature, and she encountered resistance from key department employees in trying to build a more diverse workforce. She was gone by the middle of Jay's second year as governor.

His next appointee, a bright young man with good intentions but little administrative experience, was the one who had fallen victim to the computer chaos. Now, with just one winter before his reelection campaign, Jay's directive to me was: "Fix it and get the department off the front pages." The top managers in the department were equally embarrassed about the prior winter's disaster. I told them of Jay's directive and gave them wide latitude to steer our way out of the mess. They knew what to do, and with extra resources I obtained from the Department of Labor, the problem was solved by October. The only stories about the department that made the front pages the following winter were about the department's efficiency in paying claims.

The department's negative reputation had a kernel of truth to it. Some of its employees had been there too long and had burned out, a hazard in any government agency that deals with the public on a daily basis. Most of its employees, though, were smart and dedicated and simply needed to be treated with respect. During my eighteen months as commissioner I visited every office in the state and met regularly with field office employees to hear their concerns. At the suggestion of several employees, I allocated a limited amount of money to spruce up each field office in any way the local employees chose. Although the budget was too tight for salary increases, these small things, along with the department's improved performance, made a huge difference in employee morale. It became easier for them to endure the public criticism that often accompanies working for a public bureaucracy and to accept the emphasis I tried to place on building a more diverse workforce.

I had promised Jay that I would give no hint of my plans to leave the department until after the elections of November 1980. But in the summer of 1980, with the divorce plans on hold, I began to think seriously again about work options in D.C. One option involved returning to work for John Hutchinson, with whom I had remained in touch. He'd won election to a third term as mayor in 1979, and in early 1980 he'd been elected to Congress to fill the vacant seat of Representative John Slack, a fixture in West Virginia's Third Congressional District until his sudden death. John Hutchinson was running for a full term in November 1980, and I anticipated being asked to join his congressional staff. A second option involved the vacant position of States' Washington Representative at the Appalachian Regional

Commission (ARC), representing the governors of the thirteen Appalachian states, including West Virginia, in ARC-related matters. I had been Jay's representative to the ARC when I headed the Governor's Office of Federal-State Relations, and I was familiar with its inner workings and knew many of the staff members. Jay was enthusiastic when I mentioned this option to him, and he suggested I talk with Dan Green, then his representative to the ARC. Dan had been one of the key managers in the Governor's Office of Federal-State Relations during Arch Moore's tenure, and I had come under intense pressure from one of Jay's aides to dismiss him when I took over in 1977. I had resisted because Dan had a strong reputation for competence and objectivity. As a result, Dan and I had become close, and he had subsequently become a close confidante of the governor.

Dan supported my candidacy for the position, but advised me that the deadline for applications was November 1, a week before the election. I told him of my pledge to Jay not to give any hint of my departure until after the election, and if I submitted an application prior to the deadline, I risked breaking that pledge. So Dan, with Jay's assent, arranged to have the application deadline moved to November 15. On election day, Jay was easily reelected, but in a major upset characterized by extremely negative campaigning and clouded by charges of voting fraud, John lost his congressional seat to a Republican challenger. The following day, I submitted my application for the vacant ARC position. With Jay's strong support, including calls to other governors touting my credentials and talents, I was offered and accepted the position, effective January 1981.

IX

Pursuing Our Dreams

Dreams and aspirations can illuminate our journey through life; they can give our life meaning and direction. But we cannot follow our dreams blindly. Circumstances change; we change. Our ability to adapt our dreams to such change rather than to be discouraged by change can determine how fulfilling our journey ultimately is.

Leaving West Virginia was bittersweet. During my nearly fourteen years in Beckley and Charleston, I had found the excitement and fulfillment that I'd dreamt of while still teaching school. I'd grown from a naïve and radical community organizer into a mature (though perhaps I should leave that judgment to others), committed public official, and I'd had tangible successes with the RCCAA, with the textbook crisis, with John Hutchinson, and with Jay Rockefeller. I'd confronted racism in a very personal way. I'd gotten married, had a son, raised three children, and made lifelong friends in West Virginia. And I loved the mountains. West Virginia felt more like home now than New York did. On the other hand, I dreamt of living in Washington, D.C., where key policy decisions are made and political intrigue is the dominant topic of discussion. I'd also come to love the area, the beautiful downtown greenery, the majesty of the monuments, the cultural dynamism, and the wonderful restaurants. And the Metro, which was under construction and coming soon, would simplify travel in and around D.C.

The most important reason for moving to D.C., though, was the chance to try to save our marriage. This attempt was driven largely by the children's pleas and our desire not to abandon our dream, that there was a "place for us," without a fight. Maybe, we reflected, if we were both in D.C., we could rekindle the flame. I bought a townhouse near the house in which Tempie and Arnya were living in Silver Spring, Maryland. We decided to rent our home in Charleston for the time being. Perhaps we wanted to hang on to some of the good memories of the past or to preserve the possibility of returning to Charleston as a family. Our ability to keep the house was another example of the white privilege I enjoyed and the significance of the wealth gap that is such a huge legacy of our nation's history of racial oppression. Without selling the Charleston house, I could not come up with the down payment for the Silver Spring townhouse. But my mother had substantial assets, left behind by my father despite his oft-repeated philosophy, "Being of sound mind and body, I spent it all before I left." I borrowed the money from her. But when Tempie had moved to D.C., she had no one to turn to for help. She struggled to rent a small house while still helping her parents pay the mortgage on their small house in Clinton. While I was able to use my mother's money to substantially increase my assets, Tempie had no such luxury.

I settled in, and we worked toward reconciliation. We agreed informally that Ian would split his time between us, and we enrolled him in a private Montessori school nearby so there wouldn't be an issue with public school attendance districts. We ate dinner together when we could. We talked about the issues that had created tension: finances, career ambitions, communication, our different backgrounds. We sought professional guidance from a psychotherapist. Nothing helped, however. There was little anger between us, but the spark was gone. The tensions that characterized our last years together in Charleston had been exacerbated by the separation, and our dream had dried up. With some sadness and trepidation, we divorced in September 1981. There was no contention between us; we even used the same lawyer.

We did not consciously attribute the failure of our marriage to racial factors. Household pressures, external pressures, child-rearing philosophies, financial disagreements, and career clashes are not unusual areas of conflict in any marriage. Yet our tensions were clearly aggravated by the way skin color determines how we are treated in society. Household pressures took on added intensity because of our concerns about the treatment of our children in school, and during the textbook crisis because of our concerns for our family's safety. Our conflicting child-rearing approaches were shaped largely by our own parents' approaches and by the different environments in which we grew up. Tempie's mother based her rigid disciplinary philosophy on the sure knowledge that her children would have to be especially well-behaved in order to survive in our white-dominated society. My parents' more relaxed and democratic disciplinary philosophy reflected no such worries. Our financial disagreements and career clashes stemmed largely from the enormous gulf between our early economic backgrounds, backgrounds that had been shaped by the racist policies of our society. Both of us struggled regularly to understand the other's outlook and behavior.

Being married to a black woman enabled me to get closer than most white people ever can to what it feels like to be black every day in American society. I do not carry the painful memories of a childhood in the segregated South, nor have I experienced the stress that comes with the daily encounters of which every black person must be wary. Prince Edward County had been a powerful experience that brought me face-to-face with racism, and the deaths of James Chaney, Andrew Goodman, and Michael Schwerner had scared me. But I'd been able to compartmentalize those experiences in my mind and go about my privileged life in white America. The stress I felt during virtually every day of my marriage to Tempie penetrated far more deeply. Being alert to potential pitfalls and trying to discern the good guys from the bad guys had been daily tasks. Surely that stress, not to mention the additional stress Tempie felt from constant stares and questions, contributed to our separation. Of course, many interracial marriages do endure. Our bond was simply not strong enough to survive the accumulated stresses.

We agreed to joint custody of Ian, who was nearing his ninth birthday, and we agreed to continue living in close proximity to each other to facilitate that joint custody arrangement. The girls were both in college, so they did not present a custody issue. During our first two years in D.C., Ian spent alternating two-week periods with each of us. When Tempie got re-married in 1983 and moved to an adjoining county, the arrangement changed. Ian spent alternating years with each of us; weekends were spent with the parent who did not have custody during the week. He spent Easter and Christmas Day with Tempie, Thanksgiving and Christmas Eve with me. The adjustment was probably more difficult for Ian than it was for Tempie or me.

Ian and I had established a stable routine in Charleston. We had spent all of our free time together. I had coached his T-ball team, he had jogged with me every evening, he had begun to take guitar lessons, and one of his closest friends had lived just a few doors from us on the same street. When he had a day off from school, he often came with me to Employment Security headquarters, where he quickly became a favorite of most of the employees. We'd arrive at 9 a.m., and he'd head down the hall to visit people. I might not see him until lunch, and afterward, he'd be off again until it was time to leave. People throughout the building were extremely tolerant, surely in part because Ian was the commissioner's son, but also because he was a charming kid and our employees were good people. The issue of skin color never came up, at least not in my presence. Our move to the D.C. area tore him away from everything familiar. He was resilient, though, and it didn't take him long to adjust. The relative amicability of the divorce helped.

Even the division of our possessions was amicable. Tempie and I had divided up almost everything—furniture, kitchen items, and so on—before Ian and I left Charleston. When I moved into my townhouse, there were only two major items about which we were undecided, our dining room set and a

Yamaha piano we'd bought years before so the girls could take piano lessons. Tempie wanted the dining room set, and I was happy to keep the piano, which still sits in my living room today. I reasoned I could easily buy a new dining room set, but if I gave up the piano, I'd probably never buy another one. I could read music from childhood clarinet lessons, and I could play simple melodies on the piano. The idea of having the piano around for the occasional musical interlude, for me as well as for Regina and Arnya, and someday for our grandchildren, was appealing. My mother, who rarely minced words regardless of the subject, had a different opinion. On a visit shortly after the move, she noticed the empty dining room. "What happened to the dining room set?" she inquired. Without going into detail, I explained that Tempie had taken it and I'd kept the piano.

"That's the stupidest thing I've ever heard," she snapped at me. "Why?" I asked, taken aback by her strong reaction. "Why? Because you can't eat off a damn piano."

Politics was not the only thing about which she felt strongly.

Despite the personal strains, I was excited about my job at the Appalachian Regional Commission. Since its creation in 1965, the ARC had made a huge difference in West Virginia, as it had in all thirteen Appalachian states. It had provided millions of dollars for sewer construction, job training, school and housing rehabilitation, and health clinics, among other things, all with an eye toward creating jobs and training local people, both white and black, to fill those jobs. Perhaps most importantly, it had provided hundreds of millions of dollars for highway construction in an attempt to relieve the isolation of people in the mountains and make the state more attractive and accessible to tourists and potential employers. There were other regional commissions, such as the Coastal Plains and Ozarks Regional Commissions, but none had received nearly as much money from Congress as the ARC, and none had been as effective. Having West Virginia's courtly senior senator, Jennings Randolph (D-WV), chairing the Senate Environment and Public Works Committee was a big advantage. His legendary commitment to West Virginia was humorously acknowledged by former Senator and Vice President Walter Mondale when he spoke at a 1977 banquet in Charleston that I had organized.

> I want you to know that despite Senator Randolph's reputation for bringing home the bacon to West Virginia, I've witnessed firsthand how fair-minded he is. When the Chairman is dividing up the money behind closed doors, he is scrupulously even-handed. It's one dollar for West Virginia and one dollar for the rest of the country, one dollar for West Virginia and another dollar for the rest of country.

The audience responded with knowing laughter. They recognized how successful Senator Randolph had been in steering money to West Virginia.

Even before I served as Jay's representative to the ARC in 1977, I'd come in contact with the Appalachian Regional Commission. During our skinny city efforts at the Tech Foundation, I'd approached the commission for a grant and received an enthusiastic response from key staff members, who thought our idea represented a potential model for what they called "inter-local cooperation." But in the commission process, the governor has the last word on projects in his or her state, and Arch Moore's opposition to skinny city doomed any chance for ARC money. I didn't like it, but I had to acknowledge that this unique federal-state partnership made more sense than the normal top-down process in which federal bureaucrats make grant decisions. At the ARC, 50 percent of staff salaries are paid by the federal government and 50 percent by the states, so staff members are equally accountable to the feds and the states. From the day I arrived at the ARC, I argued that despite swirling rumors about the budget-cutting intentions of the new Reagan administration, the ARC would be spared because its federal-state partnership was the kind of program Republicans advocated. The first Reagan budget proposal, authored by the infamous

David Stockman, disabused me of that notion. Without citing any evidence, he described the ARC as ineffective and wasteful and proposed its immediate elimination.

The responsibility of persuading Congress to reject the administration's proposal regarding the ARC fell to my office, since it was 100 percent funded by the states and since all thirteen governors (nine Democrats and four Republicans) supported the continuation of the commission. The influence of Senator Randolph would be important. But crucial support would have to come from two highly unlikely allies: Senate Majority Leader Robert C. Byrd (D-WV), a former Ku Klux Klan member, and Representative Jamie Whitten (D-MS), chair of the House Appropriations Committee, whose northeast Mississippi district was part of Appalachia. During the 1960s, he'd been known as one of Mississippi's most virulent racists. Without the lessons I'd learned in Charleston, I doubt I could have handled the challenge of building an alliance with these men. However, I had learned to be wary of judging people too quickly from my experiences with Mayor Hutchinson, his appointed members of the Charleston Urban Renewal Authority, Governor Rockefeller's administration, and our friends in Charleston. I'd learned that preconceived notions that paint people as either good or evil without acknowledging a middle ground or people's ability to grow can preclude potentially valuable alliances and stifle social change.

It had been more than fifteen years since the height of the civil rights movement, and the views of Senator Byrd and Representative Whitten had evolved. Byrd had renounced his brief dalliance with the KKK, and Whitten had been reelected eight times with strong black support since the enactment of the 1965 Voting Rights Act. They were different men than they had been, and they became strong allies for us. With their leadership and the support of many Republicans, we were able to build a strong bipartisan coalition in Congress that sustained the ARC throughout the Reagan and Bush administrations and that continues to sustain it today.

It was quite an evolution for me, as well. I had gone from a campus civil rights activist to a position representing the governors of the thirteen Appalachian states, from western New York to northeast Mississippi. At one time in the 1980s, I represented both New York governor Mario Cuomo and Alabama governor George Wallace, simultaneously. I learned that with some notable exceptions, this nation is not divided into good people and bad people (or, for that matter, into blue states and red states); it is just a nation of people who are the products of vastly different environments. I learned that none of us have a corner on wisdom and that people cannot always be judged solely by the views they hold or once held. Rather, what is most important is the sincerity and integrity with which they hold those views, their willingness to learn and grow, and the respect they accord others with differing views.

It was during this time that I came to know William Winter, the governor of Mississippi from 1980 to 1984 and, in my opinion, one of the South's great unsung heroes. He is a perfect example of why we must be careful not to make premature judgments about people. Born and raised in Grenada, Mississippi, Governor Winter graduated from the University of Mississippi and its Law School and went to work for Senator John Stennis, a vociferous defender of the "southern way of life" and an avowed opponent of the 1954 *Brown v. Board of Education* decision. He then joined the law firm of Senator Stennis's son in Jackson, Mississippi. He was elected to the state legislature and to the position of state auditor, and he won the governor's chair on his third try. He came from the more moderate wing of Mississippi's Democratic segregationist establishment, and he had tried to calm passions during the violent resistance to James Meredith's attempt to integrate the University of Mississippi in 1962. But although he'd received a significant number of black votes in his gubernatorial victory, he could hardly have been seen as a devoted ally by most black Mississippians.

Yet Governor Winter invited Mississippi native Leontyne Price to sing at his inauguration. The Metropolitan Opera star was the first black person to participate in the inauguration of a Mississippi governor since Reconstruction. She was also the first black person to stay at the Governor's Mansion, which she did that night. Governor Winter appointed the state's first black department heads and the state's first black judges. He had the statue of racist former Senator Theodore Bilboa moved from its place of prominence on the Capitol grounds, and he honored the widow of slain civil rights leader Medgar Evers at a formal dinner at the Governor's Mansion. At that dinner he told Mrs. Evers that her husband had not only helped to free black people in Mississippi, but that he had helped to free white people from the chains that had kept them securely shackled to an immoral past. The governor made speeches about the need for racial healing, and he became an aggressive leader in the effort to keep the ARC alive.

Perhaps most importantly, over strong opposition, Governor Winter successfully fought for legislation mandating kindergarten programs for all Mississippi children. The primary beneficiaries of this legislation were black children. Constitutionally prohibited from seeking a second term, he did not weary of the battle, nor did his family. His children were among the very few white children to attend Jackson's public schools, and his wife, also a lifelong Mississippian, became a driving force in Jackson's Habitat for Humanity. We sorely missed his leadership when his term ended. To my good fortune, he entered my life again in 1997. By then, he was well into his seventies, and had become a driving force behind the creation of President Clinton's Initiative on Race, as well as a member of the President's Advisory Board on Race.

Meanwhile, despite the pressures of my job, I had not forgotten that admonition on the plane ride years earlier: "Don't let it happen to you." Regina had been in college at North Carolina A&T University when we moved to D.C. Arnya left for North Carolina Central University in Durham the next September. But Ian had just turned eight years old when we moved. While he enjoyed having more time with his mother, I was determined to nurture the special bond he and I had developed during the past two years in Charleston. When he was with me, I turned down all invitations to evening receptions, which were plentiful in the nation's capital. I attended every school event in which he was involved, coached his baseball team, and went to all of his football practices and games. I arranged my schedule so that most of my business trips would occur when he was with Tempie. When I couldn't do that, I tried to take him with me, even if he had to sometimes miss school.

During one business trip in 1983 or 1984, we got hooked on racquetball at our hotel. Once we got home, we began playing three or four evenings a week. We teamed frequently with Leon Met, a white former Queens College classmate whose son Jamie was Ian's age. Leon and his family had moved to the D.C. area in 1984. Leon and I would play against Ian and Jamie. For several years we beat them handily, but as they grew bigger, stronger, and quicker, the games became more competitive. Then the boys began to beat us regularly. Shortly before they both headed off to college, they joked that they could beat us playing on their knees. Leon and I looked knowingly at each other, and the regular racquetball games between a pair of aging and relatively non-athletic dads and their pair of growing and quite athletic sons ended.

Ian and I also became passionate enthusiasts of whitewater rafting. Both of us felt a real rush when, as part of a group of eight to ten people, we'd paddle successfully through the rapids on a bright, sunny spring day. We began on the relatively undemanding Shenandoah River, and eventually conquered the far more challenging Tygart and Gauley Rivers in West Virginia. A surprise thunderstorm in the middle of one four-hour rafting trip nearly shattered our enthusiasm for the water. On another trip, I fell out of the raft as we negotiated a set of rapids. The current nearly took me over a waterfall. It was a small one, by waterfall standards, but nonetheless potentially deadly for an individual with nothing but a life jacket and helmet to protect him. The guide pulled me back into the raft just prior to my impending demise, and the avoidance of a catastrophe only increased the rush I felt. Ian, at eleven or twelve years old, felt invincible and never gave the dangers a second thought. At one point, totally obsessed, we decided we'd try to raft every river in the Northeast. We got as far north as the Kennebec River in Maine and as far south as West Virginia's New River before tossing in the towel on the idea.

I arranged my summer vacations to take one—or two-week father-son trips. On one such trip in 1982, Ian and I spent time at a personal growth workshop in the Adirondack Mountains facilitated by Sid Simon, my old Queens College professor, and two of his adult sons, John and Doug. Sid facilitated the adult workshop, and the sons facilitated the youth workshop. Arriving at the workshop, I encountered a former Queens College classmate named Hanoch McCarty. He had been known as "Fred" in college, before he officially adopted his Hebrew name, and he had been part of the civil rights contingent at Queens College. He now was a professor of education at Cleveland State University and the divorced single father of two children, Shayna, who was a year older than Ian, and Ethan, who was a year younger. We started planning vacations together.

Our most ambitious adventure was a month-long cross-country camping trip in August 1984. We both purchased pop-up trailers, and our two-car caravan headed west from Hanoch's Cleveland home. Our first major destination was Rapid City, South Dakota, where we camped at a dude ranch and explored the unique Black Hills and Mount Rushmore. Several days later we headed to Yellowstone National Park and the only potential danger we encountered on that trip. A backpacker had recently been killed by a bear in Yellowstone, and the warnings about bears were everywhere, reminding us how to keep food out of their reach, where not to go, how to scare them away with lots of noise, and so on. On our first night in the park, I awoke with a pressing urge. As I got up to head to the bathroom, I heard a rustling just outside the trailer. The urge suddenly seemed less pressing, and I stayed put. In the morning, some overturned items confirmed that a bear had wandered within a few feet of the trailer. We cut short our stay, but not before visiting Old Faithful and the hot springs, going horseback riding, and driving through most of the park as the kids excitedly pointed out—from the safety of the cars—every animal they saw, from bears to moose to prairie dogs. Ian and I and Ian's cousin Aaron, who accompanied us on the trip, even found time to raft the Snake River, although Hanoch and his kids demurred.

The next leg of the trip took us through Grand Teton National Park and to Jackson Hole, Wyoming, for a couple of days of respite from camping in a local motel. Our time together ended with a rodeo in Cody, Wyoming. After nearly three weeks on the road, Hanoch headed southeast to visit his brother in Oklahoma. Ian, Aaron, and I headed southwest to Arizona and the Grand Canyon. To ease the stress on my aging Datsun 500, we drove through Utah without air conditioning, even as the temperature soared beyond a hundred degrees. We stopped for a cold drink at every general store we passed on the sparsely populated route. After a day at the Grand Canyon, we concluded the trip with a stop in New Orleans to visit my sister and brother-in-law, and then wound our way home through Arkansas, Tennessee, and Virginia.

We had covered close to 4,000 miles in four weeks. We had seen spectacular sights and shared unforgettable experiences. Ian and I had bonded in ways that would endure for a lifetime. In fact, we still talk about the trip today. And despite my anxiety about being a white man traveling to unfamiliar places with two black children, we encountered not a single racial problem on the entire trip. Neither did we encounter racial problems on subsequent trips with Ian and Jamal, Beverly's son and one of Ian's closest friends, to Lake George, New York, and Denver, Colorado. In fact, Jamal, now in his late thirties and a successful advertising executive and entertainment promoter in Atlanta, has said that those trips, particularly the one to Denver, inspired him to raise his aspirations. We stayed at an upscale resort while I attended a National Governors' Association meeting, and he saw possibilities that he'd never before dreamed could be available to him.

At home, however, the racial challenges remained. Blatant instances of racism were infrequent, but life for a black child pursuing his or her dreams produced stress that white children rarely encountered. Perhaps the most egregious incident resulted from an out-of-the blue request. When he was about ten years old, Ian asked if he could take horseback riding lessons. Having been born in Brooklyn and raised both in Brooklyn and in the New York City suburbs, I'd seen horses only in cowboy movies or under a policeman in Manhattan. Ian had never been any closer to horses himself. He was interested in sports, and unlike his father, a good athlete; he was a slick-fielding, singles-hitting second baseman in baseball and a wiry, fleet wide receiver and defensive back in football. The idea of horseback riding had never come up. However, the Montessori school he was attending was located on farmland, and the students took care of the horses. Ian loved it. After quizzing him for a few minutes about how serious he was, I agreed to the lessons. We found a stable about thirty minutes away, and Ian embarked on his new-found love. To use a well-worn cliché, he took to horses like a duck takes to water. Before the end of his first year of lessons, he had begun equestrian riding and show jumping. By the end of his second year, he was encouraged by Kathryn, his teacher and the twenty-something daughter of the stable owner, to try out for the stable's junior equestrian team, which competed in an eight-team league. He made the team, and before the end of the season he had become so good that Kathryn suggested he try out for the senior team, which competed in a more advanced league for older students.

Then came an accident that almost ended Ian's riding career, and very nearly his life, while at the same time demonstrating just how committed he was to the sport. In 1986, just before tryouts for the senior team, Ian decided he wanted to spend the summer working at the stable, mucking out stalls and taking care of horses in return for free riding lessons. Every morning I drove him to the stables before heading downtown, and in the evening I picked him up after leaving the office. One evening about midway through the summer, I pulled into the stable's parking lot at about 6:30 p.m., and a girl who rode with Ian came running out to greet me. "Don't worry, Mr. Wenger, Ian is okay." I shuddered and fought back the alarm. "What do you mean, he's okay?" "Well, he got kicked in the face by a horse, but he's fine."

I rushed into the stable to find Kathryn applying cold compresses to his right cheek. "He got a bit careless and walked behind the horse," she said as she looked up. "But it missed his eye, and it doesn't feel like anything's broken." Off we rushed to the emergency room. Ian was calm, but his face was ugly. The horse had missed his eye socket by a fraction of an inch, and the hoof had landed squarely on the fleshy part of his cheek. His teeth had been protected by his braces—never before had orthodontia seemed like such a good investment—but the force of the horse's hoof had enmeshed the inside of his cheek with his braces. So, in a maneuver during which I came to more clearly understand how a parent can feel a child's pain, I tightly gripped both of Ian's hands as the nurse stuck her finger in his mouth and separated the skin from the braces. I nearly cry as I write this now, but Ian never shed a tear. Two days later, with his cheek still grotesquely swollen, he returned to the stable. When he made the senior team that fall, he was not yet fourteen years old.

His team of eight riders won the league championship. Ian, the first and only black child to ride for any team in the league, was the third-leading rider in total points in the entire league of forty-eight riders, and he was the second leading rider on his team. He'd been accepted by both his teammates and the league without incident—or so it seemed. As the evening for the league banquet approached, Ian's excitement grew. We had been told that the six leading riders in the league would receive trophies, as well as the two leading riders on each team and all members of the championship team. Ian was in line for three trophies. His Brooklyn-born-and-bred father could not have been prouder. The dinner was the usual at such gatherings, chicken and string beans, and uneventful as everyone waited for the awards ceremony that would begin after the ice cream was served. When the league's president rose to begin the ceremony, Ian sat up a bit taller in his seat, as did I, awaiting the recognition he had earned with his blood and sweat and his father's tears. The president droned on for a few minutes thanking appropriate officials. "Now," she finally intoned, "come the awards for our young riders. First, the awards for the league's leading riders." Ian smiled bashfully. "Unfortunately, this year we had funds for trophies for just the two leading riders. And so, I am pleased to recognize . . ."

I didn't hear the rest of that presentation. I looked at Ian, and my momentary surprise turned to anger. I turned to Kathryn. "I don't understand." "I don't either," she replied. "I'll find out as soon as the ceremony is over." Ian said nothing. I turned back to the podium. The president was now announcing the two leading riders on each team. Because his was the championship team, she came to Ian's team last. But again, Ian's name was not called. Now I was seething. I turned to Kathryn as she, clearly angry, rose and approached the podium to talk with the president. When she returned, she whispered, "They made a mistake in adding up the points totals. Ian will get his trophy as the second leading rider on the team." "When?" I hissed. "When there's no one around to see that a black child won an award."

Ian says today that he doesn't think about the incident anymore. I do think about it, and a good part of my pain results from the powerlessness I felt. It reminded me of the feeling of powerlessness on that night years earlier when Tempie and I had waited in vain to be served at the West Virginia Turnpike rest stop. This sense of impotence may be the hardest feeling with which to deal. At the rest stop my anger took control, and I smashed that glass. This time I exercised greater control over my emotions, but to what end? I couldn't do anything except get angry, raise my voice, and take my frustration out on Kathryn, who was innocent. It was like spitting in the wind, because the league officials simply said, "Sorry, it was just an honest mistake." Really?

Ian was welcomed by his coach and his teammates even before they realized how good he was. We encountered no flak from any of the parents, and he was included in all of the team's socializing without incident. He rode competitively and successfully in a sport where judging is notoriously subjective. In fact, I cannot remember a single time when the issue of skin color came up, prior to the banquet. Twenty years earlier, it would have been a battle for Ian to just be allowed to take lessons, let alone be invited to try out for the team. Barriers had clearly dissolved. And yet, when it came time for the league to publicly recognize Ian as more talented than a white child, the line seemed to have been drawn. He could participate, compete, win, and even socialize, but he could not be publicly acknowledged for his achievements. He had earned those trophies fairly by working harder than he'd ever worked for anything and enduring hardship and pain. Yet it wasn't enough. There was no escape then, and there is no escape today from the racism that continues to permeate our society.

Ian is a strong-willed individual, and he has not let the experience deter the pursuit of his dreams. But when you wonder why it is difficult at times to break through the iciness we whites sometimes encounter from black people, think of Ian and his missing equestrian trophies. Then multiply that by the years of daily stresses that black youngsters face, stresses foreign to white youngsters. And then imagine you are the parent of a black youngster. Am I being too harsh? Am I seeing racism where there was just an honest mistake—or two? You can make up your own minds. But even if you give the league authorities the benefit of the doubt, they had to be aware of the potential racist implications of denying Ian the awards he had earned. And they didn't seem to care. That, too, is part of the problem.

More subtle were Ian's school experiences. When he finished the sixth grade, Tempie and I decided to enroll him in Sidwell Friends School, a Quaker school in D.C. with an outstanding reputation. Ian was among the few black children at the school, and he prospered. He was smart, sociable, and athletic. There were challenges, particularly as Ian became more aware of society's view of skin color and went through a brief period of discomfort about having a white father. Before one school event we were planning to attend together, he asked plaintively, "Do you have to go with me?" Being a black child with a white father made him different, and he didn't want to attract that kind of attention. But he was well-liked by most of his classmates, and he had several good friends, mostly white, including one who a decade later would become a young colleague of mine at President Clinton's Initiative on Race. Yet one day toward the end of his tenth grade year, Ian announced that he wanted to leave Sidwell for public school. Mature and insightful, he explained his reasoning. First, he was beginning to sag under the pressure of being the only black student in most of his classes and being asked by teachers to explain how black kids felt about Black History Month, about a holiday to honor Martin Luther King Jr., about school bussing, and so on. "I don't even know how I feel about these things. How should I know how other kids feel about them?" Second, he felt somewhat overwhelmed by the family wealth of many of his school friends, the large houses in which they lived, the fancy cars their parents drove, the exotic vacations they took. He wanted to be in a more diverse economic environment where there were more kids from families like his own. Third, his interest in girls was emerging, and while he had many white female friends, dating white girls seemed off-limits.

Despite misgivings, but confident that he had a good educational foundation, Tempie and I allowed him to transfer to a public high school in Prince George's County, Maryland, where both of us now lived. When he returned home from his first day of school in September, he reported that he'd been placed in a vocational track. We thought back to Regina's experience in Charleston. As Yogi Berra might have said, it was "déjà vu all over again." The next day, we went to the school. His guidance counselor, a middle-aged white woman who was as stunned at my skin color as was the Charleston guidance counselor who had informed Regina of her alleged shortcomings, told us that placing Ian in a vocational track was to ensure that he could be successful. Again, as with Regina, we insisted our child be placed in the college preparatory track. This time, more than a decade later, and in a more urban and diverse environment, we met with even greater resistance. When she finally capitulated, the guidance counselor said she could "take no responsibility for Ian's future" because we were overriding her professional advice. Ian, to the surprise of very few who knew him, graduated from both high school and college with honors and has built a successful career as a television producer. Were it not for his stubborn and persistent parents, his level of achievement might have been far different.

I do not want to leave the impression that having low expectations for black students and the consequent tracking of black students into vocational programs is the standard operating practice of all public schools today. Despite current data showing that black children are tracked disproportionately into vocational or special education programs and punished more severely than white children for identical rule infractions, many public schools do an excellent job educating students, irrespective of skin color. And there are countless teachers and guidance counselors who demand and receive high levels of performance from all students.

The point I want to make is that high expectations are generally a given for white students. Not so for black students. If parents are not vigilant, low expectations can have a devastating effect on their children's futures. These incidents with Regina's junior high school guidance counselor, Arnya's first grade teacher, and Ian's high school guidance counselor, among many others, caused Tempie to make a surprising pronouncement one day. She suggested to me that despite the reality that our children attended better-equipped schools in a physical environment far more conducive to learning than she'd experienced in the segregated schools of North Carolina, she was not sure how beneficial school integration was to black children. Her teachers had often been better qualified than the average teacher because they were highly educated individuals who, due to their skin color, had been unable to find professional jobs except as teachers. They had high expectations of their students, and when students did not meet those expectations, the teachers were not shy about contacting parents, who would inevitably deal effectively with their children's performance. Except for the inferior facilities, the lack of books and supplies, and the inadequacy of the equipment in segregated schools, it sounded much like the environment in which I had attended school.

Nonetheless, despite the challenges, we were shepherding the children successfully through school. Regina graduated from college in 1983. For her graduation present, I took her with me to a conference in West Berlin, with a stop in Paris to visit my cousin Allan, Uncle Sam's son, who still lives in Paris. Arnya graduated from college in 1987. Both found jobs quickly, Regina inspecting restaurants and health facilities in Atlanta, and Arnya working for the House Budget Committee in Washington, D.C. Ian was growing and maturing each day as he steered his way through high school. And I was beginning to contemplate life without children at home. I dreamt of remarrying, of having a love partner to share both the joys and stresses of daily life. I dated regularly, but had not found anyone with whom I wanted to settle down. Abruptly and unexpectedly in 1988, I did find someone.

Years earlier, when Sally Richardson and I were colleagues in the Welfare Department, Sally had entrusted the installation of the Management By Objectives (MBO) program, her major priority, to Jackie Simmons, a young white woman from Rhode Island. She had come to West Virginia after college, worked in several local welfare offices, and then went to the University of Tennessee to obtain a master's degree in Social Work. Because the Welfare Department paid her tuition, she was obligated to the department for two years. Sally thought her youth and background would make her an effective MBO ambassador, especially with the younger and more diverse group of field workers we were hiring. Since field operations were my responsibility, Jackie and I spent time together strategizing and sharing ideas.

At twenty-nine, she was seven years my junior. She had been through a brief and abusive marriage and then divorced shortly before leaving for graduate school. Her tender, compassionate personality masked a will that had enabled her to be the first of her siblings (two sisters and a brother) to leave Rhode Island. She had survived a disastrous marriage, flourished in graduate school, and traded the Catholicism of her youth for a commitment to evangelical Christianity. I'd known many strong women, but Jackie had a feminine side not always present in women with such uncommon strength.

After Tempie left Charleston, Jackie and I would occasionally go on pizza and bowling dates that included Ian. After I moved to Washington, D.C., we saw each other when I returned to Charleston on business, but after a couple of years, we lost touch. In the latter part of 1987, I had occasion to call the Charleston banker who held the mortgage on the home Tempie and I still owned. He had been a friend of Jackie's, so I asked if he ever saw her. "I thought you knew," he replied. "She moved to Washington, D.C., about a year ago. She's working at Georgetown University Hospital." I was surprised she hadn't contacted me.

After a few days, I called her. "Mike," she admitted, "I wanted to call you, but I didn't know what to say. And I was afraid we'd start something that couldn't go anywhere because of our religious differences." We met for dinner at a restaurant overlooking the Potomac River on a beautiful snowy evening in January 1988. We watched the snow fall, brought each other up to date, and assured each other that we were interested only in being friends. Less than ten months later, religious barriers notwithstanding, we were married.

Divorce is difficult for children, and the remarriage of a parent can be even more traumatic if not handled well. I did not handle the situation well. The children had seemed to accept Tempie's remarriage, but I was anxious. Ian and I had become a twosome, two guys living together in a bachelor pad. He had liked our Friday night dates in Charleston, but back then Jackie and I were just friends and he was just a child. Now on the edge of manhood at fifteen, how would he react to Jackie's intrusion into the comfortable routine of our lives? With the girls, my anxiety was different. They were both now college graduates living independently. As the relationship between Jackie and me grew more intense, I worried they might be angry at the idea of another woman intruding into our lives, and shun Jackie out of loyalty to their mother. I also worried they might feel alienated because I was marrying a white woman. The fear of losing them had haunted me since before Tempie and I divorced. I had been Tempie's partner in raising them and I loved them dearly, but our culture fosters racial divisions. When their mother and I separated, I feared, without justification, they would feel the need to choose sides. Now, my impending marriage to a white woman reignited that fear. Because of my anxieties, I'd subconsciously avoided involving the children in my social life, and I'd laid no groundwork for remarriage.

In August 1988, I announced our marriage plans. Ian and Arnya were, as I feared, hurt and furious. Regina was a bit more even-handed. "Well," she said, "it's your decision and your life." My anxiety over losing them seemed to be a self-fulfilling prophecy. Things calmed down as the October 29, 1988, wedding day approached. All three children, along with Regina's best friend Brenda, participated in the service on that crisp fall day at the beautiful chapel on the campus of Mount Vernon College for Women. Jackie and I honeymooned for a week in London, visiting museums and secondhand bookstores, eating in ethnic restaurants, and seeing a different play each evening. The tension that had preceded the wedding seemed a distant memory. That is, until we returned home and discovered that while we were gone, Ian had moved out of my townhouse and moved in with Tempie and her husband. I was surprised, hurt, and angry. My attitude toward Ian turned cool, and we talked only infrequently in the ensuing months. Tension with Tempie rose. Although this hadn't been Jackie's fault, I was angry at her also. I wasn't sure our marriage could survive my losing the children. We sought counseling, and even coerced the children into attending a counseling session with us. But it seemed hopeless. The children hadn't tried to stop the marriage, but they didn't want to accept it. They'd be civil to Jackie and me, but that was it.

That first year was torturous, and only the solemn vows we'd made on our wedding day kept us together. Before our marriage, we'd bought a larger, newly built home that could more easily accommodate the children and the grandchildren we anticipated in the not-too-distant future. Because we couldn't find a home to our liking at a price we wanted to pay in Montgomery County, Maryland, the predominantly white county where I had been living, we purchased a home in Prince George's County, the wealthiest predominantly African American county in the country. It was identical to a house we'd seen by the same builder in Montgomery County, but the price was 20 percent less, a difference attributable to the lower property values in the predominantly black county, with their accompanying effect on schools and other important community amenities. We moved in February 1989 and spent our spare time furnishing and organizing the house to our taste. My heart wasn't in it, though. It seemed empty without the children, and I felt empty.

Suddenly, about a year after the wedding, Ian showed up at our front door, suitcases in hand, and moved in with us. He offered no lengthy explanation, but our bond forged through the years of baseball, whitewater rafting, camping, and mutual love and respect, had held. I would not have to experience the pain I'd seen on my former acquaintance's face on that plane ride fifteen years earlier. Ian finished high school while making our house his home, and his basement "suite" remains intact for when he and his daughter visit from Los Angeles (although our oldest granddaughter, Arian, who graduated from high school in June 2010 and enrolled in a college just blocks from our house, laid claim to the suite temporarily). Ian's action began a thaw with the girls, and the initial tension gave way to a warm and loving relationship between Jackie and all three children and an even tighter relationship between our four grandchildren and "Grandma Jackie."

Arnya got married not long after we did, moved to a home near ours, and her first daughter, Arian, was born in 1992. Alexis followed in 1994, and Grandma Jackie has been a major care-giver to both of them. Regina moved back to D.C. not long after we got married, and her presence in the area provided an opportunity for the three of us to build a closer and stronger relationship. In 2000, after Regina's return to D.C. from jobs in Hawaii and San Francisco, she became pregnant and moved into the basement suite during the last several months of her pregnancy. Since the birth of Michael Ian (I need not say how proud both Ian and I were when she surprised us with that name), she has relied heavily on Jackie and me for caregiving assistance, and we've been grateful to have him as such an important part of our lives. We've also established our own traditions as a family, such as our Christmas Eve celebration, which includes Tempie and all of the children and grandchildren, and our Christmas dinner, for which we all gather at Regina's house.

In the fall of 1990, Ian and I began visiting colleges in anticipation of his high school graduation. With Jamal accompanying us, we visited Rutgers University in New Jersey and St. Johns University in New York. Later, Ian and I visited Boston University, where he was heavily recruited by a black woman in the admissions department. He was overwhelmed, as Tempie and I had been years earlier, by the Harvard Book Store, and as we returned home he was leaning heavily toward attending Boston University. Then we headed south for our last visit, to Morehouse College, an HBCU in Atlanta. In contrast to the other places we visited, Morehouse was a spare and dusty campus in the middle of a rundown section of Atlanta. It boasted graduates like Martin Luther King Jr. and Spike Lee, among many others, but the facilities—the classrooms, dormitories, library, book store—could not match those of the other schools we had visited. And yet, when we finished the visit, Ian announced he was going to Morehouse. When I asked him why, he simply said he felt more comfortable there.

I had tried to be noncommittal, telling him the choice was his. Privately, I applauded his decision. At predominantly white colleges like Rutgers and Boston University there are diverse student bodies but little true integration; I feared he would face the choice of associating primarily with black students and being accused of self-segregation or associating primarily with white students and being accused of being an "Oreo": black on the outside and white on the inside. Furthermore, in his classes and in other campus activities, he probably would be one of the few black students, as he had been at Sidwell. At Morehouse, he would confront none of those issues. He could be himself and be "judged by the content of his character and not by the color of his skin." For essentially the same reasons, both Regina and Arnya had also attended HBCUs. Regina graduated from North Carolina A&T University in Greensboro, North Carolina, and Arnya graduated from North Carolina Central University, just down the road in Durham, North Carolina.

As his sisters had at their respective HBCUs, Ian received a high-quality education at Morehouse. He emerged as a well-educated, supremely confident, highly capable young man with a strong sense of self-identity and the necessary preparation for successfully confronting the job market. The lack of resources at Morehouse compared to the major predominantly white universities was more than offset by his professors' interest in his growth and by the freedom he enjoyed to be himself. The easy camaraderie and sense of community that existed on campus were obvious to Jackie and me when we delivered him to campus at the beginning of his freshman year. Ian seemed totally in his element. And as the Morehouse dean of students promised in his welcoming speech to parents of incoming students, Ian went on to become a proud Morehouse Man. When he graduated as one of 500 young and proud black men who defy the negative stereotype too many people hold about them, he was prepared to conquer the world.

Attending a predominantly black college, however, did not shield him entirely from society's challenges. One afternoon, he and two friends were walking in Atlanta's downtown area. They were not talking loudly, or carrying boom boxes, or wearing baggy jeans, or sporting Afro hairstyles. They were three middle-class college students looking for a way to spend some of their parents' money. (I can vouch for the fact that at least one of them succeeded in doing just that.) A white woman was walking toward them on the same side of the street. When she saw them, she crossed the street. When she was at what she apparently considered a safe distance past them, she crossed back. Ian recounted the story to me with a combination of confusion and anger. Given the rather sheltered life he'd led up to that point, it was a new experience for him. "What did she think we were going to do to her? If we'd been white, she wouldn't have given us a second look. It just makes me angry that she figures she knows us when she's never seen us before." I tried to explain that the woman may have been afraid because of the negative stereotype of young black men that is promoted by our culture, by the media, and by other institutions in our society. She probably had not had enough meaningful experiences with people from different racial backgrounds to counteract that stereotype. Ian was not placated. His confusion and anger, and that of his friends, help to explain the self-fulfilling distrust that white people often encounter from black people.

But there is something more deeply foreboding about the incident. This woman did not live in a vacuum. Suppose, for example, she were a retail store clerk. How would she treat young black men when they shopped in her store? If she were a schoolteacher, how would she be likely to treat young black males in her classroom, and what would she likely communicate to white students about young black males? If she worked in the personnel department of a large company, how likely would she be to hire a young black male, no matter how well-qualified he might be? Suppose she were in law enforcement or suppose she were simply a housewife with young children? The examples are endless. When she crossed the street, she denied herself an opportunity to challenge a negative racial stereotype that she likely carried. In the process, she probably reinforced that stereotype. And what I have labeled the self-perpetuating cycle of negative racial stereotyping continued unabated (more about this later).

More scary was an incident that occurred when Ian was driving home from Morehouse on one Christmas break. His car had broken down at about 5:30 a.m. on a cold night in southern Virginia. Since none of the auto repair places was open at that hour, he sought temporary refuge at a local McDonald's. It wasn't scheduled to open until 6 a.m., but the manager was inside getting ready, so Ian knocked on the door and asked to wait inside. The manager, a young white man whom Ian described as looking terrified of his black face, refused to unlock the door. Feeling cold, alone, and somewhat fearful, Ian called us, but we didn't hear the phone and only discovered his panicky voice mail message when we awoke at about 8 a.m. Fortunately, by the time we connected by phone, he'd located a friendly automobile repair shop. But the panic in his message was a clear reminder that his skin color made him considerably more vulnerable to danger.

As his college career wound to a close, I, like most parents, began to worry about what came next. He was an English major, but he didn't seem to have a clear direction in mind. "I don't know," he'd say when I asked him what he wanted to do. "I'll think of something." I knew he would, but his answer left me frustrated. At about 11 p.m. on a February evening during his senior year, the telephone rang. It was Ian. "Hey, Pop, what's going on in the world?"

"Um, would you like to give me some context for that question?"

"Well, I've got an interview at NBC tomorrow, and I figure they'll ask me questions about current affairs."

Ian had been working part-time as a sports writer for the *Atlanta Journal-Constitution* as his graduation approached (perhaps the apple really doesn't fall far from the tree). His English professor had taken an interest in his work and referred him to a friend, a black woman who headed NBC's Atlanta bureau. She had encouraged him to apply for a position as a news associate, or intern, at NBC in New York. Of the 500 college students in the country who applied, Ian was one of twenty-two selected to be interviewed for nine available positions, and NBC was flying him to New York for the interview. After a brief conversation, I advised him, "Pick up a copy of the *New York Times* at the Atlanta airport and read it cover to cover on the flight. If you can remember what you read, you should be able to answer virtually any current events question." After he had been offered a news associate position, he told me, tongue in cheek, that it was the best advice I'd ever given him. "Every question in the interview came from one of the articles in the *Times*. It was magic."

His graduation day was magic, as well. As Ian and his 500 fellow graduates marched down the aisle on a sweltering Atlanta day in June 1995, moisture was coming not only from my perspiration. It was coming from my tears of joy. The young man who had struggled to fit in at Barrie Day School and at Sidwell, who had endured the disappointment of the equestrian awards ceremony, who had been tracked into a vocational program by the high school counselor, and who had endured his share of difficult experiences due to negative racial stereotyping, was on his way to a successful career as a producer at NBC, first for *Dateline NBC* and now for the *Today Show* out of the Los Angeles studios.

Meanwhile, Arnya had married and started a family, and Regina was building a successful career as a quality control manager for major corporations. She spent two years as the quality control manager for a Hawaii cruise ship company, and then moved to San Francisco to take on quality control responsibilities for the five west coast kitchens of a major airline-catering company. But she dreamed of settling down and starting a family, as well. She fell in love with a man who worked in the Atlanta office of her company and decided to relocate to Atlanta to be with him. Because the company looked askance at employees dating each other, she resigned her position, confident that her excellent resume and recommendations would get her a job anywhere. Shortly after arriving in Atlanta, she responded to an advertisement for a position as a quality control specialist at a rapidly growing national fast food chain. Within a few days, she received a telephone call from the head of personnel, who gushed over her resume and asked her to come in immediately for an interview. And then they saw her, a tall, dark-skinned woman, and instantly concluded, "We've made an unfortunate mistake. The job was filled." "They didn't even want to shake my hand," she lamented. Shortly thereafter, the love relationship fell apart. She returned to D.C., personally and professionally devastated.

Being resilient, she recovered. Today, she is the proud mother of the smart, personable, and caring eleven-year-old Michael Ian. And after several years of floundering in a dead-end job, she found a highly responsible position with a major corporation. She owns her own home and recently started her own consulting business. The delay in her dream of starting a family had nothing to do with race, but the job disappointment and career detour were additional examples of the challenges black people face in pursuing their career dreams. It was another time when I felt an acute sense of powerlessness about trying to help one of my children overcome a challenge that is foreign to white people. But I was shortly to carve out a new career path that would offer the opportunity to address some of these challenges.

X

A NEW CAREER PATH

As fulfilling as my professional career had been, in my heart I'd never truly left the civil rights movement behind. (Ian chides me occasionally that I'm still mired in the 1960s.) My personal journey had only stoked my passion to be more professionally involved in combating racism. The opportunity for that involvement came with President Clinton's Initiative on Race. It began with a telephone call to my ARC office from White House Deputy Chief of Staff Sylvia Matthews at about 10 a.m. on Friday, February 28, 1997, approximately three and a half months before the President announced his plans for such an initiative. She invited me to a meeting at the White House on the following Monday to "discuss what President Clinton might do about the issue of race in his second term." She promised to fax materials later in the day in preparation for the meeting. The fax arrived at about 3:30 p.m., labeled "Information for 5:00 mtg on March 3 in Roosevelt Room." I flipped over the cover sheet and gasped. Attached was *my* concept paper, a proposal I had prepared three months earlier for the creation of a President's Council on Racial Reconciliation. I had given it to Governor Winter, who had promised to try to get it to the President. Now, here it was, clearly stamped, "The President Has Seen—2/7/97," and it was to be the basis for a White House meeting!

The paper emerged from a discussion Jackie and I had had while driving back from a trip to Hilton Head, South Carolina, in November 1996, just a few days after President Clinton had been reelected. I'd given a speech about regional economic development in Appalachia. In the speech I had referred to the dramatic demographic shifts taking place in the country, the value of racial and ethnic diversity in economic development, and the persistent racial tensions that continued to thwart economic growth in some Appalachian communities. I'd been speaking about this and the intersection of poverty and race with increasing frequency and frustration since the middle of the Reagan years, which, I felt, had noticeably set back race relations. In 1987 I had even formed a nonprofit corporation, TREASURE-America (*To REA*waken the *S*pirit, *U*nited for *R*acial *E*quity in *America*), and unsuccessfully sought foundation grants to pursue a change in the nation's racial climate. I had seen the election of Clinton, a former southern governor with an obvious concern for racial equity, as a promising harbinger of positive leadership to counteract the damage of the prior twelve years. But I was disappointed by his first term. "Now that he doesn't have to worry about reelection," I observed to Jackie as we sped north on I-95, "is there anything you think President Clinton can do that will make a difference in race relations?" I was more hopeful than optimistic.

She answered with a question of her own. "What would you like to accomplish?"

"To change the racial climate in the country as a prerequisite to enacting policies that can make the playing field more level." Two years earlier, the Republicans, under the leadership of Newt Gingrich, had taken control of the U.S. House of Representatives. The anti-government, racially divisive tone that characterized both Reagan/Bush rhetoric and the Gingrich takeover seemed to be sweeping the country, making it impossible for government to seriously address racial disparities in access to education, employment, justice, affordable housing, and quality health care. We needed to confront this negative tone, I believed, before it would be possible to adopt meaningful policies to address the disparities. I ruminated about the bully pulpit of the presidency, the power of the media to influence public debate, the need for a more accurate and inclusive American history curriculum in public schools, and the potential value of partnerships with major employers.

"You know," Jackie finally said, "what you're talking about sounds a lot like what the President's Council on Physical Fitness was about. Before it started, most people, besides athletes, were not really concerned about being physically fit. There were no health clubs, no joggers, and little effort by schools to emphasize good physical conditioning. The Council on Physical Fitness literally changed the nation's outlook on the issue, largely with help from self-interested companies: insurance, athletic apparel, sneaker companies." The concept paper I prepared when we got home proposed a President's Council on Racial Reconciliation, to be modeled after the President's Council on Physical Fitness. I sent it to Governor Winter with whom I'd remained in touch. He called to say he supported the concept and would send it with a personal letter to the President. The governor had been a mentor to Clinton during the President's early years as governor of Arkansas. In writing the paper, I had decided to leave my name off the title page, because few, if any, people at the White House would have recognized my name. I reasoned that if White House officials thought the paper had come directly from Governor Winter, it would get more serious attention. I did note, in eight-point type at the end of the paper, that it had been "prepared by Michael R. Wenger, States' Washington Representative for the Appalachian Regional Commission." The tactic worked. Despite Governor Winter's disclaimer that I, and not he, had authored the paper, White House officials gave credit to the governor. That was fine with me if it got us in the door. The governor and I also enlisted the support of newly appointed Transportation Secretary Rodney Slater, a Clinton confidante whom I had come to know when he headed the Federal Highway Administration and was involved in the development of the Appalachian Regional Highway System.

Now, three months after I'd first sent the paper to Governor Winter, it was the basis for a policy agenda meeting at the White House. Wow! I probably should have wondered how much serious thought the White House had given to the issue, since they sent out the paper without changes or comments, but all I could think of was that President Clinton had actually seen my paper. During March 1997, I attended five meetings at the White House, most of them in the West Wing's Roosevelt Room. Sylvia chaired them. A number of key White House staff attended the meetings, though not always the same ones. The only outsiders in attendance, besides me, were Governor Winter and former White House staffers Chris Edley and Bill Galston. Edley, a distinguished legal scholar who is African American, taught President Obama at Harvard Law School and is now dean of the law school at the University of California at Berkeley. Two issues consumed the discussion at every meeting. One was whether a presidential initiative should focus solely on race or encompass other oppressions, as well, particularly those related to sexual orientation. The divisions at the meetings were predictable. People of color and many white women argued for a focus on race, because to do otherwise would allow us once again to avoid confronting the issue directly. Most white men (of course excluding Governor Winter and myself) argued for a broader approach precisely because it minimized the focus on race. The other issue was whether the initiative should focus primarily on research, essentially examining the Kerner Commission Report[1] thirty years later, or whether it should be more action-oriented. The divisions on this issue were similar: most of the other white men argued for a research focus; the rest of us argued that race had been researched to death and we needed action. Since attendees varied from meeting to meeting, both issues were revisited at each meeting without final resolution.

---

[1] The National Advisory Commission on Civil Disorders was appointed in 1967 by President Johnson and chaired by then Illinois Governor Otto Kerner. Its charge was to analyze the specific triggers for the recent race riots in several major cities, the deeper causes of the worsening racial climate, and potential remedies. The commission issued its report in 1968.

On March 25, 1997, the group, along with several cabinet secretaries and key White House staff, met in the Cabinet Room with the President and the Vice President. The meeting was scheduled for 4 p.m. I had a speaking engagement at a Bethesda civic club on the topic of racial stereotyping at 7 p.m., but since the meeting was scheduled to last one hour, I presumed I'd have plenty of time to make the thirty-minute drive from the White House. On the morning of the twenty-fifth, however, the meeting was moved to 5 p.m. As I walked with Governor Winter to the White House, I told him I was a bit anxious about making it to my speaking engagement, and I wondered whether I could leave the meeting early, if necessary. "Mike," he said with a smile, "nobody leaves a meeting with the President early. I'm sure your hosts will understand if you're a bit late because of a meeting with the President of the United States."

The seating was prearranged. Cabinet secretaries had designated seats at the table. Key White House staff also sat at the table for this meeting. So did Governor Winter. The rest of us sat against the walls. I sat in a chair directly behind Sylvia Matthews. We were in our seats by 4:55 p.m., but as we waited for the President, and the minutes passed, I grew more anxious about making it on time to my speaking engagement. The President, who had hurt his leg, hobbled in at 5:30 p.m. and sat directly across the table from Sylvia. By then, I'd concluded that I'd be late to my speech (this was the pre-cell-phone era). Despite my anxiety, though, I was awestruck by the circumstances. I was one of about thirty people sitting in the Cabinet Room in the West Wing of the White House with the Vice President and the secretaries of Transportation, Housing and Urban Development, and Labor, among others, and I was sitting right across the table from the President of the United States. It was a far cry from my days as a civil rights activist and antipoverty community organizer.

The agenda was simple. Designated members of our group would present the two issues that had consumed our Roosevelt Room discussions. Chris Edley made a powerful presentation in support of focusing the initiative on race and the President strongly agreed, simply saying, "This must be about race." On the second issue he reserved judgment, but seemed to be searching for a middle ground. I marveled at his intricate knowledge of the issue and the depth of his engagement in the discussion. As the discussion continued, I wanted to be part of it, to suggest the concept of a President's Council on Racial Reconciliation as the possible middle ground he was seeking. But I didn't know the protocol. If I was not sitting at the table, was it appropriate for me to speak? I tapped Sylvia on the shoulder. "Is it appropriate for me to say anything?" She didn't answer. After the next speaker had finished, she interjected: "Mr. President, Mike Wenger, who has worked with Governor Winter, would like to make a comment."

I stood. "Mr. President, along with Governor Winter, I prepared the paper I believe you saw on the concept of a President's Council on Racial Reconciliation."

"Yes, I remember that," the President replied. "I liked that idea."

I don't remember what I said after that, nor do I recall what the President said. All I could remember was that the President liked my idea. When the meeting ended at 6:45 p.m., Governor Winter approached the President, shook his hand, and motioned me to join him.

"Mr. President, this is Mike Wenger. He is the brains behind the idea of a President's Council on Racial Reconciliation."

I blushed, we shook hands, and the President reiterated that he liked the idea. I thanked him and told him I had a speaking engagement on racial stereotyping immediately after this meeting.

"That's great," he replied. "I remember making lots of those speeches when I was governor."

I arrived in Bethesda at 7:30 p.m. and explained that I'd been at a meeting with the President. No further explanation was needed, and my speech seemed to be received with somewhat greater respect.

I had no further communication from the White House until the President announced the creation of his Initiative on Race in June. It bore little resemblance to my concept paper, but it did focus exclusively on the issue of race, and it was a mixture of research and dialogue on race, perhaps the middle ground for which the President had been searching. Governor Winter was one of the seven people announced as members of the Advisory Board to the President's Initiative on Race. Two months later, I was appointed as deputy director for outreach and program development, and I embarked on what was both the most exhilarating and most frustrating experience of my professional career. It was exhilarating because I was at the world's power center. Except for having to show identification, I had virtually unrestricted access to the West Wing. I routinely attended meetings in the Roosevelt Room just across the hall from the Oval Office. Although I rarely interacted with the President, I interacted regularly with some of his closest advisors, people most Americans see only on television. I contributed my views to decisions about the President's agenda on race relations, spoke as the White House representative on programs with civil rights legends like John Lewis, now a distinguished Congressman from Georgia, and occasionally was invited to attend the chief of staff's 7:45 a.m. meetings, in which discussions centered on where the President would be that day, the primary message of the day, and planned activities that might impact the message or otherwise draw press coverage. It was heady stuff.

My frustration arose from a realization that, despite the promise of the Initiative, we would fall far short of achieving the President's vision of "one America, respecting, even celebrating, our differences, but embracing even more what we have in common." The Initiative succeeded in generating substantial public discourse about persistent racial discrimination. It energized antiracist activists who had become discouraged by the nation's racial climate, inspired new activities designed to narrow racial divisions in many communities, and raised the nation's consciousness about the need to heal these divisions. Ultimately, though, White House divisions about the likely political consequences of the Initiative made it impossible to overcome the political partisanship and unrealistic expectations in which it became mired.

The divisions among the President's advisers during the initial Roosevelt Room meetings persisted throughout the Initiative. Virtually all the people of color and many white women in the White House supported the Initiative as a way to both help white people become more aware of our nation's continuing racial shortcomings and strengthen the Democratic Party's base of support among people of color. They had tasted oppression, some more than others, and they knew instinctively that until we confronted the issue directly, race would continue to tear at the nation's fabric.

Those who opposed the Initiative, several of them in positions of considerable influence, saw the Initiative as a political albatross. It would, they argued, create unrealistic expectations among the Democratic base, alienate white political allies, and exacerbate racial divisions. Ignore the issue of race, they advised. Concentrate instead on incremental, race-neutral improvements in education and other areas of social concern that would affect a much broader portion of the population and would incidentally help black people. From my perspective, their views reflected the privileges of whiteness and maleness that they had enjoyed their entire lives, privileges that tend to anesthetize people to the oppressive conditions others confront daily. Unfortunately, once the Initiative was underway, President Clinton seemed unwilling or unable to resolve this dispute, and it paralyzed the Initiative, dooming it to disappointment.

The fine hand of the opponents was clearly visible in two requirements that wreaked havoc on our efforts: budget neutrality and time frame. We were told at our first Roosevelt Room meeting, and reminded at subsequent meetings, that what we recommended could have no budget impact, because that would conflict with the President's commitment to a balanced budget. The consequences of this limitation were far-reaching.

Key leaders in the civil rights community were not invited to our meetings out of fear that they would put pressure on the administration to be more aggressive than it deemed politically prudent and that they would push for actions that would cost more money than the administration was willing to spend. To the best of my knowledge, none of these leaders was consulted until key decisions about the shape of the Initiative had already been made. Whether this was the President's direction or the handiwork of Initiative opponents within the administration was never clear to me. At several of the meetings, concern about the absence of these leaders was raised. How, several of us asked, can a potentially far-reaching initiative on race be planned without input from the people who have the most experience with and deepest knowledge of the issue?

The people in our meetings were well-meaning, but except for Chris Edley, most were not major players on issues of race. It seemed ludicrous that leaders of such organizations as the NAACP, the National Urban League, the National Council of La Raza, the Leadership Conference on Civil Rights, the National Congress of American Indians, the Rainbow Coalition, and others, most of whom were strong Clinton supporters, were not being consulted. I was told that some consultation did eventually occur before the announcement of the Initiative, but it was not until plans were in place. What was possibly the most consequential effort ever made by a President to address our racial divisions was planned largely without the input of the people most knowledgeable about the subject. Not only did this mean that their ideas were not considered, it also made these leaders wary of the Initiative and reluctant to provide significant visible support for it. "At least do no harm," was a biting comment made by one of these leaders.

Budgetary concerns also made the White House fearful of an independent commission that might make recommendations inconsistent with the balanced-budget goal. Thus, there emerged the convoluted structure of a President's Advisory Board on Race with no independent power of its own, and an initiative staff that was to work with the Advisory Board, but that was hired by and directly responsible to the White House chief of staff, Erskine Bowles. Only the civility and loyalty of advisory board members like Governor Winter and the chairman, the eminent historian Dr. John Hope Franklin, and the flexibility and civility of Erskine Bowles, avoided potentially embarrassing public disputes between the Advisory Board and the White House.

This arrangement hit its first snag when the Advisory Board was advised of White House plans to hire a staff director for the Initiative who was close to White House staffers but inexperienced with issues of race. Pressure from the Advisory Board and from initiative supporters inside the White House scuttled that decision. With less than a week to go before the Advisory Board's first scheduled meeting in early July 1997, nearly a month after the Advisory Board had been appointed amid great fanfare, the staff director position was offered to the highly qualified general counsel of the Department of Education, Judith Winston. After a brief hesitation, she accepted the position, but she was put in the uncomfortable position of having to admit at that first meeting that she had just been hired and had little to say. I had not yet been hired, but I attended the meeting as Governor Winter's guest. The disorganization alarmed me, and the press pounced on it. That negativity set the tone for how the press viewed the Initiative and from which the Initiative never fully recovered.

Because she had to wind up her affairs at the Department of Education, our executive director did not assume her position until early August. She then had to hire staff with a key constraint: she had to focus on hiring staff who could be loaned to the Initiative from other federal agencies without budgetary implications. I was the only top staff member hired from outside the government. I was offered the position after an interview with Judy that was arranged by Governor Winter. I explained the role I had played in the White House discussions. "I definitely need you," she said, acknowledging that she was unclear about the White House's intent. But I had to wait anxiously for several weeks after the interview while she persuaded the White House that I was worth the expenditure and while Senator Rockefeller, whom I'd used as a reference, and Governor Winter convinced them I wasn't a zealot. Unfortunately, Judy had to turn down a number of well-qualified applicants from outside the federal government because their salaries would have depleted the initiative's minimal budget. I was able to hire several young, relatively inexperienced people from outside the government only because their salaries were low.

A potentially embarrassing public dispute arising from the no-budget-impact requirement was avoided when White House staff caved on an initial edict that the Advisory Board was not to issue a public report. They were told to confine themselves to a summary letter to the President describing the board's year-long activities. This battle, mostly hidden from public view, came to a head in the spring of 1998 when Dr. Franklin simply dismissed the White House edict and directed the staff to prepare a full report. Even then, however, White House staff hovered over initiative staff as they prepared the report, trying to ensure that the report and its recommendations would be "safe" and without budgetary impact. To the degree that the report did not break new ground, one should credit the White House staff, who quaked at the possibility of costly or controversial recommendations.

Perhaps even more damaging than the no-budget-impact requirement was the declaration at that first meeting in March 1997 that the Initiative would be limited to one year. The declaration was greeted incredulously by some of us, and until the Initiative closed its doors at the end of September 1998, we attempted to extend its life. But key White House staff argued that they did not want to mire the administration in "race politics." The message to the outside world, particularly to the press, was that the administration was not serious about dealing with the issue of race. What, people asked, can possibly be accomplished in a single year? Justifiably, they argued that on an issue that has inflamed emotions for centuries, that requires the unlearning of enormous amounts of misinformation, that demands careful long-term planning to constructively engage large numbers of people, a one-year effort can barely scratch the surface. The time limit was a disaster. First, it put enormous pressure on a staff that was not even fully hired until the Initiative was nearly four months old. The Initiative was announced on June 14, 1997. Judith Winston assumed her position in early August without any clear direction from the White House other than the President's initial announcement. I and her other two deputies arrived in September, although I had taken time from the ARC in August to interview and recommend potential staff.

Few of the staff, including me, had ever worked in the White House or in an environment remotely similar to such a pressurized situation. We needed time to acclimate to the intense scrutiny the Initiative was under and to figure out how to proceed, especially without a clear mandate from the White House. But with the one-year limit looming large, such time was a luxury we could not afford. So, rather than taking time for careful planning and for outreach to build a base of support and an infrastructure to sustain ongoing dialogue and action, we had to do everything at warp speed. Rushed planning, an attempted big press splash that did not materialize, and minimal follow-up became the norm for virtually every event. It hardly seemed the right way to address persistent racial divisions and inequalities.

As the disarray at the Initiative became more evident, the White House ratcheted up the pressure and tightened its control, rather than increasing flexibility to ease the pressure. White House staff had to approve the location for every advisory board meeting, making sure that each meeting was in politically friendly territory. Despite an initial promise to hold four town hall meetings, the President held only one such meeting during the Initiative. Before its location, Akron, Ohio, was finalized, I attended at least a dozen meetings in the West Wing to discuss the political pros and cons of a half-dozen proposed locations. Had the jurisdiction voted for the President? Did it have public officials supportive of the President? Was the local press friendly? Were there enough local supporters that a large and friendly audience could be assured? These questions were vetted through the Offices of Political Affairs, Intergovernmental Affairs, Public

Liaison, Communication, and the Chief of Staff. The White House, to ensure the meetings did not generate controversy or embarrass the administration, had to approve the agenda and panel participants for each advisory board meeting. Given the choice between substance and political comfort, political comfort always triumphed.

At times this tight control backfired. The meetings tended to be bland, broke little new ground, and were not particularly newsworthy. In some cases, such as a meeting in Denver where protests broke out over the absence of an American Indian on the Advisory Board—an unfortunate oversight the White House could easily have corrected but chose not to—White House staff disregarded our advice to reach out to the protestors in advance.

The most significant and damaging result of the one-year time limitation was that it fueled cynicism in the press. White House efforts to calm troubled waters rather than address the root cause of the cynicism only exacerbated the problem. The press constantly asked what the Initiative had done and what it would accomplish in the remaining (fill in the blank) months. At that first Advisory Board meeting in July 1997, the press's refrain was, "The twelve-month Initiative now has eleven months to go, and they still don't have an executive director in place." To illustrate the administration's sincerity, both the President and Vice President attended the next advisory board meeting in September 1997. But the initiative's full complement of staff still wasn't in place, and little was accomplished. This time the press's refrain was, "The twelve-month initiative now has nine months to go. What have they done in their first three months?" (Not very much.) "What will they do in their remaining nine months?"

Concern at the White House deepened. Their response was to insist on more events, irrespective of their superficiality. The press recognized the strategy and further pilloried the Initiative and the White House. Much of the pressure fell on me, as the deputy director for outreach and program development, and I was ill-prepared for it. I wanted to take the time to build a solid foundation that could endure beyond the life of the Initiative and the administration, but the White House wanted "events" that would generate positive press. I kept thinking of the familiar Billy Crystal quote: "It is better to look good than to feel good."

The politically driven time pressure and the superficiality it inevitably produced led to press encounters that further exacerbated the situation. To support their skepticism, the press looked for signs of dissension within the ranks and sought controversial quotes. If they couldn't find anything, some of them would not hesitate to manufacture something. At our November 1997 meeting at the University of Maryland in College Park, Maryland, we focused on the issue of diversity in higher education. We'd purposely not invited divisive political figures, because we didn't want attention distracted from the core issue by superheated rhetoric. But some members of the press were not satisfied. As I stood in the back of the room at the press briefing, a reporter from the *New York Times* asked Dr. Franklin why affirmative action opponent Ward Connerly, author of referenda opposing affirmative action in California and elsewhere, had not been invited. Dr. Franklin responded that he did not want to be distracted by a politically contentious debate over affirmative action. The reporter pressed him, and Dr. Franklin gave essentially the same answer. On the reporter's fourth or fifth try, Dr. Franklin, tired and impatient, responded that Connerly had not been invited because, "He didn't have anything to contribute to this discussion." The reporter had what he wanted, and the *New York Times* headline the next day trumpeted Dr. Franklin's comment about Ward Connerly.

The press certainly had a right, even a responsibility, to pry into the workings of the Initiative. But if they had been more conscientious and less interested in needling Dr. Franklin or other members of the Advisory Board into providing negative headlines, they could have played a far more constructive role in informing the public. In all fairness, I should note that several reporters were diligent and thoughtful in their coverage. And several people more familiar with the workings of the press than

I am have suggested that reporters were less to blame than were the organizations for which they worked, some of which sought to marginalize the Initiative for their own reasons. I leave that judgment to others.

Overall, the budgetary and time-frame requirements imposed by the White House, largely demanded by administration officials unscathed by racial or gender oppression, turned many of us into little more than event planners. We lurched from one monthly advisory board meeting to the next, with forums for corporate and religious leaders stuck in between. There was little time for anything but superficial pre-planning, and no time for substantive follow-ups. The overriding goal of each event was to attract positive press attention and to avoid controversy. The National Day of Dialogue, which we had suggested as a vehicle for raising public awareness about issues of race, became a campaign to get as many governors as possible to sign a watered-down pledge of support. We had suggested The Campus Week of Dialogue as a vehicle for engaging college students in meaningful learning and action on issues of race; instead, it turned into a campaign to sign up as many colleges as possible so there would be an impressive number to report to the press. With each day, my frustration over lost opportunities increased. I knew what was happening, but like other initiative staff members, I felt powerless to change the dynamic. When I suggested that we not water down the resolution simply for the purpose of getting as many governors as possible to sign it, I was dismissed as politically naïve. When I asked about a meaningful follow-up to the Campus Week of Dialogue, I was told we didn't have the resources. When I objected that race-neutral education legislation would not address the disproportionately negative treatment of black students, I was accused of being a "fuzzy-thinking liberal."

These frustrations were exacerbated by the brutal pace of the Initiative. In the rarified atmosphere of the White House, where everything we did was carefully and closely scrutinized and any misstep could mean political disaster, each meeting required pre-meetings and post-meetings. Pre-meetings were to set the agenda and ensure there would be no surprises; post-meetings were to review what had been said and what was to be done next. Decisions made at one meeting often got revisited and reversed at the next meeting. Chaos was the prevailing atmosphere. Weekend respites were infrequent. While all of us felt the intense pressure, we were insulated from the worst of it by executive director Judith Winston. She took most of the heat and protected the rest of us from the wrath of those who wanted instant successes and no negative press. I've often thought that during the period of August 1997 to September 1998 she had the most difficult, pressure-packed, thankless job in Washington, D.C. She took heat from all sides for the frustrations associated with the Initiative, yet she was denied the authority to address the causes of those frustrations. It was a classic no-win situation, and she bore it with incredible grace.

Grace of a different kind came from Jackie, who endured my crazy hours and allowed me to vent to her on the infrequent occasions that I had time to do so. Without her forbearance, I doubt I could have made it through that year.

Despite the frustrations and disappointments, looking back at the experience with the benefit of time, one can analyze the Initiative with some degree of objectivity and learn some helpful lessons. At least three lessons about a President's ability to heal racial divisions and promote racial justice did emerge. These lessons can help all who seek to foster such change.

1. While talking is not enough in itself, it is an essential tool for promoting good race relations.
2. There are limits to the White House's power to foster racial justice.
3. Despite these limits, presidential leadership is crucial to both racial justice and racial healing.

First, despite the fears and emotions that are ever-present in discussions about race, there is an abiding hunger in the country to learn to talk constructively about healing our divisions. Wherever we went during the year, people clamored to be heard. Black and white, they wanted to share their stories and their pain. Once people felt they had been heard, they were more willing to listen. The Initiative produced a One America Dialogue Guide, the product of collaborative efforts between seven nongovernmental organizations we convened. The guide remains in use today. We convened well-attended and thought-provoking meetings of religious and corporate leaders. We organized the Campus Week of Dialogue, with the active participation of 600 college campuses, and a National Day of Dialogue, with the active participation of well over one hundred communities. We also identified 350 community-based promising practices for racial reconciliation.

Never was the value of talk more clear than at a forum in which we participated at the University of Mississippi in March 1998. Sparked by the presence of Governor Winter, an Old Miss alum, on the Advisory Board, Chancellor Robert Khyaht hosted the forum and invited our participation. There was to be a public forum in the evening and a lecture by Dr. Franklin the following morning. The forum idea was conceived by Susan Glisson, a white native of south Georgia and an Old Miss graduate student focused on the study of southern culture. In advance of the forum, she convened a series of local committees to examine issues ranging from education to job access, with the findings to be presented at the forum by the committee chairs. Prior to the forum, Governor Winter invited us to visit a local integrated elementary school, where he proudly introduced us to his grandson. His grandson was about the same age as Ian had been that day I held my breath and fought paralyzing fear as we traveled through the state on the way to Louisiana. It was nearly twenty years later, and we had come a long way.

On the evening of March 17, an integrated crowd of 900 people, a mix of students and community residents, braved a driving rain to pack the Fulton Chapel for the forum. The location was just a few feet from where two people had been killed in 1962 when James Meredith became the first African

American to enroll at the university. Perhaps the most dramatic moment of the evening, and perhaps of the entire year, came when a young white man rose to loudly proclaim his right to fly the Confederate flag at Old Miss football games. When he sat down, two young women, one black and one white, both students at the university and obviously friends, rose to respond. Holding hands as they spoke, the young black woman explained that the flag to her represented racial oppression and the pain she felt for her ancestors who had been among the enslaved; the young white woman explained that the flag represented the pain she felt as the descendent of slave owners. They returned to their seats still holding hands as the audience sat in stunned silence. The young man had been touched. He had not, he said later, understood the anguish that the flag caused. He did not intend to cause pain, and he would no longer fly the flag at football games. It was a small step toward racial healing, to be sure, but not an insignificant one.

The following morning, a similarly large and integrated audience, this time primarily students, packed the Fulton Chapel to hear eighty-three-year-old Dr. Franklin, still in robust health, share some of the painful experiences of his long and fruitful life, and discourse about our nation's history of conquest and oppression. At lunch that day, someone suggested the creation of an Institute for Racial Reconciliation and Civic Renewal at the University of Mississippi. With the enthusiastic support of Chancellor Khyaht and the strong leadership of Governor Winter, the Institute was born. Now named the William Winter Institute for Racial Reconciliation in honor of the man without whom it would not exist, it is an active and productive part of the university community and an influential voice for racial justice and healing throughout the state, and increasingly throughout the nation. It is led by the same Susan Glisson who organized the forum and went on to earn her Ph.D. at the university. This all came from "talk."

Less dramatic, but equally significant steps occurred throughout the year due to initiative-inspired dialogues on race in communities across the country. Clearly, there are limitations to just talking. In some cases, talking is simply a way to avoid difficult decisions. But we came to realize that talk informs people, clarifies misunderstandings, and builds bridges. Often, it is the key first step to engaging people in action to heal racial divisions. In the long run it is not enough only to talk, but the importance of constructive dialogue as a tool to widen the circle of allies for racial justice, especially under relatively unpressurized circumstances, should not be minimized.

Second, despite the awesome power of the White House, there are limits to a President's ability to foster racial understanding and impose racial justice. Clearly, a President can effectively enforce civil rights legislation and promote government policies to narrow racial disparities in education, economic empowerment, the administration of justice, and access to affordable housing and quality health care. But beyond the sense of white privilege that surely fed the reluctance of some in the White House to address the issues, partisan political pressures and competing national priorities also placed enormous restrictions on the President's ability to encourage and advance racial justice and healing activities in communities. It is doubtful that President Clinton was any different in this respect from other Presidents. Nonetheless, had key White House staff been more committed to the success of the Initiative, it would have been helpful. When I was accused of being a fuzzy-thinking liberal, I was too intimidated by the power of the accuser to respond. In retrospect, I wish I'd argued that increasing white people's awareness of the legacy of our history and of the reality of persistent racial discrimination would win over many who support the principles of fairness and justice, and thus, would strengthen the Democratic Party.

Had more key White House staff been in tune with their boss, the President, the Initiative would have demonstrated far more clearly the third lesson we learned, that Presidential leadership is crucial to achieving racial justice and racial healing. The country's willingness to support equitable and vigorous enforcement of civil rights laws, back policies and budget expenditures that redress past racial injustice, work to narrow racial divisions in communities and neighborhoods, and confront both negative racial stereotypes and racial discrimination (whether subtle or blatant), as well as privilege, all depends on the extent of the President's visible commitment and leadership.

President Eisenhower remained silent on the Supreme Court's *Brown v. Board of Education* decision to outlaw the *de jure* segregation of public schools. The result was divisiveness and violence perpetrated by those seeking to resist the decision. Had the President visibly backed the *Brown* decision from the beginning, the violence that enveloped the South—from Little Rock, Arkansas, to Cambridge, Maryland—might have been substantially diminished. When Presidents Kennedy and Johnson both spoke with passion about the importance of racial justice, the country followed their lead. On the other hand, as I've asserted earlier, negative leadership from Presidents Reagan and George H. W. Bush inflamed passions, stoked fears, and divided the country.

President Clinton, despite his divisive use of race in his 1992 campaign and his early missteps as President, spoke clearly and passionately during most of his administration about the damage that racial discrimination inflicts on all of us and about the importance of building a unified nation, "One America" as he called it. And he did more than talk. Even after the Initiative ended, in separate meetings he brought together corporate leaders, religious leaders, and attorneys to urge them to develop specific action plans to promote racial justice and racial healing in their respective sectors. The result was to alter for a time the political climate regarding race and to raise public awareness of the need to close the gap between our creeds and our public deeds. Unfortunately, the infrastructure necessary to sustain the dialogue and to nourish a positive racial climate fell victim to budget priorities and the politically induced time limit. It was a missed opportunity of tragic proportions.

I learned one other thing that seems relevant now, as people question the number of vacation days taken by Presidents George

W. Bush and Barack Obama. Irrespective of political persuasion, the President and his staff work harder than any group of people I've ever encountered. They need frequent vacations simply to maintain their perspective and judgment. When they are tired, which is far too often, they are more prone to make bad decisions that affect all of us negatively. We should encourage rather than discourage them to take time off.

I had felt incredibly privileged to serve, but as the Initiative wound down, I was emotionally exhausted. It was an experience I would not trade for anything, and also one I would not want to repeat under any circumstances. I wasn't sure what adventure would be next, or even if there would be a next adventure. But my goal of returning to the struggle for racial equity and healing had been achieved, and whatever the future held, the direction of any new professional pursuit was clear.

One of the initiative's more important accomplishments was the identification of approximately 350 promising practices for racial reconciliation in communities across the country. The White House wanted us to identify 1,000 to make a bigger press splash, but we had neither the time nor the resources to oblige. One of the common complaints of even the most successful community-based antiracist activists was the sense of isolation they felt from others engaged in similar work. They had no easy way to communicate with fellow activists in other cities, to share ideas, to learn from the experiences of others, or to provide support in difficult times. This limited their success and hastened their frustration and burnout. Finding a way to connect these local activists was near the top of my list of potential follow-up activities.

In early July 1998, I received a phone call from Eddie Williams, then president and CEO of the Joint Center for Political and Economic Studies. The Joint Center, as it is commonly referred to, is a think tank in Washington, D.C., focused on issues of particular concern to the African American community. Started in 1970 by presidential advisor Louis Martin and prominent social psychologist Dr. Kenneth Clark, it was initially affiliated with Howard University. Its purpose was to assist newly elected black officials who were beneficiaries of the Voting Rights Act of 1965. The 1968 election of Richard Hatcher as mayor of Gary, Indiana, and Carl Stokes as mayor of Cleveland raised the visibility of black elected officials, and at the same time revealed that information and training resources traditionally available to white elected officials were not readily available to black elected officials. The Joint Center sought to fill that gap.

Eddie Williams became the Joint Center's president and CEO in 1972. He built it into an influential organization highly respected for both the objectivity of its research and its relationship with black elected officials, who have grown in number from a few hundred in 1965 to more than 11,000 today. He moved the Joint Center away from Howard University to an independent status, and he gradually changed its mission from providing training and technical assistance to research and public policy analysis. Today, the Joint Center is a significant player in public opinion research focusing on the black community and in analyzing the impact on African Americans of policies related to voting rights, employment, health care, housing, asset-building, new technology, and education. Among the prominent scholars who were tapped early and often by the Joint Center was Dr. John Hope Franklin. His son, John Whittington Franklin, subsequently served on the Joint Center's board of governors.

I had met Eddie Williams in the early 1990s through a good friend who worked at the Joint Center. Our mutual concern about the direction in which Presidents Reagan and Bush had taken the country and our hope that Bill Clinton would be different led us to explore ideas for working together. When the invitation came to join the Initiative, we put our talks on hold. Eddie's July telephone call led to my joining the Joint Center as a program consultant to explore ways to build on the work of the Initiative.

After a much-needed ten-day vacation with Jackie at the aptly named Tranquil Inn on the Outer Banks of North Carolina, during which I regained some of the ten pounds I had lost due to the brutal pace of the Initiative, I arrived at the Joint Center on October 15, 1998. Within six months, the W. K. Kellogg Foundation had approved a one-year planning grant to explore ways to overcome the sense of isolation felt by community activists. Using contacts I'd developed at the Initiative, we formed a steering committee of nine major racial justice organizations focused on race relations activities to help guide our planning. Together, amid great anticipation, we developed a comprehensive plan for a nationwide online network of community-based racial justice and racial healing organizations. Early in 2000, we applied to the Kellogg Foundation for a five-year, $5 million grant to implement the network and make it self-sustaining. Unfortunately, beset by dwindling resources in a sinking stock market, Kellogg could provide only an additional $150,000 to sustain us until we could find alternative funding. I also tapped my former colleagues at the Appalachian Regional Commission for a grant to examine what lessons we could learn from the response of the city of Clarksburg, West Virginia, to a Ku Klux Klan threat. This latter grant enabled me, on the recommendation of former Initiative colleague David Campt, to hire Maggie Potapchuk, an award-winning antiracist activist from St. Louis, to examine the Clarksburg experience.

From my experience in West Virginia, I was no stranger to Clarksburg, a medium-sized central West Virginia city with a 95 percent white population and a form of government in which elected city council members appoint the mayor. Although I didn't know any of the political or community leaders in the area, I had visited it several times during my tenure with West Virginia state government in the late 1970s. In the early 1990s, Reverend David Kates, who had unsuccessfully sought election to the Clarksburg city council several times before, finally won a narrow victory and became the first African American elected to the city council. His victory was due in large part to the efforts of former mayor and then council member Jim Hunt. To promote racial unity in the community, Hunt led a successful effort to have Reverend Kates appointed mayor. Someone alerted the KKK, which announced plans for a rally in Clarksburg.

Hunt and Kates could have ignored the rally, hoping it would be a one-time event without lasting impact. But they chose instead to confront the situation directly. They swiftly organized a counter-rally involving the business community, public school system, and city employees. About twenty people showed up to support the Klan, while about 500 people showed up to support racial unity. Encouraged, Hunt and Kates developed a joint presentation on the value of racial diversity, piloted it in Clarksburg's schools, and then offered it to schools throughout the state. Maggie's research led to a book that chronicled the events and lessons learned in Clarksburg and suggested a workshop format to help public officials promote racial unity in their communities. Jim Hunt later served a term as president of the National League of Cities, and he continues to lead efforts to engage cities throughout the country in racial healing activities.

As the Clarksburg project drew to a close, my mother, whose health had been declining for several years, died at the age of eighty-six. As her health had deteriorated, she had become increasingly unhappy. Six years earlier, fearful of her forgetfulness and of living alone, she had moved from New York to an assisted living facility in Florida near my sister and brother-in-law. Used to being in control, she hated what was happening to her. I flew to Florida to be with my sister as my mother's death neared. A couple of days later, Ian made plans to fly down from New York. He and his grandma had had a close relationship, and he wanted to say goodbye. His plane was scheduled to arrive at 4 p.m. on a mid-October day. That morning, the doctor told us my mother had only a few hours left. We asked him to try to keep her alive until Ian arrived. Ian arrived on schedule and spent an hour alone with his grandma. She was in a coma by that time, but as my sister and I watched from the hallway, we had the feeling that she knew he was there. Ian felt the same way. She died at about 7 p.m.

The funeral was held in New York, and all of the cousins, as well as Ron Pollack, my long-time friend from Queens College, eulogized my mother. They talked primarily about her political activity and lifelong commitment to justice. Arian, then seven years old, wrote a brief statement about how much she loved Grandma Rose and would miss her, and she asked me to read it. Ian had chosen not to say anything, perhaps out of fear that he would break down. But as the last scheduled speaker concluded, he rose and walked to the podium. "I wasn't planning to say anything, but the wonderful eulogies I've heard don't describe the grandmother I knew. I admire what everyone has said about her—her commitment to principles, her political activism, even her salty tongue—but to me, she was just simply grandma, warm and fuzzy, kind, generous, spirited. A little old woman with gray hair, wrinkled skin, lots of freckles, and arms that always drew me in. That's who I'll miss." It was a poignant illustration of how our unique perspectives shape our views of people, and it reinforced a lesson I'd been learning, that people are multidimensional, and we should be careful about drawing conclusions based on limited evidence.

At a conference in Washington, D.C., early in 2000, I encountered Hodding Carter, Jr., son of a famously progressive and courageous newspaper editor in Greenville, Mississippi. Hodding had been the spokesperson at the State Department during the Carter administration and was now the head of the Knight Foundation. I had met him previously and he asked me what I was doing now. He listened intently as I explained our vision of a network of community-based racial reconciliation organizations, and then said, "You know, Mike, this sounds like something we should fund. Why don't you submit a proposal?" In October 2000, the Knight Foundation approved a grant of $900,000 over three years that we would have to match with $300,000 from other sources. It wasn't sufficient to put the network on solid footing, but it was a terrific start. We expanded the steering committee to more than twenty organizations, set goals and objectives, and named the organization NABRE (pronounced "neighbor"), an acronym for Network of Alliances Bridging Race and Ethnicity.

For three years, NABRE flourished. We developed a membership of 200 organizations and operated an interactive website that quickly became one of the Joint Center's most visited sites. We hosted regular chat rooms and discussion boards on key topics: fund-raising, recruiting and managing volunteers, dealing with burnout, and so on. We launched a demonstration project with support from the AOL-Time Warner Foundation to examine how to turn online discussions into action, we held an Upper Midwest Regional Conference on Racial Reconciliation at the University of Minnesota that resulted in the creation of an Upper Midwest Racial Reconciliation Network, we helped promote the use of documentary films to generate interracial dialogue on key issues, we developed partnerships with other organizations that had a racial justice and racial healing agenda, we convened how-to forums led by Maggie to explore the interdependence of organizations that took different approaches to combating racism, and we issued several publications resulting from our work. Steering committee meetings became forums for thought-provoking discussions on key issues and helped to build relationships among organizations that had common agendas but rarely had time to talk with each other.

Twice I traveled to international conferences in Caux, Switzerland, to talk about our work. The second time, in 2002, Jim Hunt and Reverend Kates accompanied me to talk about their Clarksburg experience. Maggie participated in the United Nations Conference Against Racism in South Africa and returned to lead an emotional discussion at a steering committee meeting about the charges of anti-Semitism leveled at some conference participants. Ironically, Maggie returned from South Africa on September 10, 2001, and on the morning of September 11, we were debriefing from the conference when news arrived of the terrorist attacks on the World Trade Center and the Pentagon. The indiscriminate anger and negative stereotyping toward Arabs and Muslims that took place in the wake of the attacks gave our work added urgency. The attacks took on a more personal and chilling meaning when Ian was sent to Afghanistan for five weeks as part of a *Dateline NBC* crew embedded with the Northern Alliance fighting the Taliban.

Unfortunately, in a tight philanthropic environment, we were unable to find sufficient funds to move beyond the three-year Knight grant. At the end of September 2003, we were forced to suspend NABRE activities. I've remained at the Joint Center, serving variously as a program consultant, acting vice president for communications and acting vice president for governance and economic analysis during transition periods precipitated by the retirement of Eddie Williams. I am now a senior fellow and work on an assortment of activities with both the Joint Center's Health Policy Institute and the Joint Center's newly launched Civic Engagement and Governance Institute. I've also had the privilege of helping Dr. Gail Christopher, whom I met at the Joint Center when she headed the Health Policy Institute and who is now vice president of program strategy at the Kellogg Foundation, to develop and implement the racial equity strategic plan that led to the launching of Kellogg's America Healing initiative, which has guided many of its recent funding priorities.

Perhaps most significantly in my own continuing education about race, in September 2003 I was invited to teach a course on race and minority relations at George Washington University (GWU). The invitation arose from a guest lecture I gave about my experiences with President Clinton's Initiative on Race. I now teach both undergraduate and graduate classes on race in the Sociology Department. From my students and my class preparation, I have been learning how much I still don't know about race and the legacy of our history of conquest and racial oppression. In the spring of 2007, when prominent shock jock Don Imus referred to black members of the Rutgers University women's basketball team as "nappy-headed ho's," four African American members of GWU's women's basketball team were in my class. I was repulsed by the remarks, but personally detached from them until I brought them up in class one day and saw the pained expressions of the four young women. It was another lesson of how my white privilege insulates me from pain that is unavoidable for people whose racial backgrounds tie them to the targets of racist remarks or actions. It has become even more personal to me as our seventeen-year-old granddaughter, Alexis, a tall and lanky twelfth-grader, now plies her basketball skills on a local high school team.

As I was writing this chapter, I received an e-mail from a current student who is white. It reads in part:

> I am e-mailing you because after class yesterday, I could not stop thinking about the concept of white privilege. I realized . . . I am not "special" because I am white, and in the same way that many whites . . . reject certain people based on their color, these three African American girls had every right to be wary of me based on their past experiences with racism.

> The concept is more unconscious than I had previously conceived. I am grateful that I was able to realize this in class. I . . . now feel the weight of recognizing white privilege and . . . an obligation to work to lessen the racial divide.

> So, I just wanted to say thank you for teaching a class like this, a class that opened my eyes and gave me no choice but to think about my situation in society to date.

This e-mail eloquently explains why I treasure teaching and why it challenges me to continue learning about race and how to effectively apply what I learn.

XI

REFLECTING ON THE JOURNEY

I am embarrassed to admit it now, but when I joined the staff of President Clinton's Initiative on Race, I had no idea, despite my personal journey, how little I understood about the issue of race in the United States. I had been raised in a home where racial justice was a defining principle, I had been active in the civil rights movement in both the North and the South, I had been married to an African American woman for eleven years, and I had helped to raise three African American children. I had written a biweekly column on race for our local newspaper and had given numerous speeches about race.

I knew about Jim Crow racism in the South. I'd seen it in Prince Edward County and witnessed it personally through my wife and her family. I knew that African Americans did not have equal opportunities to succeed in school or in the workplace, that the government was not adequately enforcing civil rights legislation, and that Dr. King's dream that we should all be judged by the content of our character and not by the color of our skin had not yet been achieved. I knew our society didn't reflect the melting pot metaphor I'd been taught as a child.

But I didn't comprehend how the legacy of our history of racial oppression still haunts us today. I didn't understand the concepts of what sociologist Joe Feagin calls "undeserved enrichment" and "undeserved impoverishment," and how intentionally racist government policies in the twentieth century (policies that had little to do with the institution of slavery), particularly during the first half of the twentieth century, are largely responsible for many of today's racial divisions and disparities. I didn't appreciate the cumulative effect of racist behavior on its targets or, for that matter, on its perpetrators, over the course of a lifetime, and I wasn't conscious of the negative racial stereotypes I'd been unintentionally force-fed as a child. I was clueless about the level of privilege I'd enjoyed simply due to the color of my skin.

Accepting the invitation to teach a class on race relations at George Washington University was the height of audacity. But it forced me to confront my abysmal lack of knowledge. I hadn't been in a college classroom in years and had no idea how much my students would know or not know. I was afraid they would know more than I did. So, I read: John Hope Franklin, john powell, Beverly Tatum, Dalton Conley, Lawrence Bobo, James Jones, Joe Feagin, Gary Orfield, Jonathan Kozol, and many others. I became increasingly aware of my ignorance. Once I walked into the classroom, I realized how similarly ignorant much of our nation is, from our highest-ranking public officials to the broad swath of our population.

I don't claim to be an authority on race today. As a former colleague said, "There is no plateau of learning about race." At least now, however, I understand how little I really know, how much I still have to learn and understand, and how much I'll never be able to know. My teaching experience, has helped me to begin to integrate the experiences of my life into some moderately coherent conclusions about where our long and tortuous national journey toward "all men are created equal" has taken us.

I ask you to consider three conclusions I've drawn from my experiences:

1. Though most white Americans do not consciously engage in racist behavior, the United States of America remains a racist society.
2. While white Americans living today are not guilty of owning slaves and most are not guilty of practicing Jim Crow racism, the legacy of these and other ugly and inhumane practices remains in both conscious and

unconscious behavior, and it casts a huge shadow over the enormous progress we've made in the past half-century.

3. Finally, and most importantly, we white Americans, all of us, are beneficiaries of this legacy to a greater or lesser degree, whether or not we like it or even recognize it. Therefore, we have an obligation to follow Rabbi Abraham Heschel's dictum: "We may not all be guilty, but we are all responsible."

Most white Americans no longer consciously engage in racist behavior. Attitudes have changed significantly. Prominent Harvard sociology professor and Joint Center board member Lawrence Bobo concludes from his research that a substantial majority of white Americans now believe in the principles of justice and fair play. No longer do they support, as they did sixty years ago, the principles of segregated schools, job discrimination, or residential separation. Sociologist Robert Blauner writes:

> The belief in a right to dignity and fair treatment is now
> so widespread and deeply rooted, so self-evident, that
> people of all colors would vigorously resist any effort to
> reinstate formalized discrimination.

We see evidence of this all around us. Black students are accepted, even sought after, by private elementary and secondary schools and by institutions of higher education. The classes that I teach at George Washington University have a wide diversity of students; this was unimaginable back when I attended college. The black middle class has grown dramatically. Workplaces are increasingly diverse; in fact, major corporations actively seek diverse workforces. Several giant corporations, such as Time-Warner, Merrill-Lynch, and American Express, have African American CEOs now or have had them in the recent past. Residential integration remains a problem in many communities, but blatant resistance to black families moving into previously all-white communities has diminished. The number of black elected officials at every level of government has grown from a few hundred in 1965 to more than 11,000 today, many elected from mainly white jurisdictions.

Mississippi has more black elected officials than any other state. Most major cities, including New York, Newark, Philadelphia, Chicago, Atlanta, New Orleans, Houston, Dallas, Los Angeles, and San Francisco, now have or previously have had black mayors. Massachusetts, the first colony to legalize slavery, has a black governor, and New York State has recently had a black governor. They were both preceded two decades ago by the election of Doug Wilder as governor of Virginia, the former capital of the Confederacy. We've had two black secretaries of state, and today we have a biracial president and a black attorney general.

My own family experiences bear out this change. Despite the difficulties he encountered, Ian was welcomed at the two private schools he attended and was heavily sought after by Boston University. Tempie is now retired, but she had a successful career as a social worker and administrator. Regina has had highly responsible, well-paying jobs with major corporations, and Ian is a well-respected producer for one of the most popular news and entertainment programs on television. Arnya worked for the Budget Committee of the U.S. House of Representatives before falling victim to the 1994 Republican takeover of the House. Jackie and I live comfortably in a predominantly black community, and several of our black friends live with equal ease in predominantly white communities.

Yet we are still far from a so-called post-racial society, a term too many people hopefully but naïvely embraced in the wake of President Obama's election. For 350 years, white Americans conquered and oppressed nonwhite Americans to expand our empire, pursue prosperity, and secure our power. We justified it by convincing ourselves that the targets of our conquest and oppression were inferior, somehow less than fully human. We even developed pseudoscientific evidence to supposedly "prove" it. For example, in 1896, a Prudential Life Insurance statistician named Frederick Hoffman issued a report entitled, *The Race Traits and Tendencies of the American Negro*. This widely accepted report concluded that African Americans would eventually become extinct because of their higher mortality rates, ignoring the facts that they were less than thirty-five years out of slavery and that many were forced to live in squalid conditions in a society that was still overtly racist. In 1911, biologist Charles Davenport predicted that intermarriage would make Americans more prone to criminal behavior and insanity. It is preposterous to think we could erase the legacy of this history in only fifty years.

Imagine a marathon hurdles race as a metaphor for life's journey. Because of the legacy of our history, most black Americans begin the race several miles behind most white Americans. Black Americans then must clear higher hurdles, which makes the journey even more difficult and the results even more inequitable. For black Americans to succeed—and many do in spite of the challenges—they must be smarter, work harder, and display greater determination and perseverance than their white counterparts do. Tempie and I, like most parents of black children, told Regina, Arnya, and Ian that they would have to be twice as good to keep pace with their white peers. From my observation, that has proven to be the case. Negative racial stereotyping and a yawning wealth gap are among the most pervasive legacies of our history. They create enormous hurdles for black people. Persistent institutional policies and practices that yield racially disparate outcomes and the pervasive sense of white privilege complicate the journey.

The Self-Perpetuating Cycle of Negative Racial Stereotyping

Let's talk first about stereotyping. Do you remember that speaking engagement I mentioned in an earlier chapter—the one scheduled for March 25, 1997, right after the meeting with President Clinton in the Cabinet Room? After arriving late and making my apologies, I spoke about my experiences in an interracial marriage, bragged about my children, and cited some of the racial myths that haunt us today: most young black males are prone to violence, most young black women get pregnant out of wedlock, most black employees are less qualified than whites and got their jobs through affirmative action. The audience of approximately forty people, all white and about 90 percent male, listened attentively as I concluded by complimenting their community improvement work, challenging them to do more to narrow racial divisions, and sharing my favorite quote from Martin Niemoller, who came to understand the danger of divisiveness as a pastor in Germany during World War II:

> In Germany they first came for the Communists, and I didn't speak up because I wasn't a Communist. Then they came for the Jews, and I didn't speak up because I wasn't a Jew. Then they came for the trade unionists, and I didn't speak up because I wasn't a trade unionist. Then they came for the Catholics, and I didn't speak up because I was a Protestant. Then they came for me—and by that time no one was left to speak up.

The applause was enthusiastic, and when I invited questions, several hands shot up. "I enjoyed your speech," said a tall, distinguished man of about fifty as he rose from his seat. "And I do think we need to speak up more. But here's my question." He hesitated. "I'm not a racist. At least, I've never thought of myself as a racist. But about a year ago, I was mugged by a young black man. He came up to me on the street, stuck a knife under my chin, and demanded my money. He didn't hurt me, but he sure scared me. So now, how can I look at a young black male and not be scared?"

I swallowed my first instinct, which was to chide him about his fear and label him a racist for allowing one incident to reinforce his negative stereotype. But challenging him in that manner would have raised his defenses and slammed shut the minds of the audience to anything else I might say. I wanted to win converts, not create cynics. "You know," I responded slowly, "I can understand your fear. But let me tell you a story that may help." He remained standing and shifted his feet.

"About a year ago," I continued, "my daughter, who, as you know, is African American, was mugged by a young white man. He came up behind her at an ATM, threw her to the ground, grabbed the money from her hand, and ran off. She's fine now, although she was pretty shaken up at the time. But the incident did not cause her to look at every young white man and see a potential mugger. Why not? First, despite the fact that the percentage of young white men who commit a violent crime is comparable to the percentage of young black men who commit a violent crime, we're all subjected to the kind of negative stereotyping of young black men that our institutions, particularly our schools and the media, drill into our heads. We are not subjected to such stereotyping of young white men. Second, she knows lots of young white men, and her experiences with them in school, in the community, and in the workplace have taught her that most of them are not likely to be muggers. She recognizes that the mugger was an aberration, not representative of most young white males.

"Her reaction illustrates the importance of meaningful, regular communication and interaction across racial lines. I believe it's the only way to counteract the unrelenting negative perceptions we are fed of the 'other.' For example, when you've had the experience I did two years ago of watching my son and the 500 young black men who graduated with him from Morehouse College march proudly onto the stage to receive their degrees, you can more easily recognize that the young man who attacked you is no more representative of young black men than the young man who attacked my daughter is representative of young white men. And you'd be better able to get past your fears."

Several heads, including that of the questioner, nodded. The fear expressed by the questioner was not dissipated, but he and his fellow club members had some food for thought and were not consumed with trying to defend themselves against being labeled as racist. The fact is that although I've not always realized it, most white people I've met are like this man. We believe in the principles of fairness and justice and would recoil from thinking of ourselves as racist. We don't want to fear people from other racial and ethnic backgrounds. But most of us have not had enough meaningful communication or interaction with people whose skin color differs from our own, so when a negative incident occurs, we don't have a sufficient number of positive experiences to call on to override the negative experience. The negative stereotype is thus reinforced. Even when we have a positive experience, we tend to view it as an aberration.

We are all victims of this process. Our schools, the media, and often public officials too often bombard us with negative images of people who are not white, and simply ignore positive images of nonwhite people, making stereotyping virtually impossible to avoid. Unless we can understand and confront this concept, it is unlikely that we will ever be able to overcome the persistent racist behavior that plagues our nation. And make no mistake: virtually all white people are guilty of such stereotyping, to varying degrees. It often occurs subconsciously, despite our best intentions. Actually, negative racial stereotyping knows no color. Every racial and ethnic group does it to every other racial and ethnic group. We tend to see members of our own racial group as individuals, while a single member of another racial group is seen as representative of the group as a whole, especially when that person is engaged in negative behavior. But for now, I will concentrate on the negative racial stereotyping of black people by white people, because it tends to be more persistent, to create higher hurdles for its targets, and to be more damaging to our society, and because my journey through the minefield of black/white relations is the focus of this book.

We see it clearly whenever a major incident occurs. For example, when a tragic event like the killing of students at Columbine High School or the bombing of the Oklahoma City Federal Building occurs and the perpetrators are white, we spend an interminable amount of time agonizing over why they did it. Did their parents abuse them? Were they taunted by peers for their nonconforming behavior? Did they play too many violent video games? We don't, however, extrapolate from their behavior negative feelings toward the general population of young white men. And yet, when we hear of violence perpetrated by a young black man, we all too often associate such conduct with the majority of young black men. We do not inquire into their individual backgrounds. We simply shake our heads in disgust, even sadness, at the perceived bad behavior of others who look like them.

Several years ago, when *New York Times* reporter Jayson Blair, who is African American, was dismissed for falsifying stories, there was an orgy of hand-wringing about what was wrong with black folks. Why must *they* do such things? Why can't they be more like *us*? On the other hand, when white *USA Today* correspondent Jack Kelley was dismissed for a similar crime, we wondered what kind of pressure Kelley was under to make him do such a terrible thing. How many of us thought to wonder what was wrong with white journalists?

I will leave the authoritative explanations to experts in psychology and sociology. What I do know is that this stereotyping—dehumanizing black people—has its roots in efforts to justify slavery in the context of our founding principle that "all men are created equal." And based on my own experiences and observations, it is self-perpetuating. I call it the Self-Perpetuating Cycle of Negative Racial Stereotyping. The process starts early. Research tells us that at a very young age, infants see color differences. However, these differences have about as much meaning to them as the colors of crayons. "Nobody is born a bigot," trumpets a T-shirt I received from the National Conference on Community and Justice. My grandchildren saw skin-color differences, but at ages as late as five or six, they had little understanding of their significance. Arian is now a bright, self-assured young woman of twenty with a dry wit and a lively personality; she said some of the funniest lines about skin color when she was about five years old. She's in disbelief today when I tell these stories—"Did I really say that?"—but they illustrate what skin color means, or doesn't mean, to a little child.

One day, Jackie picked up Arian after school. As Jackie approached, one of the little girls standing with Arian asked, "Is that your mommy?" Arian, with all the indignation a five-year-old could muster, shook her head in disbelief at her friend's ignorance and replied, "No, silly. She's not my mommy. She's white. She's my grandma."

We did not allow my mother to smoke in the house. During one visit she headed to the porch for a cigarette. Arian, who also was visiting, turned to me and announced in all seriousness: "When my mommy was white, she smoked too."

Then there was the time Arian tried to explain the color differences in our family to her then-three-year-old sister. "You see, Alexis, Mommy and Daddy are black, Papa and Grandma Jackie, they're white, and Uncle Ian—well, he's all mixed up." Or the time she insisted on talking to one of Jackie's friends on the phone. Jackie handed her the phone and Arian blurted out, "Are you a brown one or a white one?"

Arian, at the advanced age of five, clearly saw skin color. But just as clearly, it held little meaning for her. Sadly, this wonderful innocence could not last. As she grew older, she began to attach social meaning to skin color. However, she is fortunate. Like her mother (the one mugged by a white man) but unlike most people, she has lived in a fairly diverse environment and had meaningful and constant interactions with people from many racial and ethnic backgrounds. Thus, she has a basis for challenging the stereotypes that bombard her in school and in the media.

Most children, though, grow up in homogeneous racial environments, and people from different racial backgrounds are relatively unknown to them. When they are bombarded by negative racial stereotypes from family and friends, from the inaccurate and incomplete version of American history taught in school, and from inaccurate portrayals by a media more interested in profit than in fairness, they do not have the knowledge or understanding to counteract the bombardment. So, they fall prey to the stereotyping.[2] Even as adults, we have precious little meaningful interaction with people from different racial backgrounds. We talk business on the job. We say hello in the supermarket or nod politely on the street. But we really don't communicate or interact. And those mental tapes from childhood keep playing over and over again, further embedding the negative messages in our brains.

These negative messages fuel fear and prejudice, which lead to discriminatory or dysfunctional behavior that is often unconscious. This makes meaningful interactions with the stereotyped group even less likely, and in turn the separation widens and the stereotype intensifies each time we observe behavior that supports it. For example, if we harbor a stereotype that most young black males are dangerous, we will avoid them at all costs. By avoiding them, we give ourselves no opportunity to counteract the stereotype, and the next time we see a violent act by a young black male, our stereotype will be reinforced and our fear and desire for separation will grow. When we do encounter a young black male, we will likely act in ways that reflect the stereotype, which further reinforces and perpetuates it.

Remember the white woman in Atlanta who crossed the street to avoid contact with Ian and his two friends? She never gave herself a chance to counteract her stereotypes, and in fact, she probably reinforced those stereotypes and fears by crossing the street. Suppose, however, she had stayed on the same side of the street and passed Ian and his two friends without incident. Her stereotype may not have changed, but at least she would have interrupted the self-perpetuating cycle for an instant. Of course,

---

[2] For those who would like to know more about the deficiencies of our American history curriculum, I recommend the book *Lies My Teacher Told Me* by James Loewen. For those who would like to know more about biased media practices, I recommend the research of Robert Entman, a professor at George Washington University.

if she'd been with us at the Morehouse graduation ceremony and had seen those 500 young black men marching to get their degrees, the experience might have sowed real doubt in her mind about the validity of her stereotypes. But alas, the people who most need these experiences are the least likely to have them. So, the vicious cycle continues unabated.

The consequences of such stereotyping for African Americans can be crippling. In his book, *Two Nations: Separate and Unequal,* Andrew Hacker writes:

> What every black American knows, and whites should try to imagine, is how it feels to have an unfavorable—and unfair—identity imposed on you every waking day.

But it's not only black people who pay a price for this negative stereotyping. We white people pay a heavy price. I don't know the white woman who crossed the street in Atlanta, but her fear of young black men may limit the places she goes, the activities in which she engages, even the comfort she feels in her own home. Her fear may even affect her health, her sense of security, her mood, and the way she reacts to people in general. Our nation also pays a heavy price, economically and politically. Negative stereotyping often causes us to avoid hiring people who could make valuable contributions to our businesses and our economic productivity. Regina's experience with that Atlanta-based fast food chain is one small example.[3] Such stereotyping contributes to the high level of unemployment for black people and to the cost of that unemployment to society: government assistance we must

---

[3]   One recent study showed that white job applicants with a criminal record were more likely to be called back for interviews than black applicants without a criminal record. In another recent study, applicants with white-sounding names (Emily and Greg) were significantly more likely to be called back for interviews than applicants with black-sounding names (LaKisha and Jamal), despite the fact that identical resumes were submitted.

provide, productivity that is lost, increased crime rates that are often a consequence of unemployment, family dysfunction that arises due to a husband or father's inability to find a good job, and the skyrocketing costs of incarceration that limit government funding for such needs as better schools. In a labor force that is becoming increasingly diverse, this situation weakens our society and our ability to compete in the global economy. It contributes to budget deficits, lowers the standard of living for all of us, and increases racial divisions.

Politically, we pay a price because we are frequently scared into electing public officials whose motivation is victory rather than good public policy. Therefore, we often end up with bad public policies that further exacerbate racial and ethnic divisions and perpetuate societal problems. Here, my partisanship shows—with apologies to thoughtful and principled Republicans. In his 1980 campaign for the presidency, Ronald Reagan stoked the fear and anger of white people by popularizing the blatantly inaccurate stereotype of the black "welfare queen" arriving in her Cadillac to pick up her welfare check. George H. W. Bush was able to succeed him as president in part because of the infamous Willie Horton ad, which was specifically designed to inflame white fear of black men. In 2006, Harold Ford Jr., an African American man, ran for the U.S. Senate from Tennessee. Then unmarried and a popular Congressman from the Memphis area, Ford was victimized by his opponent's ad implying in a sinister tone that he had eyes for white women. Politically cynical acts like these may win elections, but they strengthen negative racial stereotypes, widen racial divisions, and diminish support for public policies that address these divisions. They therefore weaken our entire society.

In the 1990s, well-known actor Charlton Heston campaigned for Pennsylvania Republican Rick Santorum, who was running for the U.S. Senate. "Rick has correctly defined the job," he asserted. "It is restoring America, taking it back to what the smart, old, dead white guys had in mind when they thought up this country.

They had it right." I doubt any of my black friends or colleagues, or for that matter any of my white friends or colleagues, would agree. I did not closely follow Senator Santorum's career in the Senate, but it is a safe bet that with that kind of support, he was not under much pressure to support policies and programs that narrow racial divisions and decrease racial disparities. And imagine if he were to be successful in his quest to become President of the United States!

Perhaps the greatest cost of stereotyping concerns the moral hypocrisy and self-deception we practice. We think of ourselves as a people committed to the principles of justice, fairness, and freedom. But each time we unjustifiably discriminate against someone, we puncture our ideals and call our values into question. The ability of some of our soldiers to treat Iraqi prisoners at Abu Ghraib prison as less than human has its genesis, in my opinion, in how we treat people who don't look like us at home. Furthermore, it's difficult to hold ourselves up as examples to the rest of the world when we do not practice what we preach, either at home or in the far corners of the globe.

The Wealth Gap

This self-perpetuating cycle of negative racial stereotyping contributes to a second crucial legacy of our history: the yawning wealth gap. Tempie's great-grandparents and their siblings spent a significant portion of their lives in slavery. When they were emancipated, they had no education and no resources. Thus, they were forced back into virtual servitude. Tempie's grandparents and parents spent almost their entire lives under the brutal and stifling reign of Jim Crow racism. The stereotypes that had been fashioned in an earlier era, combined with the determination of many white Southerners to maintain their economic power and control, limited the vast majority of African Americans to jobs as menial factory workers, servants, or sharecroppers. They were unable to build the financial stability that my parents used to send my sister and me to well-resourced schools, to buy us books that furthered our education outside of school, to take us on trips to places that gave us a wider worldview, and to lend us money to buy a house, or in my sister's case to start a business. In contrast, Tempie and I had to help her parents to buy a house, and after we separated Tempie continued to help her parents financially, thus limiting her own ability to build financial stability. When my parents passed away, my sister and I inherited a fair amount of money, a situation inconceivable for Tempie.

But it is not only the legacy of slavery and Jim Crow racism that is responsible for the wealth gap. Federal government policies in the first half of the twentieth century blatantly discriminated against African Americans. Because domestic workers and agricultural workers, largely African Americans at the time, were ineligible for Social Security when it was first enacted, Tempie's parents could not participate. They were deprived of a financial benefit that most white people enjoyed. One might call this "affirmative action for white people." During the housing boom of the 1940s and 1950s, a specific government underwriting policy viewed the presence of even one or two Negro families in a neighborhood as a destabilizing factor that would reduce property values. Consequently, most black families, irrespective of their incomes, could not get loans to purchase homes and were largely consigned to high-density rental properties in inner cities. Thus, they were unable to accumulate wealth through equity in their homes.

Many black families have remained trapped in these neighborhoods of concentrated poverty,[4] lacking access to adequate prenatal and postnatal health care, decent housing, good education, jobs that pay a living wage, nutritious and affordable foods, positive role models, basic safety and security, and important

[4] I recommend to you the work of scholars such as john powell, Melvin Oliver, and Thomas Shapiro for a fuller explanation of this situation.

social connections. Several of Tempie's cousins who are the same ages as our children grew up in inner-city housing projects in a northeastern city. They have had to confront dangers—crime, drug dealing, school-based violence—from which our children were sheltered. When we visited them, we were anxious to exit that environment and return to the tree-lined serenity of our Charleston home.

Then there was the decision by Congress after World War II to leave implementation of the GI Bill to the states, virtually ensuring racial bias in the decision-making process in southern states. When my father needed to borrow money to purchase his first hardware store, he turned to his family and to the GI bill. Many black veterans had nowhere to turn.

The research of sociologist Dalton Conley illustrates why this wealth gap is so important. Currently, the ratio of the average net worth of white families to the average net worth of black families is approximately 20-1.[5] According to Conley, when wealth or net worth is essentially equal for white families and black families, high school graduation rates for African American students are slightly higher than graduation rates for white students, and college graduation rates and income levels are approximately equal. Conley's research suggests that net worth may be the most important determinant of economic success. It's not hard to understand why. Wealthier families can live in better neighborhoods, send their children to better schools, and provide them with a slew of other advantages that enhance their development. Furthermore, they are better able to withstand layoffs and unanticipated major expenditures, such as for health problems or major housing or automobile repairs.

---

[5] When Dr. Conley published his research, the gap was approximately 10-1. The latest research indicates that the rate has doubled in the wake of the Great Recession, largely as a result of the subprime mortgage crisis that disproportionately affected African American families.

Maddeningly, however, the wealth gap is the most difficult gap to close. As the saying goes, it takes money to make money. Families with higher net worth, in addition to building equity in their homes and taking advantage of tax deductions for the interest on their mortgages, are better able to take advantage of money-making opportunities by investing in the stock market, property, or businesses. Jackie and I have invested in the stock market, and despite the recent economic crisis, our investments have grown substantially. Our house has more than doubled in value in the twenty years we've owned it. Regina owns her own home, and Ian has invested in several properties that are appreciating in value. Poor people, who are disproportionately black, do not have similar opportunities.

Unfortunately, policies that could narrow the gap and strengthen our nation, such as affirmative action, individual development accounts, or even some form of collective reparations, are rejected out of hand by most white Americans. They believe that the playing field of opportunity is essentially level, that any failure to succeed is matter of personal responsibility, and therefore that government action to move us closer to racial equity is unnecessary and undesirable. Given the whitewashed (pun intended) version of American history that we learn in school, the media's penchant for sensationalism without regard to fairness, and unscrupulous politicians whose win-at-any-cost attitudes border on the unpatriotic, our collective ignorance is not surprising.

But as global economic competition with emerging giants like China and India becomes increasingly intense, and as racial, religious, and ethnic conflicts throughout the world grow ever more dangerous, this ignorance is a major threat to our long-term economic strength and to our political and social stability. In this context, it is important to keep in mind that demographers predict that by 2042, white Americans will make up less than 50 percent of our population. For the under-eighteen population, the projected tipping point is 2023 or earlier. Today, more than 50 percent of babies born in the United States are non-white.

Institutional Policies and Practices

On average, African Americans begin life's journey several miles behind their white counterparts due to both the self-perpetuating cycle of negative racial stereotyping and the wealth gap. These disadvantages are compounded by institutional hurdles they encounter at every stage of the journey: the socioeconomic conditions into which they're born, the system of public education through which they pass, the type of employment they are able to secure, the legacy they are able to leave behind. These hurdles, arduous, relentless, and often withering to the soul, do not confront many white people as they pursue their hopes and dreams.

A disproportionate number of African Americans begin their lives in neighborhoods of concentrated poverty, with all of the disadvantages that presents. They are, therefore, not well-prepared to enter school. Too often, they fall behind early and never catch up. They are further hobbled by the low expectations of teachers and guidance counselors, as were Regina, Arnya, and Ian, by lower per-pupil expenditures in schools that are predominantly black, by an environment not conducive to learning, and by a curriculum that largely excludes the contributions of people of color to our society.

Our children were fortunate. They had educated and successful parents who would not tolerate low expectations, and they attended schools that were predominantly white, well-financed, and highly conducive to learning. They had the textbooks, equipment, and supplies they needed. The science labs were well-equipped, the libraries well-stocked, and the recreation facilities first-rate. Their teachers—negative racial stereotyping notwithstanding—were well-qualified, and class sizes permitted individual attention for students. Their school buildings were brightly lit and created a warm and inviting learning environment. Contrast this with schools in predominantly low-income communities, which are disproportionately populated by families of color. Textbooks are outdated and in poor condition, and there are not enough for every student. Equipment is limited and obsolete. Supplies are inadequate; teachers often lack such basics as enough paper to copy lessons for all their students. Class sizes are larger, so individual attention is often impossible. Teachers are less qualified and are paid less. School buildings are old and drab, in a state of disrepair, and too cold or too hot, depending on the season. Combined with the disadvantage of growing up in poor neighborhoods, these hurdles are simply too high for many children to conquer.

I have one final point about education. When I was in school, the books we used to learn to read contained nary a black face. Reading these books, one would have thought that the entire population of the United States looked just like me. Compounding the problem was the virtual exclusion of African Americans, except as slaves, from our history of nation-building. The American history I was taught barely touched on the harsh treatment of enslaved people (finally brought alive by Alex Haley in *Roots*) and their countless efforts to escape. It included no contributions by black people to the building of our country other than a line or two about George Washington Carver inventing 300 uses for the peanut. As a child, I took great pride in reading about white inventors like Thomas Edison and Alexander Graham Bell, and white pioneers like Daniel Boone and Lewis and Clark. My dark-skinned brothers and sisters had no such sources of pride. I was never taught that black people invented the refrigerator and the traffic light, discovered blood plasma, designed Washington, D.C., and built the Capitol. Neither was I taught that the concept of mandatory public education emerged from the policies of black-led governments in the South during Reconstruction. Names like Frederick Douglass, W. E. B. DuBois, and Ralph Bunche were mentioned only in passing, if at all. But emphasis was placed on the philosophy of Booker T. Washington, who was willing to accept the concept of white social superiority as the price of black job training.

Now, try to put yourself in the shoes of a black child. Imagine how it must have felt to learn, inaccurately, that your ancestors were docile in their captivity and contributed little of value to our nation's development. As a young Jewish boy, I remember being embarrassed that Jews in Germany ostensibly offered no resistance to Hitler's Holocaust. I wondered how my ancestors could let that happen without fighting back. Were Jewish people that meek and weak? Was that who I was? Of course, Jews did resist in every way they could, but I didn't know it at the time. The manifestation of my feeling that I descended from a meek and weak people could have taken many forms. It could have been a self-fulfilling prophecy, or it could have resulted in real anger and an unhealthy tendency toward violence at the slightest provocation. When I put our inaccurate and incomplete education about American history in that context, it's easier to imagine what it must be like for black children to learn about slavery, the daily humiliations of Jim Crow racism, and the lynchings designed to keep blacks in their place. Black children learning these things have to possess great strength in order to prevent internalizing the oppression visited on their forefathers, or carrying feelings of worthlessness from being taught the patently absurd concept that their forefathers contributed nothing to the building of our country, or carrying anger that might be expressed through various forms of antisocial behavior.

It is equally important to understand what the inaccurate and incomplete teaching of American history does to white people. Most people of my generation grew up believing that enslaved people were docile and for the most part happy, and that slave owners treated them well. We were taught that enslaved people infrequently revolted or tried to escape, that they contributed little to the building of the country, and that Jim Crow was necessary to keep order in a society populated by four million freed slaves and their offspring. Being taught such lies in school and having them reinforced by the stereotypes on television of dumb, lazy, submissive blacks, how could we not have internalized a sense of white superiority? Even those of us involved in the civil rights struggles who committed ourselves by words and deeds to racial equality could not avoid succumbing at times to a patronizing attitude and the subconscious internalization of such stereotypes. Things have changed; Arian took a course in African American studies as a high school senior. But most of the students in her class were black. Unfortunately, most white students perceive no need to take such classes.

The hurdles continue as one emerges from public education to either attend college or enter the work force. Getting ready for college is an exciting time for young people. After twelve years of regimented schooling, freedom beckons. They'll decide what they want to study, choose their own classes, make their own schedules, decide whether to attend or skip class, and whether and when to do their homework. And they'll be held accountable for whatever consequences their behavior yields. Black children, if they've been able to surmount the hurdles and make it this far, have the added challenge of being marginalized in a predominantly white environment, unless they choose to attend a predominantly black university.

The fact that all three of our children decided to attend HBCUs is instructive. They had options, but they did not want their college experiences spoiled by having to defend their blackness either to whites who might question their intelligence and the legitimacy of their presence, or to blacks who might question their blackness. They didn't want to have to choose sides in campus racial disputes, or experience resistance when they tried to pursue extracurricular activities. They wanted to enjoy their college experiences free of extraneous pressures that white students don't have to face. They may not have had access to some of the resources available at predominantly white universities, but academically and socially they had the kind of enjoyable and positive college experience that most white students take for granted. They emerged as well-educated, confident, highly capable young African Americans with a strong sense of self-identity and the necessary preparation to confront the job market.

Our children have been richly blessed. They were born into middle-class surroundings, they have loving and attentive parents and step-parents, and they received good educations. Ian had a job offer from NBC before he graduated, he has won several awards for pieces he has produced for *Dateline NBC* and the *Today Show*, and he did a five-week stint in Afghanistan shortly after the 9/11 attacks. Yet he has suffered the usual slings and arrows of being black in a white world. He's been mistaken for a delivery boy, experienced frustration when trying to hail a cab, and felt patronized by some who have questioned his intelligence without knowing him. But he's been more fortunate than many young black men trying to make it in the white world of work. Arnya landed a job with the Budget Committee of the U.S. House of Representatives shortly after graduation, but was a casualty of the Republican takeover of the House in 1994. Since then, she's alternated between jobs and being a stay-at-home mom, so her experiences in the work world have been limited.

Of the three children, Regina has faced perhaps the most difficult challenges in her professional career. With stellar credentials, an engaging personality, an intense dose of determination, and a conscientious work ethic, she has had a succession of progressively more responsible jobs. Nonetheless, in virtually all her jobs she has had to battle both gender and racial bias. Except for the Atlanta experience that I mentioned earlier, she has had little trouble being hired. Once hired, however, a racist and/or sexist atmosphere has more than once made her job more difficult, increased pressure on her, or eventually led her to seek new employment. When white people enter a company, they rarely worry about whether or not they will fit in. Most employees look like they do, grew up in similar environments, and share similar experiences. Rarely does a white person have the experience of going to work in a company with predominantly black employees; rarely does a white person have to adjust to being the odd person out. Affirmative action has been effectively demonized as giving African Americans, women, and Hispanic Americans an unfair advantage. From my perspective, when one is evaluating people with similar qualifications, it is a valuable weapon for confronting the ever-present good-old-white-boy network and moving us closer to a level playing field.

Unfortunately, not everyone makes it. For some, the hurdles prove too high, and somewhere along the journey, they crash. Some fall victim to racial bias in the criminal justice system. One of Regina's close friends is a bright, attractive, personable young woman. Now in her late forties, she spent a summer with us when she and Regina were in college. She seemed destined for great things. After college, she returned to her home in North Carolina, got married, had a daughter, and settled into a comfortable life. But her marriage didn't work, and she eventually became a single mother. She began dating a young man who was, unbeknownst to her, dealing drugs. One night, his car—with her in it—was stopped by the police. A search turned up a small amount of crack cocaine. He went to prison, and despite the lack of evidence connecting her to her boyfriend's drug dealing, she was sentenced to five years in prison. The judge said he wanted to teach her a lesson. Her career was interrupted, if not ruined, and her daughter was motherless for five years. Had she been white, the likelihood of her ever seeing the inside of a prison cell would have been slim. This is not to excuse her bad judgment; we all make mistakes. But when a black person makes a mistake, institutional policies and individual racism can exact a life-altering price. If you're white, you rarely pay that price.

Even African Americans who have successfully navigated the journey often pay an emotional and physical price that most white people do not pay. The effect of racism is insidious. It's like a worm coursing through your body. Gradually, it creeps through every cell and pore of your body, eating away at your sense of control over your life. Each incident can make you more wary, more suspicious, more agitated. The cumulative effect can make you seethe with resentment. You can't believe that white people are so oblivious to the indignities you endure, and it becomes difficult to view white people as friends or allies. The pressures affect both your emotional and your physical health. According to a recent study, 33 percent of African Americans suffer from hypertension (high blood pressure), which puts them at greater risk of heart attacks and strokes. Some people attribute this statistic to genetic differences. However, the same study found that only 16 percent of West Africans and 26 percent of people from the Caribbean suffer from hypertension. This strongly suggests that the stress is related to racism, as well as to the subtle yet significant consequence of white privilege.

White Privilege

You will recall the chilling experience I recounted in an earlier chapter of encountering that North Carolina billboard: "This is Klan Country. Fight integration and communism. Impeach Earl Warren. Welcome to Smithville." The terror we experienced, simply because we were an interracial couple, was palpable. Nearly forty years later, the scars of that experience remain. I have never again driven in that part of North Carolina without having a knot in the pit of my stomach. Although I've not set foot in Smithville since then, in recent years Jackie and I have stopped overnight several times at a motel in that part of North Carolina. We are an unexceptional-looking white couple. We walk the streets freely, eat in any restaurant we choose, and browse the windows on the main street without attracting attention. Yet I have found myself looking around and wondering what dangers might lurk. Had I been with Tempie or with one of my children or grandchildren, we would not have stopped there, choosing instead accommodations at an interstate exit and eating in the motel's restaurant. That's not such a big deal, you might say, and besides, the experience in Smithville was nearly four decades ago. The sign has surely crumbled, along with the attitudes that fostered it. Perhaps. But I've not forgotten the terror of that night. It is a limitation most white people will never feel.

Whether attending school, leaving home for college, seeking a job, purchasing a house, buying a new car, traveling on vacation, or simply walking down the street, my skin color is never a factor. In most circumstances it is a huge plus. In school I experienced only the normal growing-up anxiety about fitting in. My father's connections, which would have been nonexistent had his skin color not been white, were an advantage to me for obtaining summer jobs during high school. When I bought my first car, I had the security of having my father with me, confident he would not be taken advantage of because of his skin color. In seeking my first job out of college, the factor of skin color never entered my mind. After moving to West Virginia, I felt only the anxiety of culture shock in moving from an urban environment to a rural one.

Nevertheless, the concept of white privilege is an understandably difficult concept for white Americans to grasp. Most do not feel privileged in their daily lives. They rise early to endure a long commute to a job they tolerate, but may not find fulfilling. They work long hours for less money than they feel they're worth. Their income may barely be enough to make ends meet. Their credit card debt is dangerously high, and they do well to make the minimum monthly payments. These payments barely keep up with the high interest rates, so their debt grows. When they do get a salary increase, it is eaten up by rapidly rising health insurance premiums. In this unstable economy, they are unlikely to feel secure in their jobs. Economically, they may be only one or two paychecks away from disaster. They struggle to make sure their children remain healthy and get good educations. They worry about their children's grades, their children's friends, the way their children dress, what their children watch on television, and the video games their children play. They agonize that the cost of college is far beyond their financial capacity. They fear that if one of the working parents in a two-earner household were to become seriously ill, the deductible for the care they might need, even if they have health insurance, and the loss of time on the job could rip their budget to shreds. Their elderly parents live longer now and require more care. Some families confront the choice of whether to take their parents into their already crowded homes or to put them in a nursing home where they are unlikely to get the tender, loving care they'd get at home. Life is a continuing struggle, and the light at the end of the tunnel is dim. To talk about white privilege under these conditions yields an ironic laugh at best and an angry diatribe at worst.

And yet, even with these burdens, I can drive any car that I can afford and not worry about being stopped by the police. I can stop to ask directions of a police officer without concern about the officer's possible reaction. I can read about racial incidents in the newspaper almost every day and not wonder whether it will happen to me. (If anti-Semitic incidents occurred with the frequency that racist incidents do, I'd be wary of going out on the street.) I can make a fool of myself or simply be silent at a meeting without worrying that others will think my performance is reflective of all white people. Within the limits of my budget, I can travel and eat wherever I want without attracting attention. Sociologist Joe Feagin speaks of the innate confidence of being white in a white world. Jackie and I see it every day in the predominantly black community in which we live. We stand out to such an extent that one day, when we were taking a walk, a black neighbor we didn't know greeted us with a smile and the words, "Hi, white folks." We're a distinct minority in our neighborhood, as well as a minority in our county. I'm in the minority in the office where I work. Yet we know innately and instinctively that the world is ours. We see it in newspapers every day. We see it on television. We know it in the way we're greeted when we step out of our community. We know it in terms of our access to economic resources and to political power. And we know it from our government, both historically and contemporarily.

White people complain about affirmative action as an unfair, government-imposed benefit for African Americans. But government handouts that gave white people a competitive advantage over black people are an integral part of our history. For example, in the 1600s land grants were given to white people willing to brave the dangers of settling new territory. Since black people like Tempie's ancestors were still enslaved, they were unable to take advantage of this largesse or of the power and wealth that accrued. When a similar effort surfaced to give land to freed former slaves during Reconstruction, it failed due to opposition from former slave owners, many of whom had benefited from the earlier giveaway. In fact, while these slave owners rejected the idea of government compensation for emancipated African Americans, they pressed hard for compensation for the loss of their slaves, whom they considered their property.

More recent examples are the exclusion of blacks from Social Security for the first two decades of its existence, the exclusion for many years of black people from many unions, the government underwriting policy that precluded most African American families from buying homes after World War II, and the discriminatory implementation of the GI Bill. In the context of these and countless other examples, the cries of "reverse discrimination" and opposition to affirmative action seem outrageous at best and downright racist at worst. If you're black, these countless examples of racist behavior and the obliviousness of most white people to the privilege they enjoy can be infuriating.

I can never be black, and I don't pretend to speak for black people, not even for members of my own family. I don't carry the legacy of slavery on my shoulders. My ancestors were not held in bondage, brutally disciplined for stepping out of place, or sold at auction like cattle. I don't carry childhood memories of being treated differently simply because my skin was darker, or of seeing my parents demeaned and humiliated at the whim of the dominant group, or of feeling powerless to change the circumstances of my life. I don't have to endure the daily trials that factor into nearly everything my black family members, friends, and colleagues do. But my experiences have helped me to become aware of many of the elements of white privilege I enjoy.

When I begin the discussion of white privilege in my classes, students often ask why I talk about privilege. Isn't it simply another way to describe racial discrimination? In answering the question, I refer to two quotes. The first is from a speech given by then Representative Henry Hyde (R-IL) from the floor of the House of Representatives. He asserted that the idea of collective guilt for slavery "is an idea whose time has gone. I never owned a slave. I never oppressed anybody. I don't know that I should have to pay for someone who did generations before I was born." In a narrow sense, Representative Hyde was correct. But what he failed to acknowledge, or, probably, even to understand, are the benefits that were afforded him simply because he was white. His argument turns on whether or not he engaged in racist behavior. In that context, it's too easy to become defensive and let yourself off the hook by proclaiming that you don't discriminate, or that you don't have a racist bone in your body. (As an aside, I'd advise you to beware of anyone who proclaims, "I don't have a racist bone in my body," for in this culture such a claim strains credulity or bespeaks of extraordinary self-delusion.)

But when you come at the issue from the perspective of white privilege, you change the context of the argument from whether someone engages in racist behavior to whether people have benefited from the racist behavior of others in the past. Such an argument eliminates the need for people to be defensive about their own behavior and gives them the freedom to acknowledge that whether or not racist behavior still exists, the legacy of past racist behavior continues to privilege white people today.

The second quote is from an article by Peggy McIntosh, who first brought the concept of white privilege to prominence in the early 1990s. In *White Privilege: Unpacking the Invisible Knapsack,* she lists fifty examples of privileges she enjoys simply because of her skin color, and she asserts, "Describing white privilege makes one newly accountable." In other words, even if you have not engaged in any racist behavior, you clearly enjoy certain benefits if your skin is white, benefits that you didn't have to ask for and that you can't give away. Her fifty examples include these:

> If I should need to move, I can be pretty sure of renting
> or purchasing housing in an area which I can afford and
> in which I would want to live.

I can be pretty sure that my children's teachers and employers will tolerate them if they fit school and workplace norms; my chief worries about them do not concern others' attitudes toward their race.

I will feel welcomed and 'normal' in the usual walks of public life, institutional and social.

Thus, while one may not be guilty of racist behavior, understanding the privilege conferred simply because of skin color raises the question, "What will I do to lessen or end racist behavior?"

There is a third reason I believe the concept of white privilege is important to understand. When we talk about racial discrimination, we inevitably use terms such as "the oppressed" or "the victims of racism." Both terms denote weakness and a fragile state of mind, and they reinforce an inaccurate stereotype. At the beginning of this book, I referred to my former mother-in-law, who had been victimized by racism but hardly had a victim's mentality. She recognized the privilege white people enjoyed, but refused to see herself as a victim. Rather, she saw herself as persevering under some of the most difficult circumstances imaginable. This is an important distinction. When we speak of white privilege, we can avoid thinking in terms of victimhood and weakness, and we may be better able to recognize the strength and courage it takes for black people to overcome the hurdles they confront on their journey through life.

The unique diversity I've experienced in my personal and professional lives has helped me more clearly understand this distinction. I can't be black, but I can compare the experience of being married to a black woman and having three black children and four black grandchildren (Ian now has a daughter, Lana Simone, who will soon turn six) to the experience of being married to a white woman. I can assure you that the latter circumstance, which gives Jackie and me the freedom to attract attention only when we seek to do so, makes for a much more tension-free life.

You need only recall a sampling of the incidents I've described throughout this book to recognize that truth. There were the incidents before Tempie and I were married at the Glass House on the West Virginia Turnpike and with the Beckley police at my apartment, the anxiety we felt when we bought our first house in Charleston, the incident on Interstate 85 with the North Carolina state trooper, Arnya being denied her rightful place on her high school's cheerleading squad, Ian being denied the recognition he deserved for his horseback riding accomplishments, Regina being denied that job in Atlanta, and our need to be constantly vigilant in ensuring our children received fair treatment in school. Each incident increased my wariness about other incidents that were not so clear-cut. After a while, I wondered about every incident of inappropriate behavior that occurred; it was the "is-it-or-isn't-it?" syndrome. When we were seated in the back of a restaurant, was it because of the wait staff rotation or because they were purposely giving us the least desirable table? When it took longer than usual to get service, was it because the kitchen was backed up or because the server was mistreating us? When we had to wait for service in a store, was it because the clerks were busy or because they didn't want to serve us? When the kids got bad grades in school, was it because they'd legitimately earned them or because they were being treated unfairly?

Ultimately, it didn't matter. I assumed it was racism and became angry at and wary of most white folks. The fact that hypertension is more prevalent among blacks hardly surprises me. I experienced the tension daily. You get used to it, true enough. But the relaxation and security I felt as a white person before Tempie and I were married became a distant memory. Of course, I could still escape. When I was out by myself, I was still white to the people I passed. When I ate lunch in a downtown restaurant, or caught a cab, or shopped for a book or a pair of slacks, I was white. I could find relief in a way Tempie and the children could not. But my "blackness" was never far away. I still looked at most white people with suspicion. In time, I actually found myself not wanting to escape, not wanting to engage with white people; rather, I felt as one with my black family and my black friends.

Being married to Jackie for more than twenty years has eased much of the tension, even though we continue to live, and I continue to work, in predominantly black environments. The feelings of wariness and anger still return when one of my children endures racist behavior. But they are grown, they don't live with us, and they don't need the same protection they needed when they were younger. When I'm alone with Jackie, the tension is largely absent, and I have the privilege of enjoying the relaxation and sense of security with which I grew up. We don't worry about where we are seated in a restaurant or the service we receive when we shop. We don't check out vacation spots to see if there are any black people there. The anxiety, though, is never far away. Several years ago, I was watching *Soul Food*, the well-done Showtime series about three black sisters and their families. When Ahmad, the thirteen- or fourteen-year-old son of one of the sisters, is unjustly harassed by police, he becomes angry, and his father has to sit him down and explain the realities of life to him. He has to acknowledge to his son their relative powerlessness to combat such harassment. The father's frustration and embarrassment and the anger they both feel are palpable. It is an experience that white teenage boys and their fathers do not confront.

The reality hit harder more recently, when seventeen-year-old Trayvon Martin was murdered. There is little doubt that if Trayvon had been white, with his iced tea and his bag of Skittles, he would still be alive, and if George Zimmerman were black, he would have been arrested on the spot. I thought about my grandson, Michael Ian, now eleven and tall and husky for his age. Because of his skin color, he will undoubtedly face challenges that are foreign to young males with my skin color.

Over twenty years ago, I took a creative writing class and became friendly with a white woman in the class. Over coffee one day, we talked about our respective ambitions. I said that I wanted to write a book, but I despaired I'd ever get around to it or that anyone would ever publish it. I must have sounded whiny, because after a minute or two, she snapped at me. "Michael, you're a white male. You're the most privileged person in this society. You can do anything you want. So, don't complain to me." She was, of course, correct.

Beyond The Melting Pot

My life's journey has been blessed, richly blessed, by the diversity that has infused virtually every step of it. On my unique path, I have had experiences that few other people have had and gained insights not available to most other people. From the six weeks I spent in Prince Edward County, to my role as a husband and father in an interracial marriage, to my thirteen months with President Clinton's Initiative on Race, and beyond, I have seen how race-related fear and ignorance can cause excruciating pain, and how getting beyond the stereotypes our culture inflicts on us can enrich our lives with depth and vibrancy. I've developed deep and meaningful relationships with people from very different racial, ethnic, and religious backgrounds; I've seen how diverse perspectives can give us new insights and enable us to acknowledge differing viewpoints without demonizing those with whom we disagree; I've witnessed how adversity can bolster courage and determination; I've observed the capacity of people to change deeply held views when presented with new information; and I've significantly widened the options for where I can live and work without fear or anxiety. And I've also learned that I can move beyond my comfort zone and survive, even thrive. As a result, I believe I am a stronger and more sensitive individual. And I believe we are a stronger nation when we appreciate how our racial and ethnic diversity can strengthen our society and give our lives a fullness and richness that few, if any, other nations can claim.

However, despite the election of Barack Obama as President and the wishful thinking of those who heralded the onset of a post-racial society, I know—we all know if we are honest with ourselves—that we have not yet arrived at that point. The data generated by the Joint Center and other organizations confirm this. The achievement gap and the racial disparity in drop-out rates tell us that educational opportunities for students of color are far from equal. Disparate incomes and empirical evidence of job discrimination tell us that not everyone has an equal shot at jobs for which they are qualified. White flight tells us that a significant percentage of white families, while espousing principles of justice and fair play, will tolerate only a limited percentage of black families in their communities and black students in their schools before they look elsewhere to live and to send their children to school. Regular reports of police brutality and racial profiling and the disproportionate incarceration of young men of color tell us that attitudes in law enforcement and the media reflect the negative racial stereotypes that infuse our society. The higher infant mortality rate and shorter life expectancy of African Americans tell us that equal access to quality health care is still far from a reality. The wealth gap is actually growing.

In my classes I require students to select and analyze current newspaper articles illustrating the legacy of our history, the concept of white privilege, the impact of negative racial stereotyping, and the continuing patterns of individual and institutional racism. They are amazed at how easy it is to find such articles, and it illustrates the persistence of these problems. These are problems for all of us. Separate and unequal education opportunities rob our society of the potential contributions of millions of people, and create a virtually insurmountable hurdle to mutual understanding. Resistance to meaningful residential integration reinforces negative racial stereotypes and sows racial tensions. Job discrimination deprives us of enormous productivity in a labor force that is becoming increasingly non-white. The spiraling rate of incarceration costs us billions of dollars in taxes each year. Providing emergency health care to the uninsured raises health insurance premiums for the rest of us. The subprime mortgage crisis, which was largely a product of the discriminatory treatment of people of color in the housing market, has led our nation's economy into a deep and lengthy recession, and cost the jobs of millions of people of all colors and ethnicities. Yet we resist meaningful solutions to these problems on the false supposition that these inequities are the results of individual failures.

We know what it will take to address these disparities and to achieve racial equity. We know we need policies to narrow the wealth gap and to lift people from virtual imprisonment in neighborhoods of concentrated poverty. We know we need to more effectively train teachers, equalize school funding, create more positive learning environments for all children, and develop a curriculum that recognizes and integrates the contributions of all groups. We know we need to more effectively regulate mortgage lenders and more effectively enforce anti-discrimination laws. We know we need to equalize punishment for drug use in the African American and white communities. We know we need to make sure that all Americans have access to affordable health insurance and to health care providers who understand their culture and speak their language. Tragically, we do not have the political will to implement what we know will work. The debate over reforming the health care system, characterized largely by public ignorance and fear and by the pandering of unscrupulous politicians to that ignorance and fear, vividly illustrates our lack of political will. In his 1989 inaugural address, President George H. W. Bush identified domestic problems, but then claimed, "We have more will than wallet." I respectfully and emphatically disagree. If we have the wallet for a war of choice in Iraq and for defense systems that the Pentagon doesn't need or want but that members of Congress force on them for their own political benefit, then surely we have the wallet for measures that can truly strengthen our nation. It's the will that's missing.

This brings me to my core point. Ultimately, this is about each of us shedding the protective cocoons in which we live, venturing beyond our comfort zones, and finding the will to change the direction of our national journey so that equity becomes our guiding principle and the touchstone of our behavior. There are people who understand this and who toil in their communities

219

to foster racial equity and healing. During President Clinton's Initiative on Race, we identified, as I mentioned earlier, 350 such activities in communities across the country. In places as widely divergent as Richmond, Virginia, Seattle, Washington, and Philadelphia, Mississippi, people are transcending their fears and reaching beyond their comfort zones to bring us together in an atmosphere of justice and equity. In Richmond, schoolchildren can visit a Civil War museum that tells all sides of the story, take a guided walk along a slave trail, and view monuments to the struggle for racial freedom. In Seattle, both city and county governments are deeply engaged in initiatives designed to ensure equal opportunity. In Philadelphia, Mississippi, public officials and private citizens have apologized for the murders of Andy Goodman, Micchael Schwerner, and James Chaney; an interracial coalition holds regular dialogues to help promote racial understanding; and the city, which has a white majority, has elected a black mayor. In several smaller communities in the Deep South interracial groups are trying to unearth the unvarnished truth about past lynchings and to use this truth as a basis for helping to narrow racial divisions. Throughout the country, in communities large and small, courageous and patriotic citizens are undertaking similar activities.

One of the most moving and inspiring stories I've ever heard came from a white banker in Charlotte, North Carolina, about fifteen years ago. The brother of the Republican governor of the state, he was accepting an award from the Urban League for his work in promoting racial equity and healing in the community. Sadly, he was being ravaged by Lou Gehrig's disease, and when he accepted the award, he had difficulty walking and speaking. But true to his spirit and his vision, he announced his Thursday Lunch Plan. He vowed that for as long as he was alive, he would dedicate every Thursday to having lunch with someone from a different racial background so they could learn more about each other. Then he would ask each of his Thursday lunch mates to do the same thing on subsequent Thursdays. He reasoned, with a tear in his eye, that if he could somehow live long enough, he could make every Thursday an Interracial Lunch Day in Charlotte, and perhaps across the country. Doing so, he envisioned, would increase racial understanding and equity and foster an appreciation for the unique attributes that each of us, regardless of skin color, possesses. His vision was not the melting pot that has served as a metaphor for our national vision for a century. Rather, his vision was a beautiful garden with flowers of every size, shape, and color, flowers that, when cherished for their unique qualities and nurtured with affection and tenderness, grow to their full potential and together create a stunning, dynamic picture in which the interdependence of all the flowers is on vivid display. Imagine a nation in which all of us, whatever our size, shape, or color, recognize our interdependence, yet respect the unique attributes and cultural practices that each of us contributes to the strength and beauty of our nation.

My family reflects this vision. On a wall in our family room hang six pictures. One is of Jackie and me. Four are individual pictures of the grandchildren. The sixth is a picture of my father's family, taken in Poland in 1907 or 1908. In that picture my father is less than a year old, and he is surrounded by his bearded father, his mother, and seven of his siblings. Our grandchildren are fascinated by the mix of pictures, and in particular the picture of my father's family. Visitors to our home invariably look at the wall and comment on the unique mix of colors, sizes, and cultures. We represent Polish, Russian, Irish, and French immigrants, and Americans of African heritage, with a little Native American ancestry from Tempie's forefathers thrown in.

We are now uniquely American, but we are not a melting pot. Neither Tempie, Jackie, nor I gave up our individual identities when we got married. Tempie is still black and Baptist from rural North Carolina. Jackie is still a white born-again Christian of Irish and French descent from Rhode Island. I am still a culturally Jewish white man of Polish and Russian extraction from New York City. We bring to our relationships all of the experiences, pain, joy, and insights gained over lifetimes. Regina, Arnya, and Ian have inherited all of this, and have developed their own unique perspectives which they are passing on to their children. We epitomize a garden in which a variety of flowers have bloomed and formed a beautiful whole. We admire our unique perspectives and special qualities, and we are constantly learning from each other.

On a more global scale, my classes are animated by the diversity of my students. They come from virtually every corner of the globe, from Japan, China, Korea, India, and Pakistan; from Mexico, El Salvador, Colombia, Guatemala, and Brazil; from South Africa, Ghana, Nigeria, Kenya, and Liberia; from England, France, Germany, Italy, Russia, and Spain; from Israel, Jordan, and Egypt; from New York to California and from Minnesota to Texas. From each student, the class—and I, too—learn something that enriches our understanding of the practices and norms of other cultures. All the students have become part of the beautiful garden that is the United States of America.

A similar representation is on display at the Largo Community Church that Jackie attends every Sunday and that I occasionally attend with her. It was started over thirty years ago by Reverend Jack Morris, a white man from Pennsylvania with a vision for a community-based, nondenominational church. For years, its congregation was almost all white. But as Prince George's County began to change, so did the congregation's composition. Today, while Reverend Morris continues to lead the church and a number of white members remain, the diversity of the growing congregation—African Americans, Hispanic Americans, recent African and Caribbean immigrants—is striking. But all of them benefit from the church's racial and denominational diversity, and I have learned lessons from them in compassion, integrity, and strength that I have not learned anywhere else.

Such examples, however, remain too few and too isolated. If we are to pursue the vision of a nation in which we treasure and celebrate our diversity, we must adopt a different mind-set, one that acknowledges our oppressive past and its legacy, that seeks not to blame but to inspire, and that recognizes our collective responsibility and the collective benefit that awaits a nation that can achieve such a vision. We must have the courage to move beyond our comfort zone. The question we must all confront is, "What do we truly value?" To use the criteria of my old professor Sid Simon: Do we value racial equity and healing enough to act on it, not only occasionally, but to make such action a regular pattern of our lives? What sacrifices are we willing to make to achieve true equity in our society, to be loyal to our nation's founding principles of freedom and justice, to make our behavior match our principles?

When he withdrew from the 1988 Democratic presidential primary campaign, the late Senator Paul Simon observed, "Americans instinctively know that we are one nation, one family, and when anyone in that family hurts, all of us eventually hurt. There really is a yearning across this good land for leadership that appeals to the noble in us rather than to the greed in us."

There are many things we can do as individuals to reflect the noble in us,[6] though none are easy. As my friend Chris Edley says, "It's not rocket science, it's harder than rocket science." In essence, the question is whether you are willing to step out of your comfort zone for your own good and for the greater good. You can start with baby steps. One of my favorite stories involves Pee Wee Reese, star shortstop for the Brooklyn Dodgers when Jackie Robinson broke Major League baseball's color line. Reese was the team captain when Robinson took the field with the Dodgers for the first time on April 15, 1947. The Louisville

---

[6] I include, following the Afterword, a list of ten things that each of us can do to promote racial understanding and racial reconciliation. They were developed for the Clinton Initiative by my friend and colleague—and the man who inspired this book—Dr. David Campt. Also, there are any number of websites that suggest ways you can promote racial understanding and reconciliation. Three of the most prominent ones are www.tolerance.org, the website of the Southern Poverty Law Center, www.civilrights.org, the website of the Leadership Conference on Civil Rights, and www.everyday-democracy.org, the website of Everyday Democracy.

native was neither a demonstrative man nor a spear-carrier for racial integration. But he possessed an innate sense of fairness. When some of his most prominent teammates circulated a petition opposing Robinson's presence before the season started, Reese declined to sign it. On the field one day, when the racial epithets got particularly nasty, he walked over to Robinson in full view of thousands of spectators and put his hand on his shoulder. According to Robinson, Reese didn't say a word. Later Robinson described the scene: "He looked over at the chaps who were yelling at me and just stared . . . I will never forget it." Robinson's success as the first black Major League baseball player in modern times opened the floodgates for many great African American players who followed, from Hank Aaron to Willie Mays to Ken Griffey Jr., as well as for the many great Hispanic and Asian players who now dot the rosters of many Major League teams. With the simple gestures of declining to sign a petition, of putting his hand on his teammate's shoulder, Reese demonstrated the power of being willing to move beyond one's comfort zone.

In my life and in the lives of my family, we have encountered many people like Pee Wee Reese, among them Charleston's former mayor John Hutchinson and West Virginia Senator Jay Rockefeller, who without hesitation dismissed any notion that it was a problem that I was married to a black woman; Ian's equestrian coach, who made him feel totally comfortable as the first African American rider they'd ever had; William Winter, the former governor of Mississippi and member of President Clinton's Advisory Board on Race, who has taken risks that many of us can barely fathom to stand up for what he values. Each one, in his or her own way, has been willing to take a risk, to step out of his or her comfort zone in the interest of racial equity.

Each of us can find ways to do the same thing. Indeed, we must if the strength of our nation is to endure, and if we are to realize the vision of a beautiful garden composed of flowers of every size, shape, and color. If we have the courage to step up to these challenges, we can build the kind of momentum for change envisioned by that brave victim of Lou Gehrig's disease in Charlotte, North Carolina, who endeavored to make every Thursday an Interracial Lunch Day.

About eight years ago, I attended a speech by Dr. Vincent Harding, a professor of theology and a leader in the civil rights struggles of the 1950s and 1960s. "If you don't ever walk through trouble, or confront a risk, or reach beyond your comfort zone," he asserted, "you will never meet the rest of yourself." Think about it. There is an entire part of yourself, that part of yourself that shows courage and strength in the face of challenges, that you may never know unless you are willing to risk action to stand up for your values, unless you are willing to step out of your comfort zone. To paraphrase Robert Frost, join me on "the road less traveled." It will make all the difference.

AFTERWORD

THE DESTINATION

Two core beliefs, products of my white skin privilege and youthful arrogance, used to drive my idealistic zeal. First, I believed that if I worked hard enough and was smart enough, I could save the world. Second, I believed the world was divided into good guys and bad guys. The good guys were those who believed that racial discrimination and poverty were immoral and were willing to act in support of this belief. The bad guys were everybody else.

During my civil rights activities in college and my anti-poverty organizing activities in West Virginia, I operated, quite arrogantly, on the basis of those beliefs. As a twenty-one-year-old civil rights activist, I was convinced that justice for all was just around the corner, that we were the white knights who would make it happen, and that anyone who wasn't with us must be against us. As a twenty-six-year-old anti-poverty "warrior" in the coal fields of southern West Virginia, I was convinced that poverty could be abolished if the power structure were not an obstacle. Again, we were the white knights who would sweep aside this obstacle and any other obstacles in our path. The Sunday afternoon that I spent with Gibbs Kinderman, inebriated on gin-soaked watermelon and plotting how we would make West Virginia a haven for economic and racial justice, illustrates the extent of my arrogance.

I've retained the first belief in somewhat modified form. I still believe that each of us has the power to change the world, but it must be done as *we*, not as *I*, and we must do it by focusing not on the world, but each of us on our own little corner of the world. Rosa Parks' simple act of refusing to give up her seat on a Montgomery, Alabama, bus changed the nation and the world. It sparked a year-long bus boycott that yielded a significant Supreme Court decision, launched a decade of significant milestone accomplishments in civil rights and, not incidentally, brought Dr. Martin Luther King, Jr., to prominence. Rosa Parks didn't do it by herself, but her single, selfless act inspired countless others. Reverend L. Francis Griffin endured pressures that would have crushed most of us, but because he persevered, Prince Edward County today is a very different place from the racial wilderness of fifty years ago, and many residents of Prince Edward County, white and black, are very different people. Governor William Winter risked his political career, and perhaps his life, to lead Mississippi and the entire South to a brighter day, and he continues to do so at the time of this writing.

Each of us has the power displayed by Rosa Parks, Reverend Griffin, and Governor Winter. By focusing on our little corner of the world, we can inspire others, and indeed, change the world. In the final analysis, it is a matter of integrity. If we are willing to stand up for what we value, to exit our comfort zone in order meet the rest of ourselves, the difference we can make is incalculable. Famed anthropologist Margaret Mead was right:

> Never doubt that a small group of thoughtful, committed people can change the world; indeed, it's the only thing that ever has.

But changing the world, or our little corner of the world, requires setting aside that second core belief I once had. The world is not made up of good guys and bad guys. It is, for the most part, made up of people just like you and me. We have good intentions; we simply see the world from different perspectives, through both the lens of the environment in which we grew up and the lens of our own particular experiences. We are good guys (and gals) trying our best to do what's right, as we understand it. There are, of course, exceptions: the vicious racists who blew up the church in Birmingham, killing four little girls; the "law enforcement officials" who killed Andy Goodman, James Chaney, and Michael Schwerner; the three young white men who dragged James Byrd to his death in Jasper, Texas, in 1998; the three young white men who beat and fatally ran over James Craig Anderson in Jackson, Mississippi, in 2011 because they were looking for black people to harass; and some of today's most divisive talk show hosts. But the vast majority of people are like the county official I met in Raleigh County, West Virginia, and realized, much to my surprise through the fog of my youthful arrogance, that although we disagreed on how to get there, we both wanted to end poverty in Raleigh County. He was reluctant to step out of his comfort zone, but under the right circumstances he was a potential ally. He was certainly not the evil enemy I had presumed him to be. Many of the people I've met throughout my journey have had different perspectives and opinions; we've tried to be respectful in our disagreements and to find areas of common agreement wherever possible.

In October 2009, seven members of the group who went to Prince Edward County in 1963 returned for a visit and reunion, and Governor Winter keynoted a banquet in our honor. We met black people and white people, including the granddaughter of the racist former editor of the *Farmville Herald*, who were working together to build a museum that would tell the story of Prince Edward County and the racial challenges it faced. Their multiracial hunger for justice and for healing was inspiring to all of us.

If we see the world as made up of only good guys and bad guys, we limit the number of allies we can recruit, and we set up polarizing win-lose situations in which more often than not we find ourselves on the losing end. If we recognize that most people want to do the right thing and that they are often prisoners of a historically racist system, we open up a wide world of potential allies and ultimately set up potential win-win situations. Dr. King understood this, and the nonviolent protests he inspired and led uplifted a nation and motivated people throughout the country to become allies. Had he not had faith in the ultimate good intentions of people, he would likely have polarized the population, gathered far fewer allies, and not accomplished nearly as much as he did.

So, as we go forward, I still retain two core beliefs. First, I believe that we can, in fact, change the world. We have the power to do so simply by standing up with courage and integrity for what we truly believe. Our courage and integrity will inspire others, and together we will bring change. Second, I believe we must recognize that most people are potential allies, provided we treat them with respect and don't batter them with guilt, that we honor who they are and listen attentively to what they believe and why.

We are all on a journey through life. We begin at different places, we take different paths, and we confront different hurdles. But if we remain true to our own values, and if we respect the integrity of others whose values may differ, we can hasten the day when we all arrive at a common destination: a nation in which we respect and honor our differences while celebrating the common threads that bind us all; a nation in which the level of one's effort, not the color of one's skin, is the only predictor of our success in achieving our vision of the American dream; a nation that truly reflects the metaphor of a beautiful flowering garden. Then, truly, we will have arrived at the United States of America to which we pledge our allegiance each day.

POSTSCRIPT

As I was putting the finishing touches on this book, the news of seventeen-year-old Trayvon Martin's murder in Sanford, Florida, hit the airwaves. I felt angry and empty, partly because of the senseless killing of a black teenage boy armed with nothing more than some iced tea and a bag of Skittles, and partly because I knew this was not an isolated case. In June 2011, James Craig Anderson, a black man in his forties, was killed by three young white men in Jackson, Mississippi, who were looking for black people and homeless people to harass. And at about the same time that Trayvon Martin was killed in Florida, eighteen-year-old Remarley Graham, also black and unarmed, was killed in his grandmother's house in New York City by police who had entered the house illegally. There are countless other young black men who have suffered the same fate just for "living while black." Suddenly, the optimistic note on which I had finished telling my story seemed naïve. I was afraid for my thirty-nine-year-old son, my eleven-year-old grandson, and even my seven-month-old great-grandson. Will they ever be able to live freely among us without worrying about where they venture, what they wear, how they respond to people who make automatic assumptions about them simply due to their skin color?

I am somewhat reassured by the reactions of horror expressed by people of every racial background across the country when they learned of Trayvon's murder. I still believe that we have it within us to build an egalitarian society in which no one is treated differently because of skin color. But the killing of Trayvon, with all the media attention that has accompanied it, should be another wake-up call that we still have a long and painful journey ahead of us. At the same time, it represents an opportunity to move us, through both dialogue and action, closer to our ultimate destination. I pray that Trayvon's killing will not be forgotten as quickly as other so-called teachable moments, and that all of us will use this tragedy to examine our own biases and to seek ways, individually and collectively, to inform and hasten our journey.

With the inevitable delays that accompany a project of this scope, I was proof-reading the final version of the manuscript as the 2012 Presidential election returns were being reported. I make no secret of my support for President Obama. Simply put, his policies are far more consistent with my own beliefs than are the policies that Mitt Romney espoused for most of the campaign. More importantly, however, President Obama's re-election represents a victory over those who seek to divide us, who try to stoke fear in white voters by attempting to demonize our President as something other than a real and patriotic American, and who attempt to make it more difficult for certain segments of the population to vote. They are the ones who, in my opinion, are out of step with our American ideals. Thankfully, they lost. To paraphrase the words of the late Neil Armstrong: "One small step for man, one giant leap for a more just, equitable, and united nation."

TEN THINGS EVERY AMERICAN SHOULD DO TO PROMOTE RACIAL RECONCILIATION*

One of the most striking findings of President Clinton's Initiative on Race is that there are many Americans who acknowledge that racial prejudice, privilege, and disparities are major problems confronting our nation. Many of them told the Initiative they would welcome concrete advice about what they should do to promote racial reconciliation, or in other words, how they could "make their deeds match their creeds." To fill that need, the Initiative offered a brief list of actions that individual Americans could take to increase the momentum toward making us truly one America in the twenty-first century.

1. Make a commitment to become informed about people from other races and cultures.
2. If it is not your inclination to think about race, commit at least one day each month to thinking about how issues of racial prejudice and privilege might be affecting each person you come in contact with that day.
3. In your life, make a conscious effort to get to know people of other races.
4. Make a point to raise your concerns about comments or actions that appear prejudicial, even if you are not the target of these actions.
5. Initiate a constructive dialogue on race within your workplace, school, neighborhood, or religious community.

6. Support institutions that promote racial inclusion.
7. Participate in a community project to reduce racial disparities in opportunity and well-being.
8. Insist that institutions that teach us about our community accurately reflect the diversity of our nation.
9. Visit other areas of the city, region, or country that allow you to experience parts of other cultures beyond their food.
10. Advocate that groups you can influence (whether you are a volunteer or employee) examine how they can increase their commitment to reducing racial disparities, lessening discrimination, and improving race relations.

*Adapted from *One America in the 21ˢᵗ Century: Forging a New Future, The Advisory Board's Report to the President*, September 1998.

ABOUT THE AUTHOR

Michael R. Wenger is a senior fellow at the Joint Center for Political and Economic Studies and an adjunct professor in the Department of Sociology at The George Washington University. In 1997 and 1998 he served as deputy director for outreach and program development for President Clinton's Initiative on Race. Prior to joining the Clinton administration, Mr. Wenger served for more than sixteen years as the States' Washington Representative for the Appalachian Regional Commission, representing the governors of the thirteen Appalachian states. Before coming to Washington, D.C., in 1981, Mr. Wenger was deputy commissioner of the West Virginia Department of Welfare, commissioner of the West Virginia Department of Employment Security, and director of Federal-State Programs for the City of Charleston, West Virginia. He has also been a journalist and public school teacher in the New York City area and was heavily involved in the West Virginia antipoverty program in the late 1960s and early 1970s. He is the coauthor of *Window Pane Stories: Vignettes to Help You Look At and Beyond Your Experiences*, a frequent speaker on race relations, and the author of numerous articles on race relations and on rural economic development.

Mr. Wenger was born in New York City and educated at Queens College of the City University of New York, where he was a leader in the civil rights struggles of the early 1960s. He lives in Mitchellville, Maryland, with his wife, and has three grown children, four grandchildren, and a great-grandson.

CPSIA information can be obtained at www.ICGtesting.com
Printed in the USA
BVOW040232070213

312644BV00001B/12/P